ENCYCLOPEDIC HANDBOOK OF
CULTS IN AMERICA

GARLAND REFERENCE LIBRARY
OF SOCIAL SCIENCE
(VOL. 213)

ENCYCLOPEDIC HANDBOOK OF
CULTS IN AMERICA
J. Gordon Melton

Garland Publishing Inc.
New York & London
1986

Library of Congress Cataloging in Publication Data
Melton, J. Gordon.
   Encyclopedic handbook of cults in America.

   (Garland reference library of social science ;
v. 213)
   Bibliography: p.
   Includes index.
      1. Cults—United States   2. Sects—United States.
3. United States—Religion.   4. Cults—Controversial
literature—History and criticism.   I. Title.
II. Series.
BL2525.M45   1986   291'.0973   83-48227
ISBN 0-8240-9036-5 (alk. paper)

Cover design by Stan Rosinski

Printed on acid-free, 250-year-life paper

Manufactured in the United States of America

CONTENTS

INTRODUCTION

There has been a growing need in the past several years for a concise summary of the most accurate information available on the more important of the alternative and nonconventional religious movements. As the cult wars of the 1970s have waned, the groups which had been the object of so much controversy remain. They have settled into the American religious landscape and show every sign of staying in place for the foreseeable future. For that reason alone, a guide to the more prominent of the 500 plus alternatives to the more familiar churches is necessary. The controversy which surrounds each of the groups considered here reinforces that observation.

The volume is divided into six sections. Section I surveys the broad range of issues surrounding the topic of "cults," the popular label given alternative religion, and attempts to summarize the present state of knowledge. Because of the nature of the controversies concerning the cults, a number of false stereotypes exist about them. These are discussed in the appropriate succeeding chapters.

Section II discusses approximately twenty of the older, more established nonconventional religions, all of which have their origin in the nineteenth or early twentieth century. Out of the many which could have been discussed, those chosen were selected primarily on the basis of size (a major criterion of success) and the presence of continuing controversy about them. As a whole, their main opponents have been the evangelical Christian counter-cult ministries who oppose these groups for deviating in their teachings from orthodox Christianity. Several of these groups, among them, the "I AM" Activity and the Universal Peace Mission Movement, were selected as examples of still-vital movements which were at one time widely discussed but which have in recent years been forgotten.

Section III gives an in-depth treatment of the prominent and growing New Age Movement, about which very little descriptive literature exists. It has been a difficult movement to grasp because it is so decentralized and diverse. To aid readers in further research and understanding, a lengthy bibliography of New Age literature has been appended to the description.

Section IV is the heart of the volume. It discusses sixteen of the most significant "new" religions which have either emerged in America or been transported to its shores in the past few decades. For each group, as with the older cults, an attempt has been made to highlight basic data about the group's history, founder(s), beliefs and practices, and organization. An estimate of current strength is given and the recent controversies summarized.

Section V will be especially helpful to the neophyte to the cult controversies. It discusses the two main groups opposing nonconventional religions. The secular anti-cult movement appeared in the 1970s and has concentrated its attack primarily on the groups discussed in Section IV. Christian ministries, responding from an Evangelical perspective to the growing pluralism in American society, appeared earlier, after World War II. They speak to the issue of cults from a Christian theological stance. Up to now there has been little effort to compile the story of the development of this particular mission thrust and to see it as a distinct evangelical enterprise. In its developing years, the Christian ministries directed most of their energy to the older and larger groups, such as the Jehovah's Witnesses and the Mormons. Recently there has been a shift of considerable time and effort to the newer Eastern religions.

In the final section a single important issue is raised for more substantial consideration: violence. The section discusses violence inflicted upon cult groups and members as well as that initiated within a cult body. Suggestions on reducing and eliminating cult-related violence are offered.

This book is by no means the final word. A separate chapter on legal matters, from lawsuits to nonviolent crime, should possibly have been included, but not feeling sufficiently versed to offer an adequate survey, I limited my remarks to those several cases discussed in the chapters on the specific group involved. It is my hope that such a survey can be accomplished in the near future.

The information contained in these chapters is as accurate as possible. Members and leaders of the groups discussed have been contacted, as have their critics. It has not always been possible to reach an agreement on matters of fact, and I am quite sure that people will disagree with interpretations placed upon data. I welcome additional information that will correct any errors in this volume or provide important but overlooked information which should be taken into account in making an informed evaluation.

A Word About Approaching the Cults

I have been studying nonconventional religion in America for over twenty years and writing about it for over a decade. I have worked as a professional church historian while wearing a second hat as a United Methodist minister with a distinct commitment to a conservative evangelical Wesleyan Christian faith. As a youth, I became both concerned about and fascinated by the multitudinous splinters of Christianity and then intrigued with the growing presence of so many non-Christian groups. During the late 1960s, while still in seminary, I became convinced that the heterodox Christian groups and the non-Christian groups represented a phenomenon which was inadequately understood by my colleagues in church history and which was destined soon to play a much more important role in American life than any had anticipated. The cult wars and the spread of Asian religion in America in the last decade have proved my premonition correct.

However, in the 1960s, I set out to document and build a library of materials about the smaller and more nonconventional religions in America, and in 1969, with the aid of some fellow students at Garrett Theological Seminary, I founded the Institute for the Study of American Religion as an independent research facility concerned with America's less-documented religions. It began and has continued as a scholarly pursuit, and other researchers around the country have contributed their time and talent to make it the success it has been. It has deliberately remained neutral in the cult wars, though I as its director have occasionally fought a battle or two. Furthermore, it was not turned into a ministry with a prime task of evangelizing non-Christians, though this has on occasion been a by-product of counseling individuals who turned to the institute staff for assistance. Rather, the institute's role has been one of providing a resource for the church and the public from which both could draw accurate information upon which policy decisions about ministry to and relationships with the new religions could be made.

Because of the different approach that the institute took, and because for many years I did little but gather information, attend meetings of different religions, and read document after document, I have reached a somewhat different position from that of some of my evangelical Christian colleagues who helped pioneer the church's response to the cults. In particular, I feel that the church must make a much more positive approach to the presence of so many non-Christians now in our midst. Rather than simply opposing cults, I strongly believe that the church must build a widespread, loving, and evangelical ministry to non-Christians. That ministry must honor the sincerity and integrity of people who are and who will continue to be non-Christians. It should include, along with the presentation of the Christian message, time to listen and try to understand the position of those to whom the Gospel is directed. It should, in its attempt to inform church members of the nature of alternative religions, strive to present the account of their beliefs and practices with the same care that it would that of a different denomination. In that understanding, this volume is offered to the church as a tool to assist in its development of its ministry.

From this perspective, it is also felt that at least one group should not have been included in this volume. The Local Church was included because in the past few years it has fought a head-on battle with a prominent evangelical Christian anti-cult writer and most recently pursued a lawsuit which sent a well-known Christian ministry, the Spiritual Counterfeits Project, into bankruptcy. SCP had been recognized by many in this field, this author included, as the most scholarly and research-oriented of the several hundred counter-cult ministries. It played an important role in the late 1970s in opposing the use of state funds to support Transcendental Meditation programs in public schools and the Army.

This author has also undertaken a lengthy study of the Local Church and the writings of its leaders, Watchman Nee and Witness Lee. I have observed the group from time to time for a decade. I have found no evidence that it is anything but an orthodox Christian body, even though it has some unusual and unfamiliar practices, none of which detract from its Christian faith. For whatever reason, the Local Church has been branded a heretical group by, I believe, individuals, colleagues in ministry, who have misunderstood its theology. It was included in this volume only because of the controversy surrounding it and to set the record straight.

Finally, I want to thank all who have assisted in the preparation of this volume and ask that I be forgiven for not mentioning each by name. There have been so many. I am truly grateful for their assistance in providing information and checking various sections of this volume before it went to press.

I invite their continued assistance and especially invite any readers who have additional information of interest and importance to contact me through the institute.

> J. Gordon Melton
> Institute for the Study of American Religion
> P.O. Box 90709
> Santa Barbara, California 93190-0709

I.
What Is a Cult?

WHAT IS A CULT?

The term "cult" is a pejorative label used to describe certain religious groups outside of the mainstream of Western religion. Exactly which groups should be considered cults is a matter of disagreement among researchers in the cult phenomena, and considerable confusion exists. However, three definitions dominate the writings of social scientists, Christian counter-cult ministries, and secular anticultists.

Social scientists tend to be the least pejorative in their use of the term. They divide religious groups into three categories: churches, sects, and cults. "Churches" are the large denominations characterized by their inclusive approach to life and their identification with the prevailing culture. In the United States, the churchly denominations would include such groups as the Roman Catholic Church, the United Methodist Church, the American Baptist Church, the United Church of Christ and the Protestant Episcopal Church. Groups that have broken away from the churchly denominations are termed "sects." They tend to follow the denominations in most patterns but are more strict in doctrine and behavioral demands placed upon members and emphasize their separation and distinctiveness from the larger culture (frequently spoken of as a "rejection of worldliness"). Typical sects have disavowed war (Quakers and Mennonites), championed controversial religious experiences (pentecostals), and demanded conformity to detailed codes of dress, personal piety, and moral conduct (the holiness churches). Sects such as the fundamentalist Christian groups have argued for a stringent orthodoxy in the face of the doctrinal latitude allowed in most larger church bodies. More extreme sect bodies have developed patterns and practices which have largely isolated them from even their closest religious neighbors—snake-handling, drinking poison, alternative sexual relationships, unusual forms of dress.

While most sects follow familiar cultural patterns to a large extent, "cults" follow an altogether different religious structure, one foreign and alien to the prevalent religious communities. Cults represent a force of religious innovation within a culture. In most cases that innovation comes about by the transplantation of a religion from a different culture by the immigration of some of its members and leaders. Thus during the twentieth century, Hinduism and Buddhism have been transplanted to America. In sociological terms, Hindu and Buddhist groups are, in America, cults. Cults may also come about through religious innovation from within the culture. The Church of Scientology and the Synanon Church are new religious structures which emerged in American society without any direct foreign antecedents.

When social scientists began their discussion of cults in the 1920s, they were aware of only a few cult groups, well-known groups which they could not fit into their more crucial debates about churches versus sects—theosophy, Christian Science, spiritualism, and the two large Hindu groups: the Vedanta Society and the Self-Realization Fellowship. Elmer Clark's pioneering survey of *The Small Sects in America* (1949) listed fourteen New Thought bodies and thirteen Esoteric bodies, showing an awareness of some twenty-seven cults (plus a few others such as the black Jews considered in the body of his text).

A second definition of cult arose among Christian polemicists. In the early twentieth century several conservative Evangelical Protestant writers, concerned about the growth of different religions in America, attacked these religions for their deviation from Christian orthodox faith. Among the first of the prominent Christian writers on the subject of cults, Jan Karel Van Baalen described cults as non-Christian religions but included those groups which had their roots in Christianity while denying what he considered its essential teaching. According to Van Baalen, all religions could be divided into two groups, those which ascribe to humans the ability to accomplish their own salvation and those which ascribe that ability to God. The latter group is called Christianity. All other religion fits into the first group. In *The Chaos of Cults*, which went through numerous editions from its first appearance in 1938, Van Baalen analyzed various non-Christian religions in the light of Christian teachings.

With little change, contemporary Christian counter-cult spokespersons have followed Van Baalen's lead. Cults follow another gospel (*Gal.* 1:16). They are heretical. They set up their own beliefs in opposition to orthodox faith. As Josh McDowell and Don Stewart, two popular Evangelical writers assert, "A cult is a perversion, a distortion of Biblical Christianity, and, as such, rejects the historical teachings of the Christian Church."

The Christian approach to cults would include every group which has departed from orthodox Christianity (such as the Church of Christ, Scientist, the Latter Day Saints, and the Jehovah's Witnesses) as well as those groups which have never made any claim to be Christian. Individual writers disagree over the cultic nature of such groups as the Roman Catholic Church (included and then dropped by Van Baalen), or the Unitarian-Universalist Church. Little consideration has been given to non-Trinitarian Pentecostal groups.

The third definition, the one which became the dominant force in the public debates on cults in the 1970s, developed within the secular anti-cult movement. The definition has shifted and changed over the last decade. It did not develop out of any objective research on alternative religions, rather it emerged in the intense polemics of parents who had been disturbed by changes observed in their sons and daughters who had joined particular religious groups. These "cults"—predominantly the Children of God, the Church of Armageddon, the Unification Church, the International Society for Krishna Consciousness, and the Church of Scientology—had, they charged, radically altered the personality traits of their children.

Anti-cultists began to speak of "destructive cults," groups which hypnotized or brainwashed recruits, destroyed their ability to make rational judgments and turned them into slaves of the group's leader. While drawing upon Christian counter-cult literature in the beginning, the secular anti-cultists gradually discarded any overtly religious language as a means of designating cults in order to appeal to government authorities and avoid any seeming attack upon religious liberties. Thus, "cults" have come to be seen as groups that share a variety of generally destructive characteristics. While no one group may embody all of them, any "cult" will possess a majority. Marcia Rudin, a popular anti-cult writer, listed fourteen commonly accepted characteristics of a cult:

1. Members swear total allegiance to an all-powerful leader who they believe to be the Messiah.
2. Rational thought is discouraged or forbidden.
3. The cult's recruitment techniques are often deceptive.
4. The cult weakens the follower psychologically by making him or her depend upon the group to solve his or her problems.
5. The cults manipulate guilt to their advantage.
6. The cult leader makes all the career and life decisions of the members.
7. Cults exist only for their own material survival and make false promises to work to improve society.
8. Cult members often work fulltime for the group for little or no pay.
9. Cult members are isolated from the outside world and any reality testing it could provide.
10. Cults are antiwoman, antichild, and antifamily.
11. Cults are apocalyptic and believe themselves to be the remnant who will survive the soon-approaching end of the world.
12. Many cults follow an "ends justify the means" philosophy.
13. Cults, particularly in regard to their finances, are shrouded in secrecy.
14. There is frequently an aura of or potential for violence around cults.

Anti-cultists suggest that, as of the early 1980s, 3,000 to 5,000 destructive cults operate in the United States. However, no evidence of the existence of such a large number of religious groups, either cultic or otherwise, has been produced. Anti-cult literature reflects a great concern with approximately 15 groups, though as many as 75 to 100 have received passing mention. Only five groups—the Unification Church, the Children of God, the Church of Scientology, the International Society for Krishna Consciousness, and The Way International—have received consistent coverage over the years of the anti-cult movement's existence.

The discussion of cults by social scientists, Christian counter-cult ministries, and secular anti-cultists has singled out a number of groups for attention as prominent or typical examples of cults. Among these groups, some became controversial because of their divergent behavioral norms (polygamy, a leader's claim to divinity, exotic rituals, communalism). Others came into open conflict with the authorities because of violence (the black Muslims). Many groups recruited single young adults and moved them into intense religious communities against the wishes of their parents. Such groups have received the most attention in the last decade.

This handbook includes the most prominent "cults" for analysis and discussion. It is designed to provide a concise overview of each group and a summary of the controversy surrounding it. Along with the "cult," the secular anti-cult and Christian counter-cult movements are also given treatment, as they are a very active element in the contemporary milieu. This volume will cover most groups which one is likely to encounter; however, for a more complete listing of all the individual religious groups currently functioning in the United States, including a brief descriptive statement of each, the reader is referred to the author's *Encyclopedia of American Religion*, which can be found in the reference section of most libraries.

The Flowering of the Cults in the Twentieth Century

Numbers. Everyone who has looked at the cult phenomenon has agreed that the number of alternative religious groups has grown significantly during the twentieth century, particularly since World War II. Using the broad definition of the social scientists, one can find some 500 to 600 cults or alternative religions in the United States. Of these, over 100 are primarily ethnic bodies confined to first- and second-generation immigrant communities. These ethnic religions do no recruiting beyond their small ethnic base and frequently continue the use of the language of their home country, a significant barrier to their spread into the general population.

Beyond the cults, however, numerous sect groups have splintered from the large mainline denominations although they resemble each other in most ways. They affirm the Western Christian tradition but dissent on one or more significant points. When their dissent becomes extreme or centers upon some key issues of doctrine, the label "cult" is frequently applied to these groups as well. Among the sects, for example, the Jehovah's Witnesses disagree with the Christian tradition by their denial of a number of central affirmations of orthodox Christian faith—the Trinity, hell, salvation by grace alone—not to mention a number of lesser beliefs. The Witnesses placed great importance upon their predictions of the exact date of the end of the world, and they have tended to draw their members into a closed social circle. Other sects deviated by their acceptance of faith healing or glossolalia or other nonconventional behavioral patterns and thus earned the designation "cult," particularly from Christian writers.

If one adds the Christian groups which have strongly dissented from the doctrinal norms of the Western Christian tradition, several hundred more groups join the list of cultic groups. Such groups deserve attention in any survey of the cultic milieu in America as they have tended to become separatist and develop alternative social structures which become the focus of their members' daily lives. Also, the more extreme sects occasionally have developed corrupt, rigid authoritarian leadership structures. Unhampered by normal societal checks, such corrupt leadership has led to disastrous results, amply illustrated, for example, in the murders and crimes perpetrated by members of the Church of the Lamb of God. Anti-cultists draw their image of destructive cults from extreme sects as well as from those groups more normally labeled cults.

Just as there are not really so many cult groups as are frequently reported in the press, cults also lack the huge membership often credited to them. If such alleged membership, reportedly in the millions, existed, every neighborhood would have visible cult centers. Only a few of the older cults—the Jehovah's Witnesses, the Church of Jesus Christ of Latter Day Saints—have attained a broad membership throughout the nation. Of those groups formed in the twentieth century, only a few, such as the American Muslim Mission (found in 1930), can count their membership in the tens of thousands. The more famous of the contemporary cults, such as the Unification Church (with 5,000 to 7,000 members) or the Hare Krishna (with approximately 2,500 initiated members), can count their membership in the thousands. Most cults have only a few hundred members and spend most of their energy just surviving. Thus, in those several hundred groups which have become prominent during the last decades, a total of 150,000 to 200,000 would be a more reasonable membership estimate.

One cannot, however, measure cult statistics solely by membership. It must be noted that many times the number of members have had only a brief period of cult involvement. Over ninety percent of those who join an alternative religion leave it within a few years. Even larger numbers of individuals, in the process of examining a religious group, participate in some activity but never join. Over one million people took the basic course in Transcendental Meditation, but only a minority joined the TM organization, and the total American membership remains in the 10,000 to 20,000 range. Similarly, only a few of the many thousands who were initiated into the Divine Light Mission became "premies." Between thirty and forty thousand of the several hundred thousand who have taken the basic weekend introduction to the Unification Church eventually joined the organization. Of that number fewer than 7,000 remained as members as of 1984. While the cults grew appreciably during the 1970s, they still constitute a numerically small part of the American religious scene.

The Course of Growth. While the growth of cults has not been alarming, it has been noticeable and raised questions of its causes. Why has the United States experienced this sudden burst of new alternative religions with its element of Oriental religions and Christian groups which originated in the Orient (such as the Local Church)? Some researchers have pointed to the social unrest of the 1960s and the pattern of emergent religions arising in times of social upheaval. However, while this observation provided some helpful reflection on the patterns of religious diversification, it did little to explain the rise of the new Asian component. Other students, primarily critics of the new religions, claim the growth of the new religions to be a result of their use of new manipulative psychological techniques which attract and control (i.e., brainwash) youthful followers, many of whom join during the crises of adolescence. This explanation suffers from its inability to describe any demonstrably new element in the cultic conversion techniques which have been used by Evangelical Christians for generations, in spite of the use of modern psychological terminology in discussions of conversion events. A final group of observers of the milieu of the new religions, their supporters, sees these groups as the visible expression of a new religious consciousness.

More detailed and dispassionate observation has suggested that several mundane causes may underlie the seemingly sudden flowering of the new religions. First, the contemporary burst of alternative religions continues a history of growth in metaphysical, occult and Eastern religion which is at least a century and a half old. Asian religion entered the United States in the early 1800s and found an initial expression in the Transcendentalist Movement in New England. The large immigration of Asians in the last half of the nineteenth century brought the first Buddhist and Hindu teachers to the United States and threatened many West Coast residents. California could have become like Hawaii, which is one third Buddhist, during the first decades of this century, legislators passed a series of Asian exclusion acts which slowed the flow of immigrants from India, Japan, and Southeast Asia to a trickle. The natural growth of Asian religion was thus effectively stunted. Then in 1965, President Lyndon Johnson rescinded the Asian exclusion laws and raised Asian immigration quotas to a par with those of other nations. As a result, Asians have come to the United States in the hundreds of thousands and are currently reshaping urban centers by their presence. For example, census records show that fewer than 12,000 Indians were admitted to the United States prior to 1960 (though many more than that came into the country illegally). Most lived in California. By 1980 over 380,000 had been admitted. 84,000 live in New York City, 34,000 in Chicago; and 60,000 in California. Equally dramatic figures could be cited for Japanese, Koreans, and other Asians.

The Asians brought with them their teachers—swamis, Zen masters, gurus—and a zeal to spread their religions among Americans. *The new availability of Asian teachers has been the major factor in the growth of alternative religions in the last two decades.* For the first time Asian faiths have become a genuine option for religious seekers in the West.

As the Asian missionaries arrived, they found a West prepared by recent cultural events and scientific developments to receive them. Within the occult and metaphysical communities, which had grown steadily through the century, the gurus found a welcome image of the East as the fountainhead of pure wisdom. Occult/metaphysical groups, which had been the conduit for Eastern teachings, had, as a result, built a hunger for unmediated experiences under a Hindu swami or a Japanese Zen master. Such a desire for firsthand acquaintance with Eastern religion had also been created within the colleges that were offering a growing number of courses in Eastern faiths. Students wished to go beyond the academic experience.

Three significant developments within the larger scientific community also prepared the West for the burst of new religions. The emergence of parapsychology out of the older field of psychical research, the discovery and spread of LSD and other mind-altering drugs, and the rise of alternative branches of the psychological disciplines (most notably humanistic psychology and Jungian psychotherapy) established a scientific basis for the introspective search which Eastern and occult religions claimed as their special expertise. In their own differing ways, parapsychology, hallucinogenics and psychology became the legitimizing agents for mystical occultism and Eastern spiritual disciplines.

The flowering of the cults in the last two decades is best seen as the convergence and maturation of several trends which had been developing in North America for many decades. Unleashed by the demise of Asian immigration restrictions, these trends flowed into a new permissive environment. Without the many years of effort by members of alternative religions prior to 1965 and the development of the culture to receive the Eastern gospel, there would have been little response to the Eastern teachers when they finally did arrive.

Who Joins? Since World War II, America has experienced two periods of national religious revival, first in the early 1950s and again in the 1970s. In both of them, millions of Americans attained a new religious appreciation and joined a church or some religious organization. While thousands were joining alternative religions, hundreds of thousands were joining conservative Protestant Evangelical churches, especially the pentecostal ones. Many thousands of members of mainline churches formed pentecostal groups without leaving their primary affiliation. Many blacks were attracted to Moslem organizations, while many poorer whites moved to new sectarian churches. Older "cults"—Mormons, Jehovah's Witnesses—grew among broad segments of the population.

The new cults, those which experienced their first real growth in the 1970s, and many of which had an Eastern or occult orientation, grew among a very narrow segment of the population. They primarily attracted single young adults (age 18–25). The new recruits were generally drawn from the upper half of the population economically and educationally. University campuses have continued to be a favorite recruiting ground.

Members of the new cults have been drawn equally from all segments of the established religious population though some groups show a marked individual variance. Like the population, about half of the new members have a Protestant-Free Church background and another fourth are Roman Catholic. The Jewish community is the exception, being overrepresented. Nonconventional religions tend to draw a much higher percentage of their membership, particularly their leadership, from among the Jewish segment of the population than national percentages would lead one to expect. This overrepresentation of Jews in some new religions has become a matter of legitimate concern for some Jewish religious leaders though no consensus of opinion on a single method of response has emerged. Some have become leaders in the anti-cult movement while others have become equally vocal in defending the cults from what they feel are unjustified attacks by anti-cultists.

Though the great majority of people who join nonconventional religions could easily adopt the religion of their parents, only a minority are ever active in a church or synagogue as a teenager. The weak tie to the parental religion often proves unable to hold in the face of the young adult's reading books about and then visiting different religious groups available in the community. For example, the great majority of people who joined the Hare Krishna movement had done some reading in Eastern religion and had adopted vegetarianism prior to any firsthand contact with group members. Members of many new religions had participated in the drug culture and were drawn to a religious group which promised a chemical-free alternative to the psychedelic experience.

Thus, while some groups have been actively recruiting members, potential converts have also been actively searching for a group that can meet their specific needs and desires (both religious and otherwise). They will test and reject groups until they find the right one and will leave that group if it no longer fulfills their expectations.

The nonconventional religions also vary widely in their recruitment processes. Some, particularly those with Evangelical Christian roots (and a few which are Eastern, but reacting to Christian missionary activity) have an aggressive program of membership enlistment. Most others rely upon the distribution of literature or the sponsoring of introductory classes to which a potential convert must make the initial effort and attend. Many Hindu groups offer hatha yoga exercise classes out of which they recruit individuals who show an interest in more religious forms of yoga (bhakti, raja, or japa). Some of the groups that lead a more austere and demanding life, put prospective members through a testing period (similar to a monastic novitiate) before initiating them. A few, such as the Pagan and magickal groups, do not recruit at all, and prospective members must take all the initiative in locating a group (frequently a difficult process).

In return, nonconventional religions reap a small harvest from those with whom they come in contact. Of those who attend an initial recruitment event—an introductory TM lecture, a weekend on Unification theology, a Scientology personality test, a five-week hatha yoga class—less than 10% will join. Of those who do join, the overwhelming majority will stay with the group for less than two years. For example, during its first decade (1965–74), the International Society for Krishna Consciousness (the Hare Krishnas) initiated 5,000 members. An additional 2,500 were initiated between 1975 and 1983. Of the 7,500, only 2,500 remained active in 1984. Only a handful were deprogrammed; the rest simply walked away. Those who leave can move on to a new religion or remain loosely affiliated with the group. Most return to the religion in which they were raised.

Nonconventional religions, particularly those singled out as "destructive cults," have frequently been accused of engaging in deceptive recruitment practices. The charges of deception emerged from reflection upon the activities of the Oakland Family, a local center of the Unification Church headed by Rev. Sun Myung Moon. The Family operated several structures which were not openly identified with the controversial Church, and certain literature made no reference to the Church as its sponsor. Some people who eventually became members of the Church for a short period claimed that they became active in the life of the Church before realizing that it was the Unification Church with which they had affiliated. Almost all serious charges about deceptive elements in the recruiting process have stemmed from the Oakland Family in the 1970s. Complaints about deceptive recruiting have been little heard in recent years except in the most general checklists of cult practices published by anti-cult organizations.

Most groups are and have been quite open and proud of their organization, and many, particularly those whose members adopt distinctive dress, would have a next to impossible task concealing their identity. No adult would have any question about whom they were dealing with when they met a Krishna devotee on the street or visited a Krishna temple. The Church of Scientology has had a long-standing policy of having prospective members fill out a form in which they acknowledge their awareness that they are about to participate in a Scientology event. While new members may not be aware of all of the implications of joining a distinctively different religion, they do understand the basic beliefs and requirements and the identity of the group they are joining.

Life in a Cult

Once a person joins a nonconventional religious group, he or she must begin to adapt to group life. New recruits will go through a program of education in group beliefs and practices. Frequently, they will begin to master a spiritual discipline and, most perturbing to former acquaintances, they will begin to change their behavior patterns to conform to group demands.

Indoctrination. Most groups have a more or less standard program through which they process new members. The smaller and newer the group, the more informal the induction process will be. It will involve attendance at various classes and mastering of a body of information about group beliefs. Over a period of time, the classes may become quite standardized. In some occult groups, advancement in the group is through a system of degrees. All members must master a set of studies and become accomplished in the practical use of the teachings at one level before receiving the information concerning the next.

Whatever the methods used, most groups adopt an amateurish approach to training new members. Average recruit trainers receive no teacher training to assist them in the presentation of materials. Their only asset is usually a winsome personality.

Cults expend a considerable amount of time educating new members in the ways of the group. While the average new member knows some of the teachings, especially those which proved most influential in his or her decision to join, a lengthy indoctrination by the group is frequently necessary. Unlike a person moving between Christian denominations, where much of the doctrine and practice are the same, a new cult member has to learn a totally new way to be religious and to master a different religious tradition from scratch. At the very least, if a nominal Christian joined an intense Christian sect, she or he would likely spend many hours in Bible study learning a new approach to the Scriptures.

During the indoctrination period, which could last from a few months to a few years, the new recruits may spend all of their leisure time (or in the case of communal groups, all of their waking hours) in the practice of and education in their new faith. This indoctrination completes the process of religious striving which each convert began prior to any contact with the group. The early stages of religious concern in a young adult begin in a period of dissatisfaction and investigation. The events of this period may be totally internal and completely hidden from family and close friends. The internal process often becomes visible only when potential new cult members discover a group that seems to meet their religious concerns. They then begin to investigate the group, sometimes on their own or frequently through structured recruitment activities and visits to worship services. More or less gradually, the decision to join is made. That decision is often influenced by far more than the teachings and practices of the group; the friendliness of the members, the spirituality and quality of the leader(s), and the rigorousness of the demands are all elements to be considered. During the period of investigation, potential new members will adopt some outward signs of the religion, which might include uniform dress, specific religious practices (chanting, Bible reading, meditation, vegetarian diet, etc.) and changing relationships as group members take their place in the circle of the new member's closest associates (replacing former ones).

Spiritual Disciplines. Life in many nonconventional religions includes the practice of a "spiritual discipline," a specific set of exercises designed to produce various "altered" or mystical states of consciousness. While quite common to the East, such practices have not been as common to Western Christianity apart from the monastic orders. However, the normal role of a guru or swami in India is to teach a set of spiritual practices which will lead the practitioner into a state of religious enlightenment. The systems and practices vary widely from kundalini yoga to zazen to the twirling dances of the dervishes. In the West, meditation and chanting have been the most common spiritual disciplines. Loyola's Spiritual Exercises are possibly the most famous system of spiritual practice. Also in the West, the guru, i.e., the teacher of spiritual wisdom, has usually been given the more mundane title, "spiritual director."

Some critics of new religions charge that the spiritual practices that regularly produce altered states of consciousness lead to disassociative disorders. Psychiatric studies on cult members, however, find little or no evidence to substantiate such charges. Several researchers have reported a lower-than-normal incidence of psychological well-being among converts to several well-known cults, while noting a measurable improvement over the period of initial conversion and a retention of that improved state over a period of years as members. Also reported are a reduction of alcohol and drug abuse.

Psychiatrist Marc Galanter, in summarizing all of the research on cult life and psychiatric issues, notes that psychiatry has a significant problem in assessing individual cult members because the discipline has yet to develop satisfactory methodologies for understanding social adaptation to a religious group which may deviate from conventional behavior. Behavior which might signal a disorder in a person in a more conventional social setting can be perfectly normal within a cult. Psychotherapist Robert L. Moore has also reported that most of the negative symptoms reported as typical of cult members—blank stares, disassociative states, submission to a guru, etc.—are, when viewed in the context of the developmental process, perfectly normal. Individuals going through such a significant life transition as changing a religion may exhibit patterns that become pathological only if retained for an abnormal period of time—four to five years.

Social scientists have confirmed what psychiatrists and psychologists report. The nonconventional behavior reported as typical of members of new religions is a direct result of members adapting to the norms of group life and derives its meaning from the group context. Within the group, behavior that ordinarily would be strange, even weird, becomes logical and meaningful within the context of the group goals and beliefs.

Behavioral Patterns. Some sects and most cults make great demands upon their members. Sectarian groups are distinguished by their strictness in either doctrinal or behavioral standards and/or their adoption of a nonconventional pattern of worship or piety. Sect groups generally demand a greater commitment of time than the larger, more inclusive, denominations. As a corollary, sect members make a larger number of their social contacts within the group than among the general public. Church and sect groups can be placed along a continuum of strictness with the large liberal Protestant denominations (such as the United Methodist Church or the United Church of Christ) at one extreme and the small separatist sects (such as the Amish or Old Order Brethren) at the other.

Cults do not easily fit along that continuum. All demand allegiance to some belief(s) and behavior pattern(s) which strongly differ from more conventional religion. Some nonconventional religions are very loose in their structure and demands upon members. Some are so loose, for example, that their status as a religion has been questioned. Others are as demanding as any sect body. The Hare Krishnas are a semi-monastic group which adheres to a special dress, haircut, diet, and worship schedule. Other groups, less removed from secular work patterns, will ask for all the leisure time of members. A few groups will schedule meetings every evening and plan lengthy sessions for worship, teaching, and fellowship on the weekends.

Such high-demand, unconventional religions and the newer sectarian groups have been the major targets of the anti-cult movements. Their demands on members' time and almost exclusive hold on members' social contacts became the focus of parental concerns when sons and daughters joined. Critics have accused the high-demand religions of being "antifamily" as they create a barrier between members and their natural family. In the long run, such demands upon members force them to become dependent upon the group. Such dependency over a period of years may create difficulty for members in adjusting to society if either the group dissolves or they decide to leave it.

The Aftermath of Cult Life

The great majority of people who join groups which deviate strongly from societal norms or have a high disapproval level in society leave after only a short period of time, typically within two years. For these people the time in the cult was what Robert Ellwood has termed an *excursus*, a spiritual journey away from the mundane structures of established religion. For most the excursion is brief, though it might assume a vast importance in shaping the more mature long-term religious existence. Having made the journey, former cult members return to a more conventional religion or, increasingly, to no formal religious affiliation at all. They may return to a life so integrated into dominant societal patterns that little evidence of the excursion is visible to the persons' acquaintances.

A minority of persons who join a cult leave under a situation of great stress. Some leave because of a bad experience within the group. Ex-members tell of psychological and even occasional physical abuse, the bitter disappointment of discovering corruption in the leader or leaders of a group, and the inability of a cult to deliver what it had promised in spiritual values. Members who have had a bad experience leave angry and hurt and often turn with vengeance upon their former faith.

Among those who leave cults under stressful conditions are those who have been deprogrammed. Under the pain of physical confinement and strong psychological pressure, cult members have been forced to renounce their allegiance to the group and join the chorus of cult critics.

Those who leave a cult under the stress of either a bad experience or deprogramming frequently have difficulty adapting to the world again. Psychiatrists such as Margaret Singer, who has worked with many ex-cultists who left various groups under stress, have blamed the cults for a delayed stress syndrome in their clients. More recent comparative studies have shown, however, that the delayed stress syndrome is almost exclusively limited to those ex-cult members who have left under stress (i.e., deprogramming). The great majority of people who leave simply because the group no longer meets their needs show no pattern of psychological disturbance.

A small percentage of those who join a cult will remain in it for many years, even a lifetime. For these few, the cult provides a satisfactory structure within which to discover a meaningful existence. It may motivate individuals to make significant contributions to life and culture. While cults and cult members may appear to be withdrawing from society, especially during the first generation of the group and its newest converts, in the long run, alternative religions that have survived their formative period have generally integrated themselves into American culture and added greatly to its richness.

A Perspective on the "Cults"

Much of the contemporary debate about alternative religions revolves around the basic doubts concerning the legitimacy of nonconventional religions. They appear strange and foreign. They challenge the status quo, particularly the religious hegemony enjoyed by the more established religions. In their zeal and organization, cults often seem, to outside observers, to be accomplishing far more than they would claim for themselves. The proliferation of alternative religions and the obvious impossibility for any individuals to become acquainted with more than a few of them calls for some kind of overall perspective.

Critics of the cults have proposed programs for the elimination of cults. Secular critics have tried to mobilize public opinion against those cults they consider to be intrusive harmful elements in the social order. Cults destroy families, harm individuals who join them, and threaten society. Christian critics, for somewhat different reasons, also view cults negatively. They see them as illegitimate parodies of God's true religion and a Satanic plot to lure people away from the pure faith. Both secular and Christian critics agree that efforts should be made both to discourage people from joining and to reclaim people who have joined.

This criticism has not slowed the growth of alternative religions, which have steadily increased in both numbers and percentage in Western society during the twentieth century. On the other hand, the massive criticism of the new religions has widened the rifts in the social fabric which have divided families and even communities along religious lines. The cults, the nonconventional religions, have developed deep roots in the American soil and are well on their way to becoming established elements in the social order. Such groups as the Church of Christ, Scientist and the Church of Jesus Christ of Latter Day Saints have already created a secure niche for themselves in both the religious and secular realms. The emergence of the radically pluralistic society suggests that not a continuation of hostilities but an attitude of acceptance and understanding of a new religious social order is needful. The United States, as is true for all of the West, is becoming home to Hindus, Buddhists, Sikhs, Muslims and a variety of psychic-occult religions just as it has been home to Christians and Jews.

Viewed parochially, cults can appear to be the strange activity of cultural outcasts, those small groups always on the edge of culture, always dissenting, always strange, sometimes sinister. If, on the contrary, one assumes a broader more historical approach, cults take on a quite different appearance. During the nineteenth century, riding the tide of colonial conquests, Christianity spread from Europe around the world. It swept across North America, Africa and Latin America and made a significant penetration of Asia. On the heels of the Christian expansion, non-Christian religion began to come into the West. Its first significant appearance was in New England where Hinduism greatly influenced the Transcendentalist Movement. By the end of the century, groups of Asians began to bring their faiths, primarily Buddhism, to Hawaii and the West Coast. Then in the twentieth century, returning upon the ships and planes that brought Western culture to the East, Asian and Middle Easterners came to America to establish now thriving communities. They brought their religion and their often exotic culture. All the while, occult religions which had all but disappeared in the eighteenth century made their comeback.

The progress of Christianity in the East and the spread of Eastern religion in the West accelerated after World War II. What has been viewed as the rise of cults in America is actually but a single phase of a total global shift in world religion. The basic component of this shift in recent decades has been the very visible penetration of Asian religion in unprecedented proportions in the West. This massive migration of people and ideas is far larger than the momentary success of one single religion and far more significant than the human frailties of an individual guru. A microcosm of world religion is being created in the West. Instead of the twenty or thirty Christian denominations from which eighteenth-century Americans could choose, those living in the next century will be able to pick from over a thousand Christian denominations and literally hundreds of non-Christian alternatives.

Given the change that is occurring in the West, approaches to nonconventional religions which attempt to comprehend their dynamics and build structures for people of diverse religious backgrounds to co-exist in a high degree of social harmony offer a far more healthy and rewarding approach than those which perpetuate hostilities built upon an incorrect perception of the larger impact of the so-called cults.

Thus, this volume intends to provide an introduction to the world of unfamiliar religion. It will introduce the more important of these faiths that are challenging the hegemony of the established religions of America and offer information about others which are also making their impact. While this volume is not a substitute for the detailed studies of individual groups, it should provide a point from which indepth investigation can begin. Most importantly it will furnish an overview and set the context for the understanding of any particular group.

Sources

This chapter has tried to summarize briefly the best current data on the major questions about contemporary nonconventional religions in America. Space has not allowed extensive footnoting, hence, a list of the most essential literature has been selected and listed at this point. These volumes (1) represent the range of scholarly opinion on the cult controversies and (2) draw from the most articulate critics of the nonconventional religions.

Not included in this list are a number of important articles from scholarly journals, the one exception being the article by Galanter (9) which is the best comprehensive survey of the psychological literature. To list all the important articles would have increased the size of this volume excessively, and in most cases the journal articles provide the substance from which the books are constructed. Currently, the Institute for the Study of American Religion is overseeing the production of a set of booklength bibliographies on the alternative religions and associated issues. All those which have appeared to date are cited in this volume, either in this list, or, in the case of those related to a single group, in the relevant chapter. The item by Shupe, Bromley and Oliver (27), one of the bibliographies, does list a number of the scholarly articles.

Also not included in this list are those items specifically related to the secular anticult movement and the Christian counter ministries, which may be found at the end of Section V.

Finally, some of the finest work on the broader cult issues has been included in books primarily about a single group, such as Eileen Barker's *The Making of a Moonie*. These items have been cited in the source material of the particular chapter to which they are related.

New material on the cults is constantly appearing, and books which should have been listed below have undoubtedly been omitted. However, the items cited will provide a broad introduction to the literature. The reader should note, as might be obvious from the range of opinion expressed in the many books on cult-related issues that (1) omission from the list below should not be taken as a condemnation of any book and in like measure (2) inclusion on the list by no means implies endorsement of the opinions and conclusions of any particular writer by this author.

1. Barker, Eileen, ed., *New Religious Movements: A Perspective for Understanding Society*. New York: Edwin Mellen Press, 1982. 398pp.

2. Bromley, David G., and Anson D. Shupe, Jr., *Strange Gods*. Boston: Beacon Press, 1982. 244pp.

3. ———, and James T. Richardson, eds., *The Brainwashing/Deprogramming Controversy*. New York: Edwin Mellen Press, 1983. 367pp.

4. Coleman, John, and Gregory Baum, eds., *New Religious Movements*. New York: Seabury Press, 1983. 83pp.

5. Creswell, Mike, *Your God, My God*. Atlanta: Home Mission Board of the Southern Baptist Convention, 1980. 172pp.

6. Ellwood, Robert S., Jr., *Religious and Spiritual Groups in Modern America*. Englewood Cliffs, NJ: Prentice-Hall, 1973. 334pp.

7. ——, *Alternative Altars*. Chicago: University of Chicago Press, 1978. 192pp.

8. Fichter, Joseph H., *Alternatives to American Mainline Churches*. New York: Rose of Sharon Press, 1983. 199pp.

9. Galanter, Marc, "Charismatic Religious Sects and Psychiatry: An Overview." *American Journal of Psychiatry* 139, 12 (December 1982): 1539–49.

10. Garvey, John, ed., *All Our Sons and Daughters*. Springfield, IL: Templegate Publishers, 1977. 131pp.

11. Glock, Charles Y., and Robert N. Bellah, *The New Religious Consciousness*. Berkeley: University of California Press, 1976. 391pp.

12. Kaslow, Florence, and Marvin B. Sussman, *Cults and the Family*. New York: Haworth Press, 1982. 192pp.

13. Levi, Ken, *Violence and Religious Commitment*. University Park: Pennsylvania State University Press, 1982. 207pp.

14. Melton, J. Gordon, *The Directory of Religious Bodies in the United States*. New York: Garland, 1977. 305pp.

15. ——, *The Encyclopedia of American Religions*. Detroit: Gale Research Company, 1984–85. 3 Vols.

16. ——, and Robert L. Moore, *The Cult Experience*. New York: Pilgrim Press, 1982. 180pp.

17. Needleman, Jacob, *The New Religions*. Garden City, NY: Doubleday, 1970. 245pp.

18. ——, and George Baker, eds., *Understanding the New Religions*. New York: Seabury Press, 1978. 314pp.

19. Raschke, Carl A., *The Interruption of Eternity*. Chicago: Nelson-Hall, 1980. 271pp.

20. Richardson, Herbert, ed., *The New Religions and Mental Health*. New York: Edwin Mellen Press, 1980. 177pp.

21. Robbins, Thomas, and Dick Anthony, eds., *In Gods We Trust*. New Brunswick, NJ: Transaction Books, 1981. 338pp.

22. Rubenstein, I. H., *Law on Cults*. Chicago: Ordain Press, 1981. 120pp.

23. Rudin, A. James, and Marcia Rudin, *Prison or Paradise?* Philadelphia: Fortress Press, 1980. 164pp.

24. Saliba, John A., *Religious Cults Today*. Liguori, MO: Liguori Publications, 1983. 48pp.

25. Shupe, Anson D., Jr., *Six Perspectives on New Religions: A Case Study Approach*. New York: Edwin Mellen Press, 1981. 235pp.

26. ——— , and David G. Bromley. *The New Vigilantes*. Beverly Hills, CA: Sage Publications, 1980. 267pp.

27. ——— , ——— , and Donna L. Oliver, *The Anti-Cult Movement in America*. New York: Garland, 1983. 169pp.

28. Stoner, Carroll, and Jo Anne Parke, *All God's Children*. Radnor, PA: Chilton Book Company, 1977. 324pp.

29. Streiker, Lowell D., *Mind Bending*. Garden City, NY: Doubleday, 1984. 218pp.

30. Tipton, Steven M., *Getting Saved from the Sixties*. Berkeley: University of California Press, 1982. 364pp.

31. Wallis, Roy, ed., *Sectarianism*. London: Peter Owen, 1975. 212pp.

32. Whalen, William J., *Strange Gods*. Huntington, IN: Our Sunday Visitor, 1981. 130pp.

33. Wilson, Bryan, ed., *The Social Impact of New Religious Movements*. New York: Rose of Sharon Press, 1981. 234pp.

34. Wuthnow, Robert, *The Consciousness Reformation*. Berkeley: University of California Press, 1976. 309pp.

35. ——— , *Experimentation in American Religion*. Berkeley: University of California Press, 1978. 221pp.

36. Zaretsky, Irving I., and Mark P. Leone, *Religious Movements in Contemporary America*. Princeton: Princeton University Press, 1974. 837pp.

II.
The Established Cults

A. CHURCH OF CHRIST, SCIENTIST (CHRISTIAN SCIENCE)

Because of its espousal of spiritual healing and its affirmation that Christian Science is incompatible with reliance upon materia medica, the Church of Christ, Scientist has been one of the most important of the nonconventional religions in America as well as a matter of intense controversy from the day of its founding.

The Founder

The Church of Christ, Scientist was founded by Mary Baker Eddy (1821–1919) who as a young woman had been continually hobbled with poor health. In 1862 she learned of Dr. Phineas Parkhurst Quimby, a mental healer in Portland, Maine. In October of that year she traveled to Portland and placed herself under his care. She soon experienced some relief of her symptoms which she ascribed to his efforts. She became his student and took the opportunity, when offered, to pass them on to others. While grateful for his help and generous with words of praise at the time of his death in 1866, she was disturbed by the periodic return of her illness and the conflicts of Quimby's ideas and those she found in the Bible.

Two weeks after Quimby's death, on February 1, 1866, she slipped on an icy pavement. Three days later while slowly and painfully recuperating, the Biblical Truth was imparted to her. Immediately her health was restored. That event marked the beginning of Christian Science. She quickly saw the conflict between the newly discovered Truth and some of Quimby's ideas and further study led her to abandon Quimby's mental and magnetic teachings altogether. She had realized that God was the only Life, and that Life was the only reality of being. There was no healing agent, as Quimby taught, either magnetic force or mind, only the unity with God in which there was no room for disease.

Within a few years she was ready to take students and began writing her first book, *The Science of Man*, and her major presentation of her teachings, *Science and Health with Key to the Scriptures*. Shortly before the first edition of *Science and Health* appeared, she was granted a letter of dismissal from the Congregational Church, in which she had been a member all of her adult life, and began the process of organizing those who were just beginning to follow her teachings.

In 1876 she formed the Christian Science Association, a fellowship of students in Massachusetts. Three years later she organized the Church of Christ, Scientist. In 1881 The Massachusetts Metaphysical College was chartered. That same year she was ordained as pastor for the Church. In 1883 the first issue of the *Journal of Christian Science* appeared, and in 1886 the National Christian Scientists Association was formed for non-Massachusetts residents.

No sooner had the movement been organized than Eddy began to doubt the soundness of the structures she had created. In 1889 she dissolved the church, the college and the Christian Science Association. The *Journal* was turned over to the National Christian Scientists Association. Only in 1892 was the church reorganized and the *Journal* reclaimed.

During this period of organizational flux, other students of Quimby, Julius and Annetta Dresser settled in Boston and began to teach mental healing following his system. They also began to attack Eddy for using Quimby's ideas while claiming them for her own. They accused her of distorting the teachings. The attack led to an often-bitter controversy between Christian Science and the New Thought movement which developed in the 1890s from the work of the Dressers and several of Eddy's former students. Eddy and her later followers have always claimed that what the Dressers saw as Quimby's highly distorted teachings were in fact Eddy's unique teachings discovered through her own study.

Eddy spent the majority of her life in perfecting the organization of the church and in clarifying and deepening her understanding of Christian Science. Her work manifested in large part through two books, *Science and Health with Key to the Scriptures* and the *Church Manual*. Each volume went through numerous editions, including several major revisions, during her lifetime. The texts were frozen at her death and remain as the authoritative documents for the Church. Also, after Eddy died, leadership in the Church passed to the five-person Board of Directors of the Mother Church in Boston, Massachusetts. They oversaw the production of standard editions of Eddy's writings, to this day the only ones used throughout the church.

Beliefs

A summary of the beliefs of Christian Science is found on page 497 of the Authorized Edition of *Science and Health with Key to the Scriptures*:

1. As adherents of Truth, we take the inspired Word of the Bible as our sufficient guide to eternal Life.
2. We acknowledge and adore one supreme and infinite God. We acknowledge His Son, one Christ; the Holy Ghost or divine Comforter; and man in God's image and likeness.

3. We acknowledge God's forgiveness of sin in the destruction of sin and the spiritual understanding that casts out evil as unreal. But the belief in sin is punished so long as the belief lasts.

4. We acknowledge Jesus' atonement as evidence of divine, efficacious love, unfolding man's unity with God through Christ Jesus the Way-shower; and we acknowledge that man is saved through Christ, through Truth, Life, and Love as demonstrated by the Galilean Prophet in healing the sick and overcoming sin and death.

5. We acknowledge that the crucifixion of Jesus and his resurrection served to uplift faith to understand eternal Life, even the allness of Soul, Spirit, and the nothingness of matter.

6. And we solemnly promise to watch, and pray for that Mind to be in us which was also in Christ Jesus; to do unto others as we would have them do unto us; and to be merciful, just and pure.

While Christian Science affirms its oneness with other Christians in that it worships the One God revealed in Jesus Christ, it departs from orthodox Christianity at several significant points. Christian Scientists believe in what they term the "allness of God" and hence the "unreality of disease, sin and death." Thus Christ does not defeat evil but demonstrates its lack of any reality beyond our belief in it.

Christian Science emphasizes the impersonal aspect of God as Principle, Mind, Life, Truth and Love, though the personal aspect of God as Father is acknowledged. It also distinguishes between the man Jesus and the eternal spiritual selfhood, Christ, Son of God, which has been expressed by men and women throughout the centuries. Humans are saved through the Christ, which was demonstrated in Jesus and has been seen in others.

Organization

Authority in the Church of Christ, Scientist is derived from the Bible; *Science and Health with Key to the Scriptures,* which sets forth its teachings and is the continuing voice of its founder; and the *Church Manual.* Authority is vested in the Mother Church and its Board of Directors. They have direct oversight of the Mother Church congregation, the various church agencies (especially the large publishing concern), and all teachers and practitioners.

Individual congregations are democratically organized and elect their own officers. There is no separate ministry in the Church and the congregation is led by the 1st Reader. All officers of the congregation must be members of the Mother Church and, thus, fall under the direct authority of the Board of Directors, who are responsible for the correctness and purity of teachings. Each congregation is also in charge of at least one reading room where Christian Science literature is made available to the public.

Healing Activity

Belief and practice in Christian Science come together most concretely in the Church's healing activity. The promise of physical healing has been the most attractive aspect of Christian Science, and the Church boasts of many cures of illnesses of all kinds. Healing is one of the natural by-products of growing closer to God.

The Church undergirds its healing program through its Department of Care of the Mother Church which accredits sanatoriums where Christian Science treatment is given. One of the sanatoriums offers a three-year nurses' training school where sanatorium staff are trained. The Church also trains and accredits practitioners, to whom members can turn for help with specific problems. A list of recognized practitioners is printed in the monthly *Christian Science Journal.*

Current Status

Headquarters of the Church of Christ, Scientist is located at the Christian Science Church Center, a complex in downtown Boston. This complex contains the Publishing Society which publishes and sells the authorized literature including the several periodicals: *The Christian Science Monitor,* a daily newspaper; *The Christian Science Journal,* a monthly magazine; the *Christian Science Sentinel,* a weekly magazine; *The Christian Science Quarterly;* and *The Herald of Christian Science,* which appears in a number of foreign languages.

The Board of Education teaches a class of thirty pupils every three years for the purpose of providing authorized teachers of Christian Science. A Board of Lectureship, made up of approximately forty members, provides free lectures on Christian Science worldwide. The Board of Publication deals with the public in correcting errors about Christian Science and the Church of Christ, Scientist and looks into charges of injustices done to Christian Scientists.

The Church does not give out membership statistics. In 1972 there were 3,237 branches or congregations, of which approximately 2,400 were in the United States. The membership and constituency was estimated at 475,000 at that time. During the two decades prior to 1972, there was an approximate 50% decrease in the number of practitioners. Between 1972 and 1982 the Church experienced an annual decline of from 1 to 2% and closed almost 200 congregations. Circulation of *The Christian Science Monitor* went from 218,886 in 1970 to 157,943 in 1981.

Controversy

The Church of Christ, Scientist, its founder, and her teachings were attacked from the moment they began to draw any attention and support. The initial attacks by the Dressers created a controversy which had lasted to the present day, especially as the New Thought Movement emerged. Critics of Christian Science have frequently adopted the New Thought perspective on the Church and see it as merely an extreme (and hence aberrant?) form of a Movement begun in the middle of the nineteenth century by Quimby. That perspective has spurred charges of plagiarism against Eddy and in one case the production of fraudulent documents by her enemies.

The New Thought Movement rightly dates its beginning from Quimby and his teachings, however, New Thought historians frequently overlook the point that until the 1880s, no movement existed. Quimby gathered only a few pupils, taught informally and never published his material. His students scattered and those that continued his work only began to gather a following in the 1880s. By that time Eddy had repudiated Quimby, published her own unique perspective to the health and religion questions with which each struggled, and had begun her own movement.

Finally, often overlooked is the role of Emma Curtis Hopkins. Hopkins, the teacher of the great New Thought leaders, from Ernest Holmes to Charles and Myrtle Fillmore, was herself an early pupil of Eddy and editor of the *Journal of Christian Science*. She remained closer to Eddy in her teaching than Quimby and helped make New Thought the uneasy synthesis of Eddy and Quimby which it is today. The tension between the two movements has (and will) continue as Christian Science repudiates the distorting mixture of Eddy's ideas with those of Quimby and hundreds of other teachers in New Thought. New Thought, which sees Eddy as a major source of their movement, will continue to bemoan Christian Science's single-minded allegiance to Eddy and *Science and Health with Key to the Scriptures*.

The major attacks on Christian Science have, however, come from outside the Church. At the time of the founding of the Church, spiritual healing was just beginning its revival. Its practice in Christian Science, as well as the other forms in Spiritualism and evangelical Christianity, received sharp criticism from a medical profession that was just consolidating its position as the normative authority in the treatment of illness in the United States. During the twentieth century, numerous court cases were fought over the rights of Christian Scientists to refrain from the use of doctors and the rights of Christian Science practitioners to care for the sick. An impressive body of legal decisions have given Christian Scientists a unique position in American life, including the right to deduct care received from a practitioner on their income tax as a legitimate medical expense.

The medical attack upon Christian Science has had inconclusive results. Critics cite many cases in which individuals, in some cases infants, have died in situations where proper medical care could have saved their lives. On the other hand, Church periodicals are filled with accounts of people, many unhelped by visits to doctors, who found health through Christian Science. Such testimonies remain the major appeal of the Church.

Almost as much as the medical controversy, charges of heresy from Orthodox Christian Churches have hounded the Church. Leaders of Christian Science insist that they are within the mainstream of Christian teachings and strongly resent any identification with the New Thought movement, which they see as having drifted far from their central Christian affirmations. At the same time, strong differences with traditional Christian teachings concerning the Trinity, the unique divinity of Jesus Christ, atonement for sin and the creation are undeniable. While using Christian language, *Science and Health with Key to the Scriptures* and Eddy's other writings radically redefine basic theological terms, usually by the process commonly called allegorization. Such redefinitions are most clearly evident in the glossary to *Science and Health* (pages 579–599). For example, the "Holy Ghost" is defined as "Divine Science; the development of eternal Life, Truth and Love."

While not as strongly organized or as large as the various groups which have come out of the Jehovah Witnesses, several groups of former Christian Scientists do exist and continue an active polemic against the Church. Some, such as the United Christian Scientists headquartered in San Jose, California, attack the Church for its undemocratic principles. One ex-practitioner, Joel Goldsmith developed a large following before his death in 1964, and his very loosely organized students continue to circulate his popular books and tapes.

Other ex-Scientists have become Evangelical Christians and have organized to oppose the Church from that position. Typical are New Beginnings (Ex-Christian Scientists for Jesus) of El Toro, California, and Christian Way of Lancaster, California.

Mary Baker Eddy, *Science and Health with Key to the Scriptures* (Boston: Trustees Under the Will of Mary Baker Eddy, 1906).

Mary Baker Eddy, *Manual of the Mother Church, First Church of Christ Scientist in Boston Massachusetts* (Boston: Trustees Under the Will of Mary Baker Eddy, 1908).

Mary Baker Eddy, *Prose Works Other Than Science and Health* (Boston: Trustees Under the Will of Mary Baker Eddy, 1925).

Norman Beasley, *The Cross and the Crown* (New York: Duell, Sloan and Pearce, 1952).

Norman Beasley, *The Continuing Spirit* (New York: Duell, Sloan and Pearce, 1956).

Charles S. Braden, *Christian Science Today* (Dallas: Southern Methodist University Press, 1958).

Stephen Gottschalk, *The Emergence of Christian Science in American Religious Life* (Berkeley: University of California Press, 1973).

Robert Peel, *Christian Science, Its Encounter with American Culture* (Garden City, NY: Doubleday, 1965).

Hugh A. Studdert Kennedy, *Mrs. Eddy* (San Francisco: Farallon Press, 1947).

Arthur Corey, *Behind the Scenes with the Metaphysicians* (Los Angeles: Devorss & Co., 1968).

B. THE CHURCH OF JESUS CHRIST OF LATTER DAY SAINTS (MORMON)

The most successful of the many groups which have been labeled "cult," the Church of Jesus Christ of Latter Day Saints has over two million members and dominates the religious life of the Rocky Mountain area from Boise, Idaho, to Phoenix, Arizona. Started in the early nineteenth century, it has grown steadily into a worldwide ecclesiastical body.

Founder and Early History

The Church of Jesus Christ of Latter Day Saints, popularly called the Mormons, was founded by Joseph Smith, Jr. (b. December 23, 1805, Sharon, Vermont). As a youth, Smith had moved from Vermont to western New York, near the town of Palmyra. Western New York was, during the early nineteenth century, one of the places in which the various Protestant churches fought vigorously over the allegiance of a largely unchurched population. Some of Smith's family joined the Presbyterians, but young Joe was partial to Methodism.

Undecided as to which group to join, Smith's problem was solved by a vision he had in 1820. God the Father and Jesus appeared to him and told him to join no church as they were all wrong. This vision was the first of a series that would lead to the founding of a new Church. In 1823 he was visited by the Angel Moroni who told him of some plates buried nearby upon which was written an account of the ancient inhabitants of North America. Buried with the plates were two stones with which Smith could translate the plates. Smith was informed of the exact location of the plates in 1827 and began the task of translating them. The translation was published in 1830 as the *Book of Mormon* (hence the popular designation of Smith's followers).

Meanwhile Smith, and an acquaintance, Oliver Cowdery, had a vision of John the Baptist who conferred upon them a restored Aaronic Priesthood which carried the authority to re-establish the true Church of Christ which had been lost and replaced by the numerous "sects." In a second vision Peter, James and John gave them the higher priesthood of the Apostles.

On April 6, 1830 Smith led a small group in the formation of the Church of Christ (a name soon changed to the Church of Jesus Christ of Latter Day Saints). Smith and Cowdery ordained each other as elders and, in turn, ordained others.

The new Church attracted a following almost immediately. In 1831 Smith moved the headquarters to Kirkland, Ohio, and the Church began construction of a Temple. Smith took control of the group as a prophet-revelator and guided the young group by his regular revelations that were gathered and published in a book—*The Doctrines and Covenants*. Unfortunately, soon after the Temple was completed, conditions necessitated a further move, and in 1838 Smith moved to Missouri. The stay was short as the governor ordered the Mormons from the state before the year was out.

In 1839 the Mormons established the community at Nauvoo, Illinois, which soon grew into the largest city in the state. A new Temple was begun, and the Church entered a growth phase. During this period the first of the European mission efforts (later a major source of members) was launched.

At Nauvoo Smith introduced the practice of polygamy and began by setting an example for the other Church leaders. The exact number of Smith's plural wives is still a matter of conjecture (estimates range from 27 to 84), but there is little doubt that polygamy caused immense problems for the Church and led to Smith's death and the destruction of the community. He lost the support of Sydney Rigdon, his prime counselor, who accused Smith of trying to seduce his daughter. Polygamy also led a group of disgruntled members to challenge Smith through an independent newspaper, *The Nauvoo Expositor*. Smith ordered the paper destroyed. The resulting controversy led to Smith's arrest and confinement in the jail at Carthage, the county seat of Hancock county. There, on June 27, 1844, a mob broke into the jail and murdered Smith and his brother, Hyrum.

The death of the Prophet threw the Church into confusion. Sydney Rigdon asserted his right to succession from his position in the First Presidency. However, the Council of the Twelve Apostles gave their support to Brigham Young, their senior member. He proved an outstanding leader and organizer and dominated the Church's life for the next thirty years.

Brigham Young (b. June 1, 1801) had joined the Church in Ohio and had become an original member of the Council of Twelve Apostles in 1835. He headed the first British Mission in 1840 and took his first plural wife shortly after his return in 1842. Within four years he had married seventeen more women.

Under Brigham Young's leadership the Mormons organized their forced exodus from Nauvoo and the migration to Utah in 1848. He was named governor of the proposed state of Deseret, a position that manifested his role as both temporal and spiritual leader of the Church and community established at Salt Lake City.

In 1852 Young announced the practice of plural marriage as public doctrine and began a battle with the United States government that was to last for the rest of the century. Young himself married nine more times. As the polygamy spread and became more openly practiced, public outrage increased. In 1862 the first federal anti-polygamy bill was passed, and efforts were increased to prevent its practice. These efforts were strengthened in 1882 with the passage of the Edmunds Bill, which disenfranchised all people living in polygamy, and the 5-member Utah Commission established to enforce the provisions.

The pressure on the Church and the disruption of secular life led Church President Wilford Woodruff to announce a reversal of Church policy toward plural marriage. Tension levels decreased greatly until 1900 when a polygamist was elected as a Congressman from Utah. He was denied his seat. In the face of renewed public hostility, the Church announced in 1904 that anyone who entered into plural marriage in the future would be excommunicated. During the twentieth century polygamy was eradicated from the Church of Jesus Christ of Latter Day Saints, but it continued to flourish in Mormon territory, especially in Mexico where it was not illegal. A large Fundamentalist (polygamy-practicing community) still exists in the Western United States and Northern Mexico (see Chapter 4).

Doctrine

The faith and life of the Church are based upon the revelations given Joseph Smith and the restored priesthood. Smith is claimed to have been given a set of gold plates written in "Reformed Egyptian" which he translated as the *Book of Mormon*, which has authority equivalent to that of the Bible for Mormons. They also accept the set of revelations received directly by Smith (and later Church Presidents) contained in the *Doctrines and Covenants*. Finally, they accept a third volume which Smith claimed to be a translation from the inscriptions on a mummy he once owned called the *Pearl of Great Price*.

Smith's authority to establish the Church came in the restored priesthood given to him and Oliver Cowdery. On two separate occasions, the two were elevated first to the Aaronic (lower) priesthood and then the Melchisedek (higher) priesthood, both believed to have been lost centuries before.

What the Church understands Smith to have revealed is summarized in their Articles of Faith:

1. We believe in God, the Eternal Father, and in His Son, Jesus Christ, and in the Holy Spirit.
2. We believe that men will be punished for their own sins, and not for Adam's transgression.
3. We believe that through the Atonement of Christ, all mankind may be saved, by obedience to the laws and ordinances of the Gospel.
4. We believe that the first principles and ordinances of the Gospel are: first, Faith in the Lord Jesus Christ; second, Repentance; third,

Baptism by immersion for the remission of sins; fourth, Laying on of hands for the gift of the Holy Ghost.

5. We believe that a man must be called of God, by prophecy, and by the laying on of hands, by those who are in authority to preach the Gospel and administer in the ordinances thereof.

6. We believe in the same organization that existed in the Primitive Church, viz. apostles, prophets, pastors, teachers, evangelists, etc.

7. We believe in the gifts of tongues, prophecy, revelation, visions, healing, interpretation of tongues, etc.

8. We believe the Bible (King James Version) to be the Word of God in so far as it is translated correctly; we also believe the Book of Mormon to be the word of God.

9. We believe all that God has revealed, all that he does now reveal, and we believe that He will yet reveal many great and important things pertaining to the Kingdom of God.

10. We believe in the literal gathering of Israel and in the restoration of the Ten Tribes; that Zion will be built upon this (the American) continent; that Christ will reign personally upon the earth; and that the earth will be renewed and receive its paradisiacal glory.

11. We claim the privilege of worshipping Almighty God according to the dictates of our own conscience, and allow all men the same privilege, let them worship how, where or what they may.

12. We believe in being subject to kings, presidents, rulers and magistrates, in obeying, honoring and sustaining the law.

13. We believe in being honest, true, chaste, benevolent, virtuous and in doing good to all men; indeed we may say that we follow the admonition of Paul—We believe all things, we hope all things, we have endured many things and have to be able to endure all things. If there is anything virtuous, lovely, or of good report or praiseworthy, we seek after those things.

Organization

The Church of Jesus Christ of Latter Day Saints is headed by the General Authorities, which consists of the First Presidency, the Council of Twelve Apostles, the First Quorum of Seventy, a Patriarch and the Presiding Bishopric. The First Presidency consists of three men, one of which is designated the President of the Church. It along with the Twelve Apostles and the Seventy (which is headed by the seven-member Presidency of the Seventy) administers the ecclesiastical affairs of the Church. The gift of prophecy is believed to reside in the President who may propound revelations binding upon the whole Church. The Presiding Bishopric administers the temporal affairs of the Church under the Patriarch and First Presidency.

The membership of the Church is organized into wards (congregations) of 300 to 800 members, and the wards are grouped into stakes which consist of 6 to 10 wards. The stake is headed by a President, two counselors and a High Council of twelve members. A Bishop and two counselors head a local ward.

Members of the Church are expected to refrain from the use of tea, coffee, tobacco, and alcohol and to tithe their income.

Of particular concern to the organization of the Church is temple worship. A Mormon temple is not a public house of worship but a space set aside for special services for members of the Church only. The main ceremony is sealing of a married couple for time and eternity, it being a Mormon belief that marriage and family life continue into life beyond death. Each place the Church settled in the nineteenth century they immediately began to construct a temple. In the twentieth century they have constructed a number of them around the world wherever they have strength.

Present Status

In 1980 the Church reported 2,632,000 members in 7,379 churches and 25,075 clergy. The line between laity and clergy is not as sharp as in some churches. All male members are expected to receive the Aaronic priesthood and most do. Most men who function in ministerial leadership positions do so on a parttime basis while earning their living at a fulltime job in the secular world.

In 1977 the worldwide Church was subdivided into eleven zones and further subdivided into 41 areas. In 1979 there were 965 stakes around the world.

Temples are located in Utah (6); Hawaii; Mesa, Arizona; Idaho Falls, Idaho; Los Angeles; Oakland; Seattle; and Washington, D.C. Outside the United States temples can be found in Alberta, Canada; Bern, Switzerland; New Zealand; London; Sao Paulo, Brazil; Tokyo; and Samoa.

Controversy

During the first generation of the Church it experienced much the same hostility which the new alternative religions were subjected to during and since the 1970s although the Mormons experienced much more violence. Joseph Smith was tarred and feathered by an angry mob in Ohio, jailed for no reason in Missouri, and murdered in Illinois. The communities in which the Mormons settled were offended by their curious beliefs, threatened by the political power they represented, and upset by the loss of family members to a new religion.

Once the Church moved to Utah, polygamy was openly practiced and became the major focus of tension with the larger society. The Church prospered only because of its distance from the major centers of population and power in the United States.

During the twentieth century, with the growth of evangelical Christians who were specialists in counter-cult polemics, Mormonism became one of several major "cults" to receive extensive attention. Numerous books, booklets, and tracts have been written to refute Mormon teachings and the authenticity of Mormon revelation.

As it is given particular attention in Mormon-antiMormon polemics, the integrity of the *Book of Mormon* has been questioned from the moment it appeared. Critics have noted its anachronisms, its verbatum quotations from the King James Bible, and the coincidence that a document proporting to be thousands of years old dealt directly with many of the issues hotly debated in western New York in the 1820s. There have been a variety of attempts to track down possible mundane sources for the *Book of Mormon*, none of them conclusive. The Church has just as stoutly defended the *Book* and supported archeological research throughout the Americas to find evidence of its truth.

During the 1970s controversy flared over the small volume called the *Pearl of Great Price*. The mummy from which Smith supposedly translated the text was thought to have been lost many years ago, however, it was rediscovered and claims were made that it was nothing but a common funerary mummy and that the inscriptions on it contained nothing related to the text Smith produced.

Other critics have questioned the Church's attitude toward blacks who have traditionally been denied the priesthood, the status and role of women, and the wealth amassed by the Church. Its very success and its strong influence in the several states in the Rocky Mountain region have given it the strength to deal with most of its critics with little effort, and individual Mormons provide a steady stream of polemic literature to answer anti-Mormon literature.

THE REORGANIZED CHURCH OF JESUS CHRIST OF LATTER DAY SAINTS

After the death of Joseph Smith in 1844, the Church he founded splintered into several groups each of which claimed to be the legitimate successor to Joseph Smith's Restorations. Of the several groups, over twenty-five of which currently exist, only one has attained a large membership. Unlike the other branches, the Reorganized Church of Jesus Christ of Latter Day Saints was formed by the coming together of a number of individuals and remnants of the Church who did not follow Brigham Young to Utah, rather than a group which formed around one leader who claimed to be Smith's successor though the story of the Reorganized Church begins with such a claimant.

The Formation of the Reorganized Church

The events leading up to the formation of the Reorganized Church began with Joseph Smith's brother, William. In May 1845, William was named Patriarch of the Church in place of Hyram Smith, who had been killed along with Joseph. William, who had had a stormy relationship with the Church, almost immediately began to claim the office of President by right of his relationship to Joseph. Eventually he was excommunicated and joined the Church of Jesus Christ (Strangite). James J. Strang welcomed William as his Patriarch, but the two argued when Strang invited Joseph Smith's son to share the post of Patriarch with William. William left Strang and in 1848 called the Church members to gather under his leadership at Palestine Grove, Illinois. In 1850 he called a conference at Covington, Kentucky to organize a Church, but by that time had significantly changed his stance. He named himself "President pro-tem," an act by which he for the first time, asserted that the real President should be Joseph Smith III. This was the first assertion that the right of succession to the Presidency was by lineal descent. Among William Smith's twelve apostles was Jason Briggs.

Jason Briggs had supported Brigham Young and the twelve apostles against the claims of Sydney Rigdon but in 1848 left Young and became a missionary for Strang in Wisconsin. He left Strang and joined William Smith. On November 18, 1851 he had a revelation that in due time God would call Joseph Smith Jr.'s son to lead His Church.

A similar experience was claimed by Zenos Gurney. A senior president of one of the ruling quorums of seventy at Nauvoo, he advocated Young's cause but then left to work for Strang. Gurney had a revelation which said, "The successor to Joseph Smith is Joseph Smith, the son of Joseph Smith the Prophet."

Briggs heard of Gurney and, upon meeting him, shared his revelation. The two decided to re-organize the work under their control and in 1853 formed the "New Organization."

The New Organization offered the presidency to Joseph Smith III but he refused the offer. However by 1859 he changed his mind and accepted it. At this same time William Marks, a onetime supporter of claimant Sydney Rigdon who had joined several of the different Mormon splinters, joined the New Organization.

At a meeting held April 6, 1860, the New Organization became the Reorganized Church of Jesus Christ of Latter Day Saints. There were about 300 members.

From the small beginning, the Reorganized Church grew as it gathered Mormons across the Midwest into membership. Much of Strang's Church was absorbed after Strang was murdered. Headquarters were established in Plano, Illinois. During the 1870s Decatur County, Iowa, on the Missouri border, became a site for gathering, and the town of Lamoni was founded. Headquarters were moved there in 1881.

The Reorganized Church also moved to obtain the property formerly owned by the Church as Temple sites. In 1880 the courts awarded the Reorganized Church the Temple lot in Kirkland. In 1891 the Church went to court to obtain the temple lot in Independence, Missouri, the site designated by Joseph Smith as the city of Zion. Though initially given the land, the Supreme Court returned it to the Church of Christ (Temple Lot), a small faction that had bought the property earlier.

Eventually, the Reorganized Church moved their headquarters to Independence and erected a large building, the Auditorium, across the street from the Temple Lot.

Doctrine

While following the teachings of Joseph Smith and basing its authority upon the revelations received by Joseph Smith and the priesthood he reinstituted, the Reorganized Church has taken pains to distinguish its beliefs from what it considers the innovations of the Utah branch of the Church. Its statement of faith affirms that the Church believes:

> In God the Eternal Father, Creator of the heavens and the earth.
>
> In the divine Sonship of Jesus Christ the Savior of all men who obey the gospel.
>
> In the Holy Ghost, whose function it is to guide all men unto salvation.
>
> In the gospel of Jesus Christ, which is the power of God unto salvation.
>
> In the six fundamental doctrinal principles of the gospel, named in the sixth chapter of Hebrews: (1) faith; (2) repentance; (3) baptism by immersion in water, and the baptism of the Holy Ghost; (4) the laying on of hands (for the healing of the sick, conferring of the Holy Ghost, ordination, and blessing of children); (5) the resurrection of the dead; (6) the eternal judgment.
>
> In the justice of God, who will reward or punish every man according to his works, and not solely according to his profession.
>
> In the kind of organization that existed in the primitive church: apostles, prophets, evangelists, pastors, teachers, elders, bishops, seventies, etc.
>
> In the word of God contained in the Bible, so far as it is correctly translated.
>
> In the willingness and ability of God to continue the revelation of his will to men until the end of time.
>
> In the powers and gifts of the gospel: faith, discernment of spirits, prophecy, revelation, healing, visions, tongues and their interpretation, wisdom, charity, temperance, brotherly love, etc.
>
> In marriage as instituted and ordained of God, whose law provides for but one companion in wedlock, for either man or woman, excepting in cases of death or when the marriage contract is broken by transgression.
>
> In the Book of Mormon declaration: "There shall not any man among you have save it be one wife; and concubines he shall have none."

The most obvious difference between the Reorganized Church and its larger cousin is in the former's denial of polygamy. The Reorganized

Church opposed polygamy from its beginning, and, in fact, the immediate occasion of its formation was due in no small part to Strang having introduced polygamy into his Church. The Reorganized Church holds the increasingly untenable historical position of denying that Joseph Smith ever taught polygamy.

The Reorganized Church has also opposed the "polytheistic" interpretation of Smith's teaching introduced into the Utah Church by Brigham Young. It holds strongly to a strict monotheism that approaches a traditional doctrine of the Trinity.

In practice, the Reorganized Church believes in a tithe, not of one's income but of one's increase, that is, a tenth of what you earn above and beyond that needed to feed, clothe, and house yourself.

Finally, the Reorganized Church recognizes the most obscure of Joseph Smith's writings, the *Inspired Version* of the Bible, a Bible with revisions given to Joseph Smith. (The Utah Church uses the King James Version of the Bible.)

Organization

The organization of the Reorganized Church follows the pattern laid down by Joseph Smith and followed by the Utah Church—First Presidency, Council of Twelve Apostles, Patriarchy, Presidency, Bishopric, stakes, and wards. It differs only in the perpetuation of the descendents of Joseph Smith, Jr., in the position of President. Joseph Smith III headed the Church until 1915 and was succeeded by Frederick M. Smith, his son. Having no sons, Frederick designated Israel Smith, his brother to the post. Upon Israel's death, since his oldest son had died and the other was disinterested in the post, Israel's half-brother W. Wallace Smith became President.

The power to receive revelation, of course, rests in the President of the Church and on occasion new revelations are received by the President and delivered to the Church. These revelations are printed in the *Doctrine and Covenants*. Thus, because of additional revelations since 1845, the editions of the book used by the Reorganized and Utah Churches differ in content. The Reorganized Church has, as have several other Latter Day schisms, produced their own edition of the Book of Mormon in which the verses are divided quite differently from the Utah edition. The Reorganized Church members also do not accept the designation "Mormon."

Present Status

The Reorganized Church reported 190,087 members, 1,056 congregations and 16,574 clergy in 1980. The Church is headquartered in Independence, Missouri. Graceland College at Lamoni, Iowa, is sponsored by the Church. Branches of the Church are found in 35 countries around the world.

The current President (1983) of the Church is Wallace B. Smith, great-grandson of Joseph Smith, Jr.

Mormons

Church of Jesus Christ of Latter-Day Saints Joseph Smith Jr., trans., *The Book of Mormon* (numerous editions).

Joseph Smith Jr., *The Doctrines and Covenants* (Salt Lake City: Church of Jesus Christ of Latter-Day Saints, 1949).

Le Grand Richards, *A Marvelous Work and a Wonder* (Salt Lake City: Deseret Book Company, 1968).

Gordon B. Hinckley, *Truth Restored* (Salt Lake City: Church of Jesus Christ of Latter Day Saints, 1947).

Reorganized Church of Jesus Christ of Latter-Day Saints

History of the Reorganized Church of Jesus Christ of Latter Day Saints (Independence, MO: Herald House, 1951).

Aleah G. Koury, *The Truth and the Evidence* (Independence, MO: Herald Publishing House, 1965).

Church Members' Manual (Independence, MO: Herald House, 1964).

Joseph F. Smith, Jr., and Richard C. Evans, *Blood Atonement and the Origin of Plural Marriage* (Salt Lake City: Deseret News Press, n.d.).

Fawn M. Brodie, *No Man Knows My History* (New York: Alfred A. Knopf, 1945).

Leonard J. Arrington and Davis Britton, *The Mormon Experience* (New York: Alfred A. Knopf, 1979).

Thomas O'Dea, *The Mormons* (Chicago: University of Chicago Press, 1957).

George Bartholemew Arbaugh, *Revelation in Mormonism* (Chicago: University of Chicago Press, 1932).

Jerald Tanner and Sandra Tanner, *Mormonism—Shadow or Reality?* (Salt Lake City: Modern Microfilm Company, 1972).

C. FUNDAMENTALIST OR POLYGAMY-PRACTICING MORMON GROUPS

In 1882 the United States government passed the Edmunds Law outlawing polygamy. Eight years later the Church of Jesus Christ of Latter Day Saints withdrew its support of polygamy and threatened excommunication to any who practiced it. In spite of the Church's stance, some Mormons continued in the practice. Many polygamists moved to Mexico because of the relative liberality of Mexican law.

Polygamy experienced a revival in the 1930s following the publication of the claims of Lorin C. Woolley. Woolley claimed that on the evening of September 27, 1886, John Taylor, President of the Church of Jesus Christ of Latter Day Saints, while staying at the Woolley home in Centerville, Utah, received a spirit visitation from Joseph Smith, Jr., the Church's founder. Smith's revelation concerned the continuance of plural marriage, and Taylor extracted a promise from all present that they would defend, sustain, and uphold the principle. The group covenanted together that no year would pass without children being born according to "the principle."

Later, according to Woolley, Taylor conferred the priesthood on five men, including Woolley and his father. At the time of the publication of the claim, all the men involved in the story except Lorin Woolley were dead. Only when he was the only one left, did Woolley assert any prerogatives based on Taylor's actions. He gathered followers and appointed a seven-member council to which he passed authority to govern the Church. Woolley died in 1934 and was succeeded by J. Leslie Broadbent. Broadbent lived only a short time before he was succeeded by John Y. Barlow.

Barlow began the polygamist colony at Short Creek on the Arizona-Utah border. An unsuccessful raid in 1935 failed to stamp out the colony, and by the 1940s it had reestablished communal living (the United Order) and reached a population of 36 men, 86 women, and 263 children. One member of the council, Joseph W. Musser, became the major defender of the polygamous tradition; he wrote several books and edited the group's periodical *Truth*.

Barlow's death in 1951 led to the first major split in the group. Joseph Musser succeeded Barlow; however, a paralytic stroke partially disabled him, causing many people to oppose his assuming an active leadership role. Opposition grew when he appointed Rulon C. Allred, his physician, and Mexican leader Margarito Bautista, to vacant positions on the council. Musser then disbanded the council and appointed a new one. He designated Allred as his successor. This action precipitated the schism.

United Order Effort

In 1936 the leaders of the Short Creek community formed the United Trust, a corporate expression of the united order which they intended to live. In 1951 those who rejected the continued leadership of Joseph Musser, a Salt Lake City resident, lived in Short Creek and remained in control of the United Trust. They selected LeRoy Johnson to lead them. He accepted only after a vision of Christ confirmed his new role. His visions have guided the community through the years, and in the over thirty years of his leadership the community has grown and prospered. The United Trust now owns most of Colorado City, Arizona (the recently renamed Short Creek) and nearby Hilldale, Utah. It also owns businesses in St. George, Utah, and other towns in southern Utah.

The United Order Effort is the most conservative wing of the Fundamentalist Movement. It allows sexual relations only for the purpose of procreation and prohibits sexual contact altogether during pregnancy, lactation (nursing) and menses. As of 1985 there are an estimated 3,000 members of the group residing in the Colorado City-Hilldale area, with several thousand other adherents who accept Johnson's leadership of the polygamy-practicing Mormons. Johnson, in his nineties, was reportedly in ill health, but no successor had been named.

Apostolic United Brethren

Approximately 1,000 Fundamentalists remained loyal to Musser and the new Council he appointed. He began a new periodical, the *Star of Truth*, which he edited until his death in 1954. After his death, Rulon Allred (1906-1977) reorganized his scattered following into the Apostolic United Order. Allred, the son of a former Speaker of the House in the State of Idaho, had joined the Fundamentalists in the 1930s. After his father's death in 1937, he moved to Salt Lake City and opened his practice of naturopathic medicine. His large suburban home became a regular gathering place of polygamists in the urban area.

Allred's real prominence in the Movement came after his arrest on March 7, 1944, during a massive anti-polygamy raid in Salt Lake City. He went to prison but was paroled on his word to refrain from either the practice or advocacy of plural marriage. In 1947 he violated his parole and fled to Mexico. He returned to Salt Lake City in 1948 but served only a few weeks for his parole violation.

After he took control of Musser's following, the Apostolic United Brethren prospered. It grew as did Allred's own family. His major losses came in Mexico, where Joel LeBaron left to form the Church of the First Born of the Fullness of Time in 1955.

The Apostolic United Order is the more liberal branch of the Fundamentalist Movement. It allows sexual relations apart from the strict purpose of procreation.

During the 1970s Allred became the target of his former follower Ervil LeBaron. Ervil, Joel's brother, had left the Church of the First Born and formed the Church of the Lamb of God. He claimed authority over all of the polygamous groups and the right to execute any who defied him. In 1972 he had Joel killed. On April 7, 1975, he sent a pamphlet, *A Response to an Act of War*, and a handwritten note to Allred. Allred ignored him. Then on May 10, 1977, two female members of the Church of the Lamb of God murdered Allred in his office in Murray, Utah. The women and LeBaron were eventually tried and convicted. LeBaron died in prison.

Allred was succeeded by his brother Owen Allred. The Apostolic United Order has approximately 5,000 members, many of whom live in the community at Pineville, Montana, and the several Mexican colonies.

The Church of Jesus Christ in Solemn Assembly

The Church of Jesus Christ in Solemn Assembly was formed by Alexander Joseph in 1974 after he left the Apostolic United Brethren in which he had been a prominent leader. Joseph has actively pressed the rights of polygamists in general and his Church in particular. Shortly after founding the Church, he attempted to homestead federal land but was denied access by court order. He moved to Glen Canyon, Kane county, Utah, and established a new town incorporated as Big Water, the current location of the Church's headquarters. Joseph became the first mayor of the town in 1983.

Joseph had 10 wives in 1983. He is the author of one book, *Dry Bones, A Resurrection of Ancient Understandings*, a commentary on *The Pearl of Great Price*, one of the Latter Day Saint scriptures.

THE CHURCH OF THE FIRST BORN OF THE FULLNESS OF TIMES

The Church of the First Born is the most successful of several churches founded by the sons of Alma Dayer LeBaron, a polygamy-practicing Mormon who lived at Colonia Juarez, a Mexican Mormon settlement where many went to escape anti-polygamy laws in the United States. His children, Benjamin, Ross Wesley, Joel, Ervil, and Alma, each became founders of a new Church.

First, in 1944 Benjamin declared himself a prophet. Several of the brother's supported his claim, most notably Ervil, but most of the family quickly recognized that his claims were mixed with some mental pathology. Few followed him and he spent much of his life in and out of mental institutions.

Next Ross Wesley proclaimed himself a prophet, specifically the "One Mighty and Strong" who would put the House of God in order as prophecied by Joseph Smith in the *Doctrine and Covenants* 85:7, and the heir to his father's patriarchal authority which the LeBarons believed had been passed through the family from Benjamin F. Johnson, A. D. LeBaron's grandfather. Ross Wesley still has a small following in Utah.

It was in the context of membership in a family within which two brothers had already claimed prophethood that Joel became the third. According to his account, in 1955 he was visited by two heavenly messengers and told that he was the "One Mighty and Strong." He incorporated the Church of the First Born of the Fullness of Times in September of that year in Salt Lake City and the next spring formally organized the new body. He appointed his brother Ervil secretary and head of the Mexican Mission.

Prior to the formation of the new Church, Joel was a member of the Apostolic United Brethren headed by Rulon C. Allred. He invited Allred to join his group, but Allred refused.

Joel propounded two unorthodox teachings. First, like his brother Wesley, he claimed a lineage of priesthood (and the office of First Grand Head) through his family from Benjamin F. Johnson to himself rather than through Lorin Woolley and Joseph Musser. He also believed that an hereditary patriarchal office existed and was held by Margarito Bautista, a Mexican leader also with Allred's group. When Bautista died, Joel appointed his brother Ervil to that post. Second, Joel taught that the law, i.e., the Ten Commandments, were the basis of political life and only when the Commandments were kept would Christ return to earth.

During the 1960s trouble developed between Joel and Ervil. Joel was attempting to develop a group that practiced the Ten Commandments. Ervil came to believe that this new order should be established by force. This disagreement and other problems led Joel to excommunicate Ervil in 1971. Ervil asserted his right to lead because of his patriarchal office and founded the Church of the Lamb of God. The next few years became ones of bitter strife as Ervil attempted to force his will upon the polygamy-practicing groups in both Mexico and the United States.

On August 20, 1972, on orders from Ervil, some members of his Church shot and killed Joel. Joel's brother Verlan succeeded him as head of the Church of the First Born.

Ervil was arrested and tried for killing Joel, but served only 12 months of a 12-year sentence. A few days after he was released, on December 14, 1973, his followers attacked and burned Los Molinos, a town in Baja California where many members of the Church of the First Born resided. Two were killed. Again Ervil was tried and convicted but served only eight months. Then on May 10, 1977, several members of Ervil's Church murdered Rulon C. Allred in his office in Salt Lake City. After a lengthy and extensive manhunt, Ervil was arrested in 1979. On May 28, 1980 he was sentenced to life imprisonment. On August 16, 1981, he was found dead in his prison cell, apparently of natural causes. On that same day, Verlan LeBaron, who had succeeded Joel as head of the Church of the First Born, was killed in an automobile accident in Mexico City.

In the midst of the troubles, Alma LeBaron, the presiding bishop of the Church of the First Born, asserted his authority to control the economic affairs of the Church in ways that were disapproved by the majority of members. Alma left and founded his own Church which he now heads.

Of the several Churches to grow out of the LeBaron family, three, the Church of the First Born of the Fullness of Times and the small bodies headed by Ross Wesley and Alma, seem to still be in existence. The Church of the Lamb of God disintegrated after Ervil's death.

Other Polygamy-Practicing Groups

Besides the several larger and more well-known groups discussed here, numerous small independent polygamy-practicing churches exist throughout the Rocky Mountain area from Montana and Idaho to Mexico. Most are confined to a single community (frequently communal in structure). Some have a lineage that can be traced to Lorin Woolley, but others have established their authority on divergent bases.

Controversy

Polygamy has produced numerous defenders and critics on both the theoretical and practical level since its widespread practice was advocated by Brigham Young in the mid-nineteenth century. Critics charge practitioners with degrading and even enslaving women. Mormons, however, claim polygamy is the answer to prostitution and lascivious behavior and provides a family context for all.

Since the rise of Fundamentalism, the Church of Jesus Christ of Latter Day Saints has been at pains to refute the claims of Lorin C. Woolley. Most recently, J. Max Anderson has examined the Fundamentalist story and found it impossible, as the journals and other records of the movement of President Taylor and those who claimed to have been present in Centerville in 1886 show conclusively that they could not have assembled at the same place on the day in question. Anderson's research adds substance to the long-standing criticism of Woolley, namely, that no account of the Taylor revelation appears until twenty-four years after the event and no published account for almost a half century.

Rulon C. Allred, *Treasures of Knowledge* (Hamilton, MT: Bitteroot Publishing Company, 1981, 2 Vols).

———, *The Most Holy Principle* (Murray, UT: Gems Publishing Company, 1970–75, 4 Vols.).

Joseph W. Musser, *Celestial or Plural Marriage* (Salt Lake City: Truth Publishing Company, 1944).

Robert R. Openshaw, *The Notes* (Pinesdale, MT: Bitteroot Publishing Company, 1980).

Stephen M. Silver, "Priesthood or Presidency," *Ensign* 2, 11 (January 1963) 1–127.

J. Max Anderson, *The Polygamy Story: Fact or Fiction* (Salt Lake City: Publishers Press, 1979).

Ben Bradlee, Jr., and Dale Van Atta, *Prophet of Blood* (New York: G. P. Putnam's Sons, 1981).

Lawrence Foster, *Religion and Sexuality* (Urbana: University of Illinois Press, 1984).

Henry W. Richards, *A Reply to "The Church of the Firstborn of the Fullness of Times"* (Salt Lake City: The Author, 1965).

Kimball Young, *Isn't One Wife Enough* (New York: Henry Holt and Company, 1954).

D. THE "I AM" RELIGIOUS ACTIVITY

The Great White Brotherhood is the name given in metaphysical/occult circles to those adepts of wisdom who have finished their earthly pilgrimages (the cycles of reincarnation and karma) and, while ascending to a higher state of existence as masters of space, time and material existence, have assumed responsibility for the cosmic destiny of the human race, both individually and collectively. Most occult groups assign a high level of importance to the Brotherhood, but some make interaction with the Ascended Masters of the Brotherhood a major focus of their existence. Of these several, two stand out as most prominent: the "I AM" Religious Activity, the original Ascended Masters group founded in the 1930s, treated below, and the Church Universal and Triumphant, founded in the 1960s, a discussion of which can be found elsewhere in this volume. The two organizations, though frequently confused in the public media, were never connected and vary widely in their teachings.

Founders

Guy W. Ballard (1878–1939), leader of the "I AM" Ascended Master Religious Activity and co-founder with his wife Edna of the Saint Germain Foundation (its corporate expression), was born in Kansas. He married Edna Wheeler (1886–1971) in 1916 and three years later their son Donald was born. After a period in the Army during World War I, he superintended his uncle's lead mine in Tucson, Arizona. Edna was an accomplished concert harpist, and like her husband, had a deep interest in metaphysics and the occult.

1930 became the turning point in the Ballards' lives. Guy Ballard, widely read in theosophical/occult literature, had heard the reports of strange occult events that had been said to occur at Mt. Shasta, a giant volcanic cone in northern California. He developed a desire to visit the mountain to investigate the rumor that a group of Divine Men called the Brotherhood of Mt. Shasta were to be found there.

One day in 1930, while hiking around the mountain he encountered another hiker, "Directly behind me stood a young man, who, at first glance, seemed to be someone on a hike like myself." The man turned out to be the Ascended Master Saint Germain. The Comte de Saint Germain was one of the most famous occultists of modern time. He had lived in eighteenth-century France, had claimed to be several centuries old, and possessed a great reputation as a mystic, alchemist and generally mysterious figure. At the time of their meeting, Ballard, thirsty from his hike, had been looking for a spring. Saint Germain offered a more refreshing drink, a creamy liquid, which had an astonishing vivifying effect upon him. Saint Germain identified the liquid as a substance coming from the Universal Supply. Over a period of time, he introduced Ballard to the astonishing powers of the Ascended Masters and led him into a number of experiences which prepared him to assume his new role as the Messenger of the Masters.

According to Ballard, Saint Germain had ascended to become a member of the Divine Spiritual Hierarchy which rules the life of the universe, and had been assigned the task of initiating the Seventh Golden Age, the permanent "I AM" Age of eternal perfection on this earth. He had searched Europe for several centuries to find someone in human embodiment through whom he could release the instructions of the Great Law of Life. Not finding anyone, he began a search in America, where he encountered Ballard. He subsequently designated Ballard, his wife Edna, and their son Donald as the only Accredited Messengers of the Ascended Masters.

As the initial experiences with Saint Germain and the other ascended beings were occurring, Ballard wrote lengthy letters to his wife in Chicago introducing her to the events. He returned to Chicago in 1931 to initiate Saint Germain's instructions. In 1932 Ballard began to release the message of Saint Germain and to bring forth the visible manifestation of the "I AM" Religious Activity. Together with his wife, he founded the Saint Germain Press and Saint Germain Foundation. Two years later, under the pen name Godfre Ray King, he published his first book, *Unveiled Mysteries* (1934), an account of the encounter with Saint Germain, quickly followed by its sequel, *The Magic Presence* (1935). He also held the first ten-day class in Philadelphia. The class was repeated in Chicago, New York, Washington, D.C., Florida and Los Angeles. To assist in the work, the Ballards designated a group of "appointed messengers" from among their most capable students. These messengers gave classes and toured the country speaking at various sanctuaries.

Through the 1930s, the other publications which were to become the major literary expressions of the Activity were released: *"I AM" Adorations and Affirmations* (1935), which gave the texts for the decrees, the affirmations and invocations regularly repeated by students of the I AM; and *"I AM" Discourses* (1936), a series of lectures by Saint Germain which contain the tenets of the Activity (1935). The Saint Germain Press also issued *"I AM" Songs* (1938), a hymnal, while Mrs. Ballard had already launched the Foundation's magazine, *The Voice of the "I AM"* (1936).

The success in Los Angeles led the Ballards to move there and establish a second headquarters. They also encouraged students to establish "I AM" sanctuaries and reading rooms to help strengthen the movement around the country. They promoted the idea of "I AM" schools, and the first one was established in Tenafly, New Jersey. Another was opened in Los Angeles. The movement grew in the face of public recognition of its unorthodox beliefs and practices and at one point claimed over a million students.

In 1939, because of attacks by the media and the appearance of hecklers in the midst of the classes and in order to keep a serene atmosphere in the classes (which had been attended by some 7,000 people in Los Angeles), Ballard discontinued the open classes. It became necessary for sincere followers to obtain a special card of admission. He continued regularly to instruct those who had become students of the teachings until his death in December 1939.

Shortly before Ballard's death, several former members of the movement became vocal critics of the Ballards. One former student, Gerald B. Bryan, wrote a series of booklets and one book, *Psychic Dictatorship in America*, attacking Guy Ballard's integrity and accusing him of plagiarizing much of the religion from old occult books. Other students initiated lawsuits against the Foundation. These suits in turn led to a criminal indictment of Edna and Donald Ballard, along with several staff members. They were charged with mail fraud, i.e., "for using the mails to operate a religion they knew to be false in order to obtain the money of their students." Overwhelmingly the student body supported the Ballards and the Foundation.

When the case finally came to trial in 1942, the Ballards were convicted. Subsequently, the Post Office Department denied the Foundation and Press use of the mails. The convictions were reviewed for the first time by the Supreme Court in 1944, and the Court ruled, in one of its most quoted opinions, that members of a new religion could not be held accountable before a judge and/or jury for the sufficiency of their faith as a grounds for continuing to propagate it. However, a lower court again upheld the conviction which was reviewed and reversed a second time by the Supreme Court in 1946.

The criminal charges behind it, the "I AM" turned to the correlative actions against the Foundation. Another eight years of legal action was required before the Post Office removed its ban on the Foundation's use of the mails in 1954. Up to that time, it had been forced to distribute literature by American Express. Finally, in 1957, the Foundation's tax-exempt status was granted.

In 1941, as legal actions proceeded, Edna Ballard moved from the hostile atmosphere in Los Angeles and established her headquarters in Santa Fe, New Mexico (though the official headquarters always remained in Chicago). A branch of the Saint Germain Press, which had just been established in Denver that same year, also moved to Santa Fe, as did the school previously opened in Los Angeles. It offered classes for elementary and high school grades. She further expanded the youth program by initiating the youth conclaves in 1943.

The rebuilding of the movement could begin in earnest, after the final dismissal of the various charges. It was done with little public fanfare. In

1948 national conclaves of the membership were resumed, and that same year a twelve-story building was purchased in Chicago's Loop to serve both the large concentration of followers there and to be a national teaching center. In 1951, a resort center, the famous Shasta Springs Water Co., was purchased, and Mt. Shasta became the scene of two annual national conclaves for both youth and senior students. The Youth Conclave featured a pageant of the life of Christ, "I AM Come!," one of the few Activity events open to the public.

Throughout the 1950s Edna Ballard expanded the Teachings, The Saint Germain Series (the basic textbooks of the Activity which currently numbers eleven volumes). She also recorded over two thousand dictations from the Ascended Masters. Her son Donald had resigned in 1957 as vice-president of the Foundation and withdrew from the "I AM" Activity. He managed his own manufacturing business but continued to handle most of the recording activity for the Foundation and Press. By the mid-1960s she was heard on twenty-five radio stations. After her death in 1971, the movement's leadership passed to the Board of Directors, which had been established in 1932 and had previously served under the Ballard's guidance.

Beliefs and Practices

Though the spiritual hierarchy, that group of beings who constitute the spiritual cosmos and are popularly called the Great White Brotherhood, have been referred to in occult texts for generations, the contact begun with the Ascended Masters through Guy Ballard led to the releasing of what the "I AM" Religious Activity believed to be a three-fold Truth not previously known outside of the Masters secret retreat centers: This Truth includes the (1) knowledge of the Individualized Presence of God which is known as the "Mighty I Am Presence," God in Action; (2) the use of the Violet Consuming Flame of Divine Love; and (3) the Ascended Masters' use of God's Creative Name, "I AM."

The Activity affirms the reality of One God who is omnipresent, omniscient, and omnipotent and who rules all creation. As the Life of the Universe, God permeates all things and is individualized for dynamic action. From the "I AM" perspective, light is the dominant form taken by divine realities. At the heart of our universe the Great Central Sun, the source of the God's power and authority, emanates forth as the "Mighty I AM Presence." As that Presence goes forth and is individualized, creation is brought into existence. Each individual begins as a spark from the divine flame. The "I Am Presence" is the light in the electron and the cells of the body; it is the light in the mind and heart. However, the misuse of the divine energy over the centuries has resulted in the present condition of humanity, manifest in discord, hate, impurities and death which hide the perfection, harmony, love, purity and life which is God and His "I Am Presence."

As the individualized "I AM Presence," God is the Master within each person, the Christ Self. God is also individualized within each of the members of the hierarchy who govern the cosmos, this planet and solar system. Members of the hierarchy are known as the Ascended Masters of Love, Light and Perfection. They are the guardians of humanity and have worked through the centuries from the invisible, as well as the physical, to awaken, bless, enlighten, and lift humankind out of the self-created situation in which it now finds itself. Once like other humans, they have, through a series of reembodiments, overcome the present condition and by atuning themselves to the I Am Presence, ascended into the light. To follow their path is the goal of each person. One of the Ascended Masters is the Master Jesus. Through His ministry and ascension, He released the Christ Light, the "Mighty I AM Presence," to give the earth the forward movement out of darkness and hate into the Light of Divine Love. A picture of the Master Jesus adorns the platform of every I Am sanctuary, next to that of Saint Germain. The emphasis placed upon his work and teaching by the Activity leads the members to affirm themselves as members of a Christian religion.

The Activity also teaches that each Ascended Master radiates a certain color, an aspect of the divine light representative of a specific divine quality. "Clean, clear, bright colors," said Mrs. Ballard, "are rivers of blessing from the realms of light, the source of all perfection." However, members generally refrain from wearing red or black or having objects of these colors in their immediate environment. Black is indicative of hate, death and destruction. Red is associated with anger, irritation and impurity. When impurity is removed from red, for example, it will be transformed instantly into gold.

Within the "I AM" Activity, contact with the Ascended Masters and cooperation with their work is a central goal of each individual's life. Through their Authorized Messengers, the Ballards, the Ascended Masters regularly communicated with the "I AM" membership. Those communications were delivered before gatherings of members, published in the monthly periodical, and the more prominent ones collected and reprinted in the textbooks. (In all, over 3,000 dictations from the Masters were received during the Ballards' lifetime.) In these dictations the Masters presented a total program of guidance for both individual development and effective action in the world.

Each person in his fullness is pictured in the chart of the "Mighty I Am Presence" which also is to be found on the platform of "I AM" sanctuaries. The individual is shown possessing a "Mighty I AM Presence," a higher self, which is the focus of the Light and Power of God within the self. The "I AM" is the designation of God's creative Word or power in action in everyone. It is pictured as a being of light surrounded by a rainbow of lights, above each person and connected to each conscious self by a thread of luminosity. The purpose of the I AM Activity is to release the I AM power within and to make it available for the student to use, in cooperation with the Ascended Masters, in the elimination of evil and the advent of freedom and justice in the world.

Each person is also shown surrounded by a violet flame, a cylinder of light created by the "I AM Presence." It is released to function whenever the individual calls forth his/her "I AM Presence" to consume discord and impurity in the world.

The most definitive activities for "I AM" members, by which they seek to attune themselves to their "I AM Presence," and thus align themselves to the path of the Ascended Masters, are (1) quiet contemplation and (2) the repetition of affirmations and decrees. Affirmations are sentences that affirm the individual's attunement to God and the blessing due to the person as a result of that attunement. A decree is a fiat spoken from the standpoint of the higher self, the "Mighty I Am Presence," and may be, depending upon the occasion, peaceful, calming or powerful in content and/or enunciation. The repetition of decrees is devotional activity, and all decrees are given in the Name of God, the "Beloved Mighty I AM Presence" and in the Name of the Ascended Master Jesus the Christ. Decrees are repeated daily for the release of the violent Consuming Flame and the dissipation of discord in the individual's environment. One typical decree, repeated in a strong commanding voice, might be:

> In the Name of God, the "Beloved Mighty I AM Presence," and in the Name of the Beloved Ascended Jesus Christ, I Am the Strength, the Courage, the Power to move forward steadily through all experiences, whatever they may be, by the glorious Presence with "I AM" "I AM" the Commanding Presence, the Exhaustless Energy, the Divine Wisdom, causing every desire to be fulfilled. The "Presence which I AM!" remains untouched by disturbing outer conditions. Serene, I fold my wings and abide in the Perfect Action of the Divine Law and Justice of my Being, commanding all things within my radiance to appear in Perfect Divine Order!.

Students are taught basic decrees from the beginning of their work in the movement, and booklets of decrees for every occasion have been published.

Freedom was a persistent theme in the teaching of the Ascended Masters, who assigned America a special role in the unfolding Plan for the coming Golden Age. As a result, the Activity and its members have become known for their patriotism and love of country. American flags are prominently displayed at all "I AM" centers, and patriotic literature is integral to all their teaching activity.

Current Status

After the death of Edna Ballard, the governance of the Saint Germain Foundation and the Saint Germain Press and the supervision of the "I AM" Activity passed to a five-member Board of Directors. That board was expanded to eighteen members in 1982. The Foundation charters the local sanctuaries, which are otherwise autonomous centers of the Activity. It oversees the work of Appointed Messengers of Saint Germain who teach the introductory classes, which are open to the public, and other classes for "I AM" Activity students, as well as the several regional counselors, field workers, and local councils. The radio programs begun by Edna Ballard have been continued and may be heard weekly across the United States.

In 1978 the headquarters of the Foundation was moved into a new Worldwide Headquarters in Schaumburg, Illinois. The Saint Germain Press moved into the new facilities in 1982, and the property in Santa Fe was sold. The Press publishes the Saint Germain Series, the eleven text-books of the Activity, and the monthly periodical, *The Voice of the "I AM."*

In 1984 there were over 300 "I AM" centers in over twenty-five coun-tries. One school owned and operated by the students of the Activity is located in Denver, Colorado.

New students in the Activity begin by reading the first three books of the Saint Germain Series and studying two series of Fundamental Lessons. After completion of these materials, the student may receive an admit-tance card to an Introductory Class, which is offered periodically in Chicago. The Saint Germain Foundation emphasizes that it does not charge for the Teaching or the classes. Students frequently make gifts to assist and support the work of the Foundation or a local sanctuary, but no charge is ever made for instruction.

Controversy

Soon after its establishment as a national movement, the "I AM" Activity came under attack. The first significant critic was Gerald Bryan, author of *Psychic Dictatorship in America* (1940). However, as soon as the Movement began to show signs of success, newspapers took a critical approach to what many saw as its very unusual teachings and frequently ridiculed the movement and its leaders. During the string of legal actions and especially the several trials during the 1940s, the sensational and hostile reporting drove many from the movement and drove the move-ment itself away from the public eye. Over the years, the leaders refrained from discussions with reporters and others who attempted to gather information about them. As a result little was written about the Activity after the lengthy chapter in *These Also Believe*, the 1949 survey of Amer-ica's alternative religions by Northwestern University professor Charles Braden.

Thus while the movement has slowly rebuilt itself into a significantly large religious organization, it has been almost totally unnoticed, and frequently reported as nonexistent. (The Foundation has a policy against advertising and promotion of itself and the Activity.)

During the decade, some recognition of the I AM Activity has come because other organizations that have derived some of its teachings and symbolism from the "I AM" Activity have received widespread media attention. One such group, the Church Universal and Triumphant, has emerged as a prominent and controversial organization. In the face of this variety of groups whose teachings resemble those of the "I AM" Activity, the Saint Germain Foundation has attempted to hold to the teachings of the Ascended Masters exactly as originally delivered by those whom they believe to be their only Accredited Messengers, the Ballards, unmixed with the teachings of other religious traditions or other Messengers.

Godfre Ray King (pen name of Guy W. Ballard), *Unveiled Mysteries* (Chicago: Saint Germain Press, 1934).

Godfre Ray King, *The Magic Presence* (Chicago: Saint Germaine Press, 1935).

Ascended Master Saint Germain, *The "I AM" Discourses* (Chicago: Saint Germain Press, 1936).

The Great Cosmic Beings, *Ascended Master Light* (Chicago: Saint Germain Press, 1938).

Ascended Master Saint Germain, *The "I AM" Discourses* (Schaumburg, IL: Saint Germain Press, 1984).

Charles S. Braden, *These Also Believe* (New York: Macmillan, 1949).

Gerald B. Bryan, *Psychic Dictatorship in America* (Los Angeles: Truth Research Foundation, 1940).

David W. Stupple, *A Functional Approach to Social Movements with an Analysis of the I AM Religious Sect and the Congress of Racial Equality* (Kansas City, MO: University of Missouri, MA thesis, 1965).

E. THE IDENTITY MOVEMENT

What has come to be known as the Identity Movement was previously termed Anglo-Israelism or British-Israelism. It is composed of those individuals and groups who identify the present day Anglo-Saxon people as the direct biological descendants of the ancient Israelites and, as such God's chosen people, the heirs of all God's promises to Abraham and his progeny. The ten lost tribes of Israel, the former northern kingdom, are sharply distinguished from Judah, the ancient southern kingdom centered upon Jerusalem, which consisted of the tribes of Judah and Benjamin and some Levites. In like measure, modern Anglo-Saxons (Israelites) are to be sharply distinguished from the Jews (Judah).

Origin and History

The Anglo-Israelite hypothesis originated with Richard Brothers (1757–1824), a Canadian-born visionary. His self-proclaimed right, as a descendant of King David, to the throne of England led to his commitment to an asylum. Dismissed as mentally deranged, Brothers found no support for his ideas before his death. They did not receive serious attention until 1840 when John Wilson published his restatement of them in *Our Israelitish Origin*. Throughout the rest of the nineteenth century, supporters of Wilson's presentation emerged in bible student circles. In England, Piazzi Smith, famous for his study of the Great Pyramid, became a believer. In America, M. M. Eshelman, author of *Two Sticks or the Lost Tribes of Israel Discovered* (1887) and a prominent minister in the Church of the Brethren, became an early exponent. He was soon joined by Canadian minister W. H. Poole, author of *Anglo-Israel or the Saxon Race Proved to be the Lost Tribes of the Bible* (1889). Both of these early authors were eclipsed by J. H. Allen, whose *Judah's Sceptre and Joseph's Birthright* (1902) became the single most important instrument in spreading Anglo-Israel thought into Adventist and independent bible student circles. Through the efforts of Merritt Dickinson, who had read and accepted the arguments in Allen, Anglo-Israel thought entered the Church of God (Seventh Day). Herbert W. Armstrong, a minister in the group, as leader of the Worldwide

Church of God, subsequently became the single most successful exponent of Anglo-Israelism.

In spite of the efforts of the early teachers, and the founding of both British and Canadian Anglo-Israelite organizations, the message did not find a large audience until the 1920s when Howard B. Rand began a small bible study group in Haverhill, Massachusetts. He began a periodical, and in 1930 organized a national convention of Identity people to be held in Detroit. At the convention he met W. J. Cameron, formerly the editor of the *Dearborn* (MI) *Independent* in which Henry Ford had originally published his infamous series of articles on "The International Jew." Cameron became president of Rand's Anglo-Saxon Federation of America. Assisted by public relations executive Clarence S. Warner, the Federation promoted the formation of Anglo-Israelite groups across the United States. Some of these groups matured into large independent congregations, which, in turn, became publishing centers for the movement.

In identifying the Anglo-Saxon people as the modern descendants of ancient Israel (as distinguished from ancient Judah) and in concentrating attention upon the promises of God to Israel, His chosen people, the Movement was inherently racist. However, while using their ideas to support Britain's colonial empire and America's manifest destiny during their first decade, American believers did not crusade against those whom God had not chosen, particularly blacks and Jews. Inevitably, as the movement gained national support, some supporters of the revived Ku Klux Klan and various neo-Nazi movements found Anglo-Israelism a very acceptable ideological system. By the beginning of World War II, most leaders of the Anglo-Israelite Movement were giving open support to racial propaganda.

Rand's Anglo-Saxon Federation of America, which had dominated the Movement, was joined after World War II by a score of new centers of activity. A new generation of leaders also emerged. Most prominent of the Anglo-Israelite leaders who gave great prominence to racial themes, was Gerald L. K. Smith. In 1947 he launched the Christian Nationalist Crusade, and its periodical, *The Cross and the Flag*, became one of the most violent anti-black and anti-Jewish publications in the United States. Smith campaigned for the deportation of Zionists, abolition of all "Jewish Gestapo organizations," shipping of all black people back to Africa, and liquidation of the United Nations.

A survey of the movement made in the early 1950s appeared in Ralph Lord Roy's *Apostles of Discord*. Roy discovered centers in every part of the United States. Among the most important were the Beacon Light Ministry headed by William Kullgren of Atascadero, California; the Prophetic Herald Ministry headquartered at Bethel Temple in Spokane, Washington, pastored by William Schiffner; Destiny of America Foundation headed by Conrad Gaard of Tacoma, Washington; the United Israel World Fellowship headed by James A. Lovell of Fort Worth, Texas; and the Anglo-Saxon Christian Association headed by H. M. Greene and Hugh C. Krum of Portland, Oregon. For a few years in the late 1940s, the movement sponsored the Dayton Theological Seminary in Ohio.

Beliefs

Members of the Identity Movement do not consider themselves a new sect or denomination, rather they believe themselves to be a group of orthodox Christians who accept the Bible as the inspired and hence literally true Word of God. While affirming their belief in God, Jesus Christ and the Holy Spirit, they generally stop short of belief in the Trinity. Their belief in the literal truth of the Bible is manifested by a firm belief in the biblical account of creation as described in Genesis, the virgin birth of Jesus, the personal return of Jesus to earth, and the final battle to be fought between the Israel of God and the enemies of Jesus. Following the tradition of free church Protestantism, two ordinances, baptism (by immersion) and communion, are practiced.

Some Identity groups have also adopted both sabbatarianism and sacred name emphases from Adventism. Joe Jeffers, head of the Kingdom of Yahweh, was possibly the first person to combine a belief in the British Israel hypothesis with the keeping of the sabbath on Saturday and the use of transliterations of the Hebrew names of the Creator and His Son (Yahweh and Yahshua) in place of God and Jesus.

The movement is most at variance with the larger body of Christians by its belief that, as Identity pastor Sheldon Emry asserts, ". . . the Anglo-Saxon, Celtic, Scandinavian, Germanic, and related peoples, often called the 'Christian nations' are the racial descendents of the tribes of Israel." The modern Anglo-Saxon nations continue those ten tribes of ancient Israel to whom the law and the promises of God were given. Israel is first of all a literal nation and then a Church. Britain and the United States possess what Israel was to possess and are doing what Israel was to do.

The New Covenant first mentioned by the prophet Jeremiah was made with Israel, and Jesus Christ came to confirm that Covenant and hence to redeem Israel. Jesus' death re-established the relationship between Israel and God broken at the time just prior to Israel's being cast out of the Holy Land (*II Kings 17*).

The perspective on Scripture and history adopted by the Identity movement has led to a distinctly pro-white racial bias and an anti-black and anti-Jewish stance that varies in militancy within various segments of the movement. Modern-day Jews, the surviving remnant of the House of Judah, are sharply distinguished from Israel, with which they have no part.

Organization of the Movement

The Identity Movement is composed of numerous independent congregations and ministries, each of which is built around one prominent minister who frequently combines the roles of congregational leader, writer and radio-TV spokesperson. Only one person, Herbert W. Armstrong, has been able to build a large denominational structure. (His Worldwide Church of God is considered elsewhere in this volume.) Though independent, various congregations form networks and distribute the literature of the movement as a whole. Among the most important centers of the movement are the following:

The Anglo-Saxon Federation of America. Founded in 1928 by Howard B. Rand, the Federation is the oldest Identity group currently operating, though its work has been considerably reduced as its leader has aged. It is headquartered in Haverhill, Massachusetts and continues to distribute Rand's books and a newsletter.

Christian Conservative Churches of America. The Christian Conservative Church of America grew out of the spiritual experience of John R. Harrell while recuperating from cancer at the Mayo Clinic. He founded the Church and donated his 55-acre estate to it in 1959. The Church suffered a major setback five years later, however, when Harrell disappeared on the eve of a scheduled IRS hearing. Arrested the following year, he was sentenced to 10 years in jail. Although paroled in 1969, he was not allowed to participate in the work of the Church until his probation was ended in 1975. He immediately began to rebuild the Church whose stated purpose was to blend Christianity and Patriotism to effectively oppose Zionism (i.e., Jews) and communism.

Harrell teaches that the present governmental systems of North America are in imminent danger of collapse, and he encourages members of the Identity Movement to band together for survival and the preservation of the heritage of the white race. He has designated an area in the middle of the United States (roughly the land between Pittsburgh, Atlanta, Lubbock (Texas), and Scottsbluff (Nebraska), which he terms the "golden Triangle," as prime territory within which Christian survivalists can defend themselves when the collapse occurs.

Associated with the Church are three auxiliary organizations. The Christian-Patriots Defense League, founded in 1977, is a dues-free organization which educates and organizes Christian patriots for the coming collapse. It is dedicated to preserving the Anglo-Saxon culture against any form of miscegenation. The Citizens Emergency Defense System is a private militia standing ready to be activated should the situation deteriorate sufficiently. The Paul Revere Club receives funds used to support the other organizations. The Church and its auxiliary organizations are headquartered at Harrell's estate in Louisville, Illinois in a full-scale replica of Mt. Vernon, George Washington's home.

Church of Jesus Christ Christian, Aryan Nations. The Church of Jesus Christ Christian was founded after World War II by Wesley A. Swift, a Ku Klux Klan organizer on the West Coast and close associate of Gerald L. K. Smith. Swift died in 1970 and was succeeded by his widow. Richard Butler, a pastor at the Church moved to Idaho and began an independent branch at Hayden Lake. Due to Butler's open identification with both Klan and Nazi groups, this branch has become one of the most notorious centers of the Identity Movement. In 1982 he organized the International Congress of Aryan Nations, which attracted numerous white supremacy groups.

The Aryan Nations describes itself as a white racial theopolitical movement whose aim is the re-establishment of white Aryan sovereignty over the lands of Aryan settlement and occupation. It teaches that the preservation of the white race is demanded and directed by Yahweh and that a battle is presently being fought between the present-day children of darkness (i.e., the Jews) and the children of light (the Aryan race).

The Church of Israel. The Church of Israel was formed in 1972 as a result of a disagreement in a small Mormon splinter group, the Church of Christ at Halley's Bluff, Missouri. That Church was, in turn, a splinter from the Church of Christ (Temple Lot) which claims to be the original church founded by Joseph Smith Jr., the Mormon prophet. During the 1960s, Daniel Gayman, one of the Church's pastors, was appointed editor of the Church's periodical. He soon began to print articles reflective of his extreme racial views and then began to use the church's youth camp as a seminary for fellow white supremicists and as a military training ground to teach weapons use and military tactics.

Tension over Gayman's activities resulted in schism in 1972 after an election in which Gayman won control of the congregation and dismissed all the members of the congregation's priesthood. Those relieved of their office sued Gayman, and the court returned almost all of the church property to their control. From 1974, following the court ruling, to 1981, Gayman's supporters reincorporated as the Church of Christian Heritage.

In place of the teachings of Joseph Smith, the Church of Israel has substituted the Identity Movement's theology and its belief in white supremacy. Gayman teaches that the British people have transmitted the apostolic succession of the early church through Joseph of Arimathea who brought it to the British Isles in the first century. Gayman has developed a theologically unique variation on the two-seed-in-the-spirit theory first popularized in the last century by Baptist minister Daniel Parker. Basing his interpretation upon *Genesis 3:15*, Parker argued that Cain and Abel represented two seeds carried within the human race, the former of Satan, the latter of God and Adam. Every person was born of one of the two seeds and was thus predestined from the beginning to be part of either God's family or Satan's. Gayman turned Parker's theories into a racial polemic against blacks and Jews. White gentiles have descended from Seth (the murdered Abel's substitute) while blacks and Jews have descended from Cain, the child of Satan's impregnation of Eve.

At the time the Church adopted its present name, it also reorganized. The Church was divided into twelve dioceses, each named for one of the twelve tribes of Israel. There is no diocese for either Levi or Joseph, but there is one for each of Joseph's two sons, Ephraim and Manasseh. Each diocese is headed by a bishop. The Diocese of Manasseh, covering the United States, is headed by Bishop Gayman. The Diocese of Ephraim covers the British Commonwealth and other dioceses have been designated for the various European countries. Only the Diocese of Manasseh has been activated as of the mid-1980s.

The New Christian Crusade Church. The New Christian Crusade Church was founded in 1971 by James K. Warner, a former member of Lincoln Rockwell's American Nazi Party. Headquartered in a New Orleans suburb, it is closely associated with The Knights of the Ku Klux Klan which uses the Church's postal box for distributing its periodical, *The Crusader*. Warner has also founded two associated structures, The Christian Defense League, an open membership organization for people who support the Church's racial policies (anti-black and anti-Jewish), and the Sons of Liberty, a publishing and literature distribution company.

The Covenant, the Sword, the Arm of the Lord. One of the most militant groups within the Identity Movement, The Covenant, the Sword, the Arm of the Lord was founded in 1976 by Rev. Jim Ellison, an independent minister from San Antonio, Texas. Following a vision of the coming collapse of American society, he established a survivalist commune, Zarephath-Horeb, near the Arkansas-Missouri border on land purchased from the Campus Crusade for Christ. The former campground is intended as a haven when the battle of Armageddon begins. The community is partially self-supporting. A farm produces its food. Education and medical services are provided by members, and residents live without either electricity or plumbing. Part of the community's income has derived from classes in military skills and survivalism at the communal site.

C. S. A. believes that the two-edged sword of God's Spirit is coming in judgment to the earth, and that God's Arm, which will administer that judgment, will soon be manifest. C.S.A. will have a significant part in the execution of God's judgment. In preparation for the difficult times ahead, the community is storing food, stockpiling weapons, and learning to live an austere life. It fully expects a major internal war in which white Christians will be set against Jews, blacks, homosexuals, witches, and Satanists, as well as foreign enemies.

Ministry of Christ Church. The Ministry of Christ Church was incorporated in 1964 and is headed by William P. Gale. The church teaches that Jesus preached the Gospel of the Kingdom and the Kingdom is a government. Further, Jesus accomplished the salvation from sin of his kinsmen, Israel, or modern-day Christians. Jesus' kinsmen are the white race, which began with Adam who suddenly appeared on earth in approximately 5,500 B.C. The black and yellow races preceded Adam by thousands of years. The Bible is the book of the "generations" (i.e., race) of Adam, the white race, who are to bring God's government to this earth. That government is present in the United States, the New Jerusalem.

The Ministry of Church is headquartered in Mariposa, California.

Other Centers. Besides these more prominent organizations in the Identity movement, a number of others publish and distribute literature and/or regularly broadcast over radio. Such organizations include The Lord's Covenant Church headed by Sheldon Emry of Phoenix, Arizona: The Church of Jesus Christ founded by Thomas Arthur Robb of Bass, Arkansas; New Beginnings headed by Eldon D. Purvis of Waynesville, North Carolina; the Mountain Church of Cohoctah, Michigan, headed by Robert E. Miles; the Gospel Temple in Hopkins, Minnesota, pastored by C. O. Stadsklev; and Your Heritage headed by Bertrand L. Comparet of San Diego, California.

Internationally, the Movement is represented by the British-Israel World Federation, headquartered in London, but with centers throughout the British Commonwealth. A similar organization, The Association of Covenant People, distributes literature throughout Canada from its headquarters in Vancouver.

Current Status

No directory of the Identity Movement has been published, and no recent survey to determine the size of the Movement has been undertaken. Churches and publishing centers can be found throughout the United States, and a great amount of literature is circulated. The Sons of Liberty catalog lists hundreds of books and tapes for sale. Among the several Identity ministers on radio, none approach Sheldon Emry, whose radio broadcast is currently heard on approximately 40 radio stations across the United States each weekend. However, most groups have only a single congregation with membership averaging in the low hundreds. A few, such as the Church of Israel and the Christian Conservative Churches of America, have several congregations.

While based in a single congregation, Identity groups have frequently sought a national following through the circulation of a periodical or the building of a national auxiliary organization, the members of which may gather for a convention annually. Among the prominent periodicals of the Movement are: *America's Promise Newsletter* (Lord's Covenant Church); the *Christian Vanguard* (New Christian Crusade Church); *The C.D.L. Report* (Christian Defense League); *C.S.A. Journal*; *From the Mountain*; *Identity* (Ministry of Christ Church); *New Beginnings*; *Our Nation* (Church of Jesus Christ Christian-Aryan Nations); *The Torch* (edited by Thomas Arthur Robb); and *The Watchman* (Church of Israel).

Apart from the Worldwide Church of God, adherents to the Identity movement seem to number approximately 10,000 to 20,000. Of these only a minority seem to be involved in the more violent Ku Klux Klan and Nazi-oriented wing of the Movement.

Controversy

From the beginning of its appearance in the nineteenth century, scholars have attacked the basic ideas of British-Israelism. They have noted that the ten lost tribes of Israel did not migrate to Europe, they were assimilated within the cultures of the Middle East. No evidence for Anglo-Saxon roots in the ancient Middle East has been found. Scholars have also refuted the particular claims of British-Israelites, such as their philology (most British Israelites, for example, derive the word British from the Hebrew "brith," i.e., covenant) and their archaeology. (Movement writers, for example, generally assert that the Stone of Scone came from the Holy Land. In fact, it came from Scotland.)

More recent criticism of the Movement has focused upon the racial teachings inherent within the Movement's basic assumptions. While less than half of those associated with the Identity Movement seem to support the overt and frequently violent racist rhetoric, the racial (antiblack and antisemitic) teachings of white supremacy pervade the Movement. Within the Movement, bitter antisemitic documents circulate freely (including the fraudulent *Protocols of the Learned Elders of Zion*), and leaders openly advocate racist and antisemitic beliefs. Several of the Identity churches keep strong ties to the Klan and the several Nazi groups. Jewish organizations, such as the Anti-Defamation League, have taken the lead in attacking the Identity Movement in this regard.

To the long-standing criticism of the racial teaching of the Identity Movement has been added concern about its potential for violence. Much of that concern centers upon two groups, C.S.A. and the Posse Comitatus, a populist organization which has become well known for its protest of the income tax system. Posse Comitatus' national membership includes members from Identity Churches, and many Posse members have formed congregations of the Life Science Church or the Basic Bible Churches of America, two churches which offer ordination by mail, merely upon application. They brought Identity beliefs into these two churches. For many years, C.S.A. used its rural location as a school for members of other Identity groups to teach a variety of courses in weapons use, military tactics, survival, and related subjects. They also deal in weapons as a means of supporting their commune.

On February 17, 1983, Posse leader Gordon Kahl was involved in a shootout in Medina, South Dakota, that left two U.S. Marshals dead and three other law officers wounded. Kahl fled but was discovered and killed June 3, 1983 in Arkansas not too far from C.S.A. The following year, in July, an Arkansas state trooper, Louis Bryant, was killed. Richard N. Snell, formerly a resident at C.S.A., was arrested and later convicted of the murder. In 1985 James Ellison, C.S.A.'s founder, and other members of the group were arrested and convicted on racketeering charges. Ellison was sentenced to twenty years in prison.

During 1975 authorities also moved against a militant semi-secret Identity group which had split off from the Church of Jesus Christ Christian, Aryan Nations, called the Order. Members were accused of a variety of crimes in the Northwest, including the murder of Denver talk-show host, Alan Berg. During the course of the investigation into Berg's death, FBI agents arrested Order-member Gary Lee Yarbrough. They found the gun used to kill Berg in his possession. In December 1984 Order founder Robert Matthews died in a siege on a house on Whidbey Island, Washington. Other Order members also in the house surrendered. In February 1985 Yarbrough was convicted of assault for shooting at the FBI agents. In early 1985, other Order members were arrested. In the fall of 1985, ten members of the Order were put on trial in Seattle and convicted of racketeering charges.

J. H. Allen, *Judah's Sceptre and Joseph's Birthright* (Boston: A. A. Beauchamp, 1930).

The Pattern of History (Merrimac, MA: Destiny Publishers, 1961).

William P. Gale, *Identity* (Glendale, CA: Ministry of Christ Church, n.d.).

C. O. Stadsklev, *Tracing the Isaac-Sons—Anglo-Saxons* (Hopkins, MN: Americas Hope Broadcasts, n.d.).

Anti-Christ vs. Christians (Hayden Lake, ID: Church of Jesus Christ Christian, Aryan Nations, n.d.).

Ralph Lord Roy, *Apostles of Discord* (Boston: Beacon Press, 1953).

Hate Groups in America (New York: Anti-Defamation League of B'nai B'rith, 1982).

Alan M. Schwartz et al., "The 'Identity Churches': A Theology of Hate." *ADL Facts* 28, 1 (Spring 1983) 1–16.

Anton Darms, *The Delusion of British-Israelism* (New York: Loizeaux Brothers, n.d.).

F. JEHOVAH'S WITNESSES

Since its founding in 1881, the organization known today as Jehovah's Witnesses has been one of the most controversial religious groups to spring up on the fertile American soil. Its roots lie in the nineteenth century Adventist movement begun by William Miller. Originally, Miller projected the imminent return of Christ in 1843. After the failure of that prediction and its revision to 1844, Adventists splintered into a number of factions, one group of which attempted to set other dates for the Second Advent. The Jehovah's Witnesses and their founder Charles Taze Russell emerged from among these people.

Charles Taze Russell (1852-1916)

The history of the Witnesses is largely told in the careers of its leaders. The first, Charles Taze Russell, was raised a Presbyterian but soon left that church. While still in his teens, he met Jonas Wendall, an Adventist minister who believed that the Second Advent would occur in 1874. Russell associated with Wendall and in 1868 formed his own Bible Study group to explore the Bible in the light of Wendall's ideas. Working with the small group, Russell developed the views with which he was to become identified. Over the next decade he began to teach that hell meant annihilation (death) not eternal torment; that humanity had been ransomed from that death, not from hellfire; and that there was no biblical basis for the doctrine of the Triune God.

Most importantly, Russell faced the fact that Christ had not returned in 1874 by announcing that Christ did, in fact, return in 1874 but as an invisible presence. He adopted the view that the Greek word, "parousia," commonly translated "coming," in fact should be translated "presence."

In 1879 Russell began to publish a magazine, *The Watch Tower and Herald of Christ's Presence*, to expound his ideas, and tracts and a booklet, *Food for Thinking Christians*, soon followed. By the end of 1880, approximately 30 groups of worshippers had formed. In 1881, Russell sent two people to England to distribute literature. From the incorporation of the Watch Tower Bible and Tract Society (originally Zion's Watch Tower Tract Society) in 1884, the work progressed steadily. Congregations of

believers led by local elders sprang up across the United States and in
Canada, Australia, and Europe.

Russell's popularity rested, in part, on his prediction that the end of
gentile sovereignty over the nations would occur in 1914. The beginning of
World War I seemed to confirm Russell's prophecy, but the War continued and the lack of supernatural intervention became obvious to all. In
the midst of the confusion, Russell died.

Joseph Franklin Rutherford (1869-1942)

J. F. Rutherford, the Society's lawyer, had joined Russell's group after
reading *The Studies in the Scriptures*, Russell's six-volume exposition of the
Bible. He became the Society's attorney in 1907 and oversaw the movement of the headquarters to Brooklyn, New York.

Following Russell's death, Rutherford was elected President of the
Society but not without a struggle and the loss of a number of congregations who opposed his leadership. No sooner had his position been
consolidated, than he had to deal with the government. He and other
members of the board were arrested and sentenced to prison for advising
men to refrain from military service. Rutherford emerged from prison in
1918 embittered by his imprisonment to lead a group discouraged by the
failure of the 1914 prediction.

Rutherford made monumental changes in the Society. He began to
weld the loosely organized congregations into a close-knit body, described
as "theocratic," whose job was to inform the world of Jehovah's reign. He
attacked the established structures of Satan's world—the Church, particularly the Roman Catholic Church, and government. Members of the
Society were mobilized to distribute the ever-growing number of Watch
Tower books and pamphlets.

Rutherford was the first popular religious leader to raise the issue of
God having a name in the Hebrew. That name, asserted Rutherford, was
Jehovah, and Jehovah's people should be called by his name. Thus he led
the members of the congregations affiliated with the Society to adopt the
new name, Jehovah's Witnesses, in 1931.

Rutherford created the strong organization he had envisioned in the
1920s. He died in 1942 as government persecution of the pacifist Witnesses
began to disrupt the international work.

Nathan Knorr (1905-1977)

Rutherford was succeeded by Nathan Knorr, the former manager of
the Society's printing plant. Knorr put his managerial skill to work in
perfecting the organization built by Rutherford, but he approached his
task in a much lower key. As in the days of Rutherford, books and
materials flowed from the Watch Tower publishing plant, but no one was
named as the author.

Knorr placed great emphasis upon training members and instituted the Service Meetings and the Kingdom Ministry School as a lay education effort to assist Witnesses in communicating their beliefs effectively. He also enlarged the international conventions, which were held in multiple locations around the United States and the world in stadiums or other large structures where crowds could gather. The same program would be held in each site.

The last decade of Knorr's tenure was filled with the expectation that the Second Advent would occur in 1975. He lived only a short time after that prediction failed, which has shaken the organization in recent years.

Fred Franz (1893–   )

Possibly the most lasting accomplishment of the Knorr years was the publication of the *New World Translation of the Holy Scripture*, which embodied all the Witnesses' ideas about translation of the Bible, especially in its use of Jehovah as God's name. However, the man generally given the most credit for the Bible was Fred Franz who succeeded Knorr as President of the Society. A scholarly man, he, even more than Knorr, was a retiring man. He has, nonetheless, kept a tight rein on the organization and done nothing to allow the strong central authority to slip, in spite of the defections of many Witnesses due to the failure of the 1975 prophecy.

Beliefs

Jehovah's Witnesses consider themselves Bible-believing followers of Christ, however, they have come to different conclusions about what the Bible teaches from those of orthodox Christianity. Their position is close to that of Arius (ca. 256–336 A.D.), a teacher whose opinions were condemned by the Council of Nicea (325 A.D.). Arius, like the Witnesses, held that Christ was not the second person of the Triune Godhead but rather the first of God's creations. Christ's death, which occurred on a stake, not a cross, was a ransom paid for obedient humanity.

Humans are saved by their faith and obedience to God (Jehovah). At death their soul (i.e., their life) ceases. They go to the grave (hell) and their hope is in a future resurrection. Humankind looks for the imminent end of Satan's reign upon earth. After his reign is destroyed in the Battle of Armageddon, Jehovah's rule will be established on earth. A select 144,000 will go to heaven and reign with Christ, while the remaining Christians will live forever on earth. Most present-day Witnesses do not expect to go to heaven. After Armageddon, the dead in Christ will be raised to enjoy eternal life.

Witnesses also believe in creation as opposed to evolution. They consider saluting the flag to be idol worship. They do not use blood transfusions because of the biblical admonition to refrain from drinking blood.

Organization

The Jehovah's Witnesses are organized as a theocracy, that is, the Witnesses see their organization under the direct rule of Jehovah through Christ. Their first alliance is to that rule, even if it conflicts with various national governments, and most especially if such governments demand what Witnesses consider idolatrous or otherwise against Jehovah's moral precepts. Jehovah's authority on earth is manifest in the Jehovah's Witnesses' organization, the Watch Tower Bible and Tract Society (and its affiliate corporations). The Society is headed by the President and Governing body of seventeen members. They have direct control of the entire organization.

The Society is divided into various zones or branches which consist of one or more countries. Literature, the distribution of which is a major item on the Witnesses' agenda, is written at the international headquarters in Brooklyn. Copies are then distributed to the branch offices. Those with their own printing presses will print the material (and translate where appropriate). Other branches will obtain their material directly from the presses in Brooklyn.

Each branch is further divided into districts and each district into circuits. A circuit will have approximately twenty congregations. Both the district and circuits are headed by an overseer appointed by the Governing Body. Each has responsibility for the congregations in their area. The congregation itself is headed by a presiding elder, under whom other elders work to distribute the literature to the public and lead the various worship and lay training sessions.

Members of the Witnesses are expected to attend Sunday worship and the several meetings each week. They are also expected to spend some time selling the Society's two magazines *Awake* and *The Watchtower* and current books. Such activity is the main source of new members. The immediate area around the Kingdom Hall, where the congregation meets, is canvased regularly by the members, each of whom is designated a minister by the organization. The Witnesses do not believe in designating a special "ministerial" class, though certain ministers are assigned the traditional ministerial tasks, such as leading worship.

Witnesses have generally disapproved of higher education, though in 1943 they founded a training school for missionaries, the Watch Tower Bible School of Gilead, at Brooklyn, New York.

Current Status

The 1982 *Yearbook of the Jehovah's Witnesses* reported 2,138,373 active "publishers" in 43,870 congregations in 206 countries. Of these 588,503 publishers in 7,590 congregations could be found in the United States. Brazil, Germany, Mexico, and Nigeria each reported slightly over 100,000 publishers. The 1970s were a decade of growth for the Witnesses. The 1972 *Yearbook* reported only 416,789 publishers in the United States, but remarkable growth occurred in countries such as Italy where the numbers went from 22,196 in 1972 to 90,553 in 1982, better than 400% growth in a decade, and Italy is by no means a unique case.

While most of the printing for the Witnesses is done in the massive plant in Brooklyn, a number of printing shops around the world provide local material, especially in other languages. The number of pieces of literature distributed annually has taken on astronomical proportions, reaching well into the hundreds of millions. The two magazines, *Awake* and *The Watchtower*, both published biweekly, are the primary items used in witnessing activity along with tracts, pamphlets and a selection of current books in print.

Controversy

The Witnesses have never been far from controversy. From the moment Russell began to teach, other Adventists warned followers of his dangerous ideas. However, his major opposition came from mainline churches after it became known that he did not believe in either the Trinity or the divinity of Christ, bedrock beliefs of orthodox Christianity. A number of Evangelical Christian groups, many made up of ex-members of the Witnesses, have arisen to counteract what they see as group heresy. Together, these groups have produced as much material as the Witnesses themselves.

Ever since World War I, the Witnesses have encountered attacks from both the community and the government. In the patriotic atmosphere of the War, their pacifist stance made the Witnesses (then known simply as Bible Students) objects of government suppression, and their refusal to salute the flag made them objects of community scorn and popular prejudice. That popular prejudice carried over into the post-war years and led many communities to attempt to prevent the Witnesses from distributing their literature. Such attempts led to a series of court battles and Supreme Court landmark decisions.

Among the most unacceptable of the Witnesses' beliefs is their refusal to allow blood transfusions. This belief also led to numerous court cases and, especially in the case of children, was often overruled.

The Witnesses faced their most severe persecution outside the United States. The Nazis were possibly the first government to attempt to destroy the organization entirely and many Witnesses died in concentration camps. The story of their perseverance in the face of such persecution is impressive to even those who oppose their religious beliefs. In more recent years other governments have attempted to limit their activities and suppress them, the most bloody persecution arising in the tiny nation of Malawi.

During the years immediately following the failure of the predicted events of 1975, the Witnesses experienced an intense period of inner turmoil. Not only did many members, citing their dislike of the arbitrary authority exercised by the leadership and the failure of the prophecy, leave, but a number of leaders resigned or were disfellowshipped. Among the most important to depart was Raymond Franz, nephew of Frederick Franz, and member of the governing body. Others included Edward A. Dunlap, head of Gilead School of the Bible, the Witnesses' missionary training center, and Canadian professors James Penton, and Heather and Gary Botting. The Bottings, Franz and Penton have all written books attacking the organization.

Jehovah's Witnesses in the Divine Purpose (Brooklyn, NY: Watchtower Bible and Tract Society, 1959.

——, *Make Sure of All Things* (Brooklyn, NY: Watchtower Bible and Tract Society, 1957).

——, *The Truth That Leads to Eternal Life* (Brooklyn, NY: Watchtower Bible and Tract Society, 1968).

——, *Organization for Kingdom-Preaching and Disciple-Making* (Brooklyn, NY: Watchtower Bible and Tract Society, 1972).

——, *Did Man Get Here by Evolution or by Creation?* (Brooklyn, NY: Watchtower Bible and Tract Society, 1967).

Alan Rogerson, *Millions Now Living Will Never Die* (London: Constable, 1969).

James A. Beckford, *The Trumpet of Prophecy* (Oxford: Basil Blackwell, 1975).

Timothy White, *A People for His Name* (New York: Vantage Press, 1967).

Chandler W. Sterling, *The Witnesses* (Chicago: Henry Regnery Company, 1975).

Edmond Charles Gruss, *Apostles of Denial* (n.p.: Presbyterian and Reformed Publishing Co., 1970).

Heather and Gary Botting, *The Orwellian World of the Jehovah's Witnesses* (Toronto: University of Toronto Press, 1984).

Raymond Franz, *Crisis of Conscience* (Atlanta: Commentary Press, 1983).

James Penton, *Apocalypse Delayed* (Toronto: University of Toronto Press, 1985).

G. ROSICRUCIANS

The Rose Cross (the juxtapositioning of a cross and one or more roses) has, since the early seventeenth century, become one of the most popular occult symbols. From its origin in Germany, it spread throughout the Western world. It entered into Freemasonry where various ritual degrees derived their name and meaning from the Rosicrucian legend. At least eight occult orders currently functioning in the United States accept the name Rosicrucian and a version of the Rosicrucian legend as their history.

According to the Rosicrucian legend, the Order began with one Christian Rosenkreuz, born in 1378 in Germany. Beginning in 1393, he visited Damascus, Egypt, and Morocco where he sat under the masters of the occult arts. Upon his return to Germany, he began in 1407 the Rosicrucian Order with three monks from the cloister in which he had been raised. He also erected the House of the Holy Spirit (the Spiritus Sanctum) which was completed in 1409. The original group was enlarged to eight. Christian Rosenkreuz died in 1484 (at the age of 106) and was entombed in the Spiritus Sanctum. Knowledge of his tomb was lost, but it was rediscovered in 1604. Its opening led to the spread of the Order anew.

Modern Rosicrucian groups have different opinions about Christian Rosencreuz. Some believe he actually existed as the early documents assert; others see the name as a pseudonym for one or more historic personages (Francis Bacon?); still others view the story as a parable, an occult legend that points to more profound truth.

Knowledge of Christian Rosenkreuz and the Order he supposedly founded was given to the world in three documents in the second decade of the seventeenth century: *The Fama Fraternitas of the Meritorious Order of the Rosy Cross* (1614); *The Confession of the Rosicrucian Fraternity* (1615); and *The Chymical Marriage of Christian Rosenkreuz* (1616 but purportedly written by Christian Rosenkreuz in 1459). While the full facts of the case may never be known, research indicates that these three documents and the idea of the Order originated with a German Lutheran pastor Johann Valentin Andrae (1586–1654). Andrae had envisioned a society for the reformation of social life—and he, with or without assistance from others, created the legend and published the documents describing it. A few have seen Rosicrucianism as a complete hoax. Most believe, however, that either Andrae formed an order combining his interest in esotericism and the reformation of society, which the documents promoted, or, more likely, Andrae wanted the documents to catalyze others to initiate the Rosicrucian work.

The response to the documents was immediate and intense. Rosicrucian societies arose, and the rose and cross symbol (which seems to have derived from Andrae's coat of arms) became popular. The Rosicrucian groups combined a vision of social transformation, the study of alchemy, Cabalism, and mysticism with otherwise "orthodox" Christian theology. The Rosicrucian groups blended into the larger community of Christian pietism which could be found throughout Germany at this time.

During the seventeenth century Rosicrucianism spread throughout Europe. It found exponents in England almost immediately in the persons of Robert Fludd (1574–1637) and Michael Maier (1568–1622). In 1616, the same year *The Chymical Marriage* appeared, Fludd published his *A Compendius Apology for the Fraternity of the Rosy Cross*. Maier, an alchemical physician, both during his years in England and after his 1619 retirement to Germany, did much to bring Rosicrucianism and alchemy together.

The mystical piety of German Rosicrucianism produced the first Rosicrucian group in America. The Chapter of Perfection, as it was called, was formed by scientist-theologian Johann Jacob Zimmerman. Zimmerman joined other pietist groups in accepting the invitation of William Penn to migrate to Pennsylvania. However, just before the group sailed, Zimmerman died. Their beliefs included a strong millennialism, and the group brought a hope for the imminent return of Christ to earth with them when they came to America in 1694. Zimmerman's role was assumed by Johannes Kelpius (1673–1708) who led the small band to Germantown where they established headquarters on the bank of the Wissahickon Creek. On top of their building they erected an observatory so as to discern the moment of Christ's second advent.

The Chapter lasted only a few years. After Kelpius' death, his successor Conrad Matthai allowed the break-up of the communal structure, and the small group became a community of mystical hermits. Several of the members worked in the community as healers and practitioners of the occult arts. They passed along their knowledge of magic and occultism to later generations and became the source of the modern hexmeister tradition.

Rosicrucianism almost completely disappeared in the eighteenth century, but in the nineteenth century was a major component of the occult revival in the West. It emerged out of Masonry. In 1866 Robert Wentworth Little (1840–1878) formed Societas Rosicruciana in Anglia, open only to Masons. A Scottish branch was formed a few years later. Rosicrucianism never completely died in France, but in the mid-nineteenth century it received a new impulse from occultist Eliphas Levi (1810–1875) who wrote three monumental works on magic: *The Doctrine of Transcendental Magic* (1855); *The Ritual of Transcendental Magic* (1856); and the *History of Magic* (1860). American Rosicrucian P.B. Randolph mentions meeting Levi on his trip to Rosicrucian gatherings in France. The renewed interest begun in Levi's time led to the formation of the Qabalistic Order of the Rosy Cross in 1888.

Rosicrucian groups are occult orders, and as such make their central and most important teachings available only to members. In like measure no examination of documents and archives is allowed, and no independent corroboration of the claims of the various groups, especially their claims to ancient origins and European alliances, is possible.

FRATERNITAS ROSAE CRUCIS

The oldest Rosicrucian body in the United States, the Fraternitas Rosae Crucis was founded in 1858 by Pascal Beverly Randolph (1825–1875). Randolph, a self-educated orphan of mixed blood, developed an early interest in the occult and in 1850 traveled to Europe and was initiated into a Rosicrucian Fraternity in Germany. On his third trip to Europe in 1858, he was made the Supreme Master for the Western World, at a Conclave headed by Supreme Grand Master Eliphas Levi. He returned to the United States and founded the Fraternitas Rosae Crucis. Two years later he returned to Europe and was initiated in 1861 in the Order of the Rose, a group headed by Rosicrucian historian Hargrave Jennings, and traveling on to Syria, he was initiated by the Ansaireh.

Randolph was succeeded by ex-Spiritualist Freeman B. Dowd (b. 1812) who had been drawn to the Fraternity by reading Randolph's writings. He established temples in Philadelphia, San Francisco, and Denver. He also formed the Rosy Cross Publishing Company in San Francisco. He retired in 1907 and was succeeded by Edward H. Brown (1868–1922). Upon Brown's death, Reuben Swinburne Clymer (b. 1878) became head of the Fraternity.

Under Clymer, the Order, whose growth had been slow and erratic, blossomed. Clymer had joined the Fraternity in 1897 and coupled his training in the occult with a career in non-conventional medicine. His career kept him in continual conflict with the American Medical Association and the government. In 1904 Clymer founded the Philosophical Publishing Company, which reissued many of Randolph's books.

Upon his assumption of the leadership of the Fraternity, Clymer established the headquarters at Beverly Hall in Quakertown, Pennsylvania. He wrote voluminously, and his numerous books remain standard reading material for Rosicrucians. He brought his healing concerns into the Fraternity, and the headquarters complex still includes a chiropractic office and a clinic specializing in natural healing methods. Upon his death, Clymer was succeeded by his son Emerson M. Clymer, the present Grand Master.

Associated with the Fraternity is the Church of Illumination, a religious body and outer court for the Fraternity. The Church defines its task as teaching the Divine Law, the exoteric teachings of the esoteric group.

The Church is the tool for bringing about the Masisis Aeon, in which the two natures in humanity (male and female) will reach a state of equilibrium.

Members of the Fraternity receive private instruction through lessons mailed from the headquarters. Teachings focus upon the transmutation of the base and inglorious aspects of humanity into the self pure and refined. Progress in the course can lead to ordination into the Council of Initiated Priests.

SOCIETAS ROSICRUCIANA IN CIVITATIBUS FOEDERATIS
(S.R.I.C.F.)

The Societas Rosicruciana in Civitatibus Foederatis was founded in 1880 as the Societas Rosicruciana Republicae Americae. Charles E. Meyer was named the first Supreme Magus. The S.R.I.C.F. originated with a group of Masons who traveled to England in 1878 and were initiated into the Societas Rosicruciana in Anglia at the college at York. They applied to the S.R.I.A. for permission to begin an American branch. Rebuffed, they turned to the Scottish branch which chartered American colleges at Philadelphia in 1879 and New York the following year. These two colleges established a High Council in April 1880 for what became an autonomous American branch. During 1880 three additional colleges were authorized for Boston, Baltimore and Burlington, Vermont.

The S.R.I.C.F. is one of the smallest Rosicrucian groups. One must be a Mason to join. The last issue of their magazine, *The Rosicrucian Fama*, published in 1973, set the membership at less than 600. In 1912 it adopted the rituals of the British and Scottish branches.

SOCIETAS ROSICRUCIANA IN AMERICA
(S.R.I.A.)

The Societas Rosicruciana in America originated with members of the Societas Rosicruciana in Civitatibus Foederatis who wished to open the Rosicrucian teaching to the general public (i.e., non-Masons). In 1907 Sylvester C. Gould, a member of the Boston college of the S.R.I.C.F., in collaboration with other Rosicrucians, began the S.R.I.A. and a periodical, *The Rosicrucian Brotherhood*. Unfortunately Gould died in 1909 and the periodical died with him. The leadership of the infant Society, however, was picked up by George Winslow Plummer (1876–1944), who had assisted Gould in its formation, and under his leadership the Society began to grow.

Plummer incorporated the Society in 1912. In 1916 he founded the Mercury Publishing Company and began issuing *Mercury*, the official quarterly for the Society. By 1920 seven colleges (including one in Sierre Leone) had been established. Two more were added in 1921. By 1930 eighteen colleges had been chartered (though not all remained active) and there were seven study groups in other cities. After his death, Plummer was succeeded by his widow, known as Mother Serena, who published much of his work in a series of booklets.

Plummer had a strong interest in Christian mysticism and liturgical religion. Intimately connected to his Rosicrucian work, the Seminary of Biblical Studies operated out of the Society's headquarters and offered lessons in mysticism. Then in 1934 Plummer was consecrated as a bishop by Archbishop William Albert Nichols of the American Orthodox Church. He formed the Holy Orthodox Church in America, also head-quartered at the Society's office. Two years later the Church reported four congregations, all located in cities which had S.R.I.A. colleges or study groups.

Plummer's widow married Stanislaus Witowski, whom Plummer had consecrated and who succeeded Plummer as head of the Church. After Witowski's death, Mother Serena became head of the Church and in 1982 was consecrated as bishop by Archbishop Adrian Spruit of the Church of Antioch.

THE ANCIENT AND MYSTICAL ORDER ROSAE CRUCIS (A.M.O.R.C.)

The largest and best known of the several Rosicrucian groups in America, the Ancient and Mystical Order Rosae Crucis, was formed by Harvey Spencer Lewis (1883–1939), a writer, artist and occultist living in New York City. In 1904 he had formed The New York Institute for Psychical Research, an occult interest group. Four years later, he met Mrs. May Banks-Stacey, a Rosicrucian who put him in touch with members of the Order in Europe. In 1909 he went to France, where he was initiated and given authority to begin an organization in America. He pulled together a group of interested occultists and in 1915 the A.M.O.R.C. was formally organized and a magazine, *The American Rosae Crucis*, began.

In 1917 the first national convention was held. The convention approved a plan for offering its teaching to individuals through correspondence lessons. These lessons, which have been widely advertised over the years, became the major tool for the rapid spread of the Order.

In 1918 headquarters of the Order were moved to San Francisco. During these years Lewis formed ties with several occult groups and in 1921 received a charter from the Ordo Templi Orientis. In 1925 Lewis moved to Florida for two years but moved back to California in 1927 and established

headquarters at San Jose, on land the Order had acquired. He re-incorpo-
rated the Order in California and incorporated the Pristine Church of the
Rose Cross, an affiliated religious group over which he served as bishop.
The Church lasted only a few years as the Order began to stress its non-
religious fraternal aspect and hence dropped its "religious" structure.

During the 1930s Lewis developed the headquarters complex which
came to include the Rose-Croix University (1934), a Planetarium (1936),
and the Rosicrucian Research Library (1939). Possibly the most famous
structure at the headquarters, the Egyptian Museum, has received wide
acclaim and become a popular tourist attraction for San Jose.

Though no membership figures are available, the A.M.O.R.C. has
spread throughout the world and has groups in most non-Communist
countries. It publishes two magazines, *The Rosicrucian Digest*, a monthly,
and *The Rosicrucian Forum*, for members only. Lewis was a voluminous
writer and the Order circulates his many books, as well as those of his son
Ralph M. Lewis (b. 1904), who succeeded him as Imperator of the Order.

The Rosicrucian Fellowship

Several Rosicrucian groups have a direct lineage from the Theosophical
Society, the largest one being the Rosicrucian Fellowship founded by Max
Heindel (1865–1919) in 1907. Heindel, born Carl Louis Von Grasshoff, was an
engineer whose occult interests led him to the Theosophical Society shortly
after the beginning of the century. By 1905 he was a theosophical lecturer.
Then in 1907 he traveled to Germany where there appeared to him several
times one whom he described as an "Elder Brother of the Rosicrucian
Order." He was sent to work with a knowledgeable teacher, believed by
most to have been Rudolf Steiner, founder of the Anthroposophical Society.

Returning to the United States, he wrote down what he had been taught
and published it as his first book, *The Rosicrucian Cosmo-Conception*, still the
major introductory text of the Fellowship he founded. The first center was
founded in Columbus, Ohio, but within a few years centers could be found
along the West Coast from Seattle to Los Angeles. In 1910, while recuperating in a hospital from his recurrent heart condition, he had a vision of the
future center on Mt. Ecclesia in Oceanside, California. That center remains
the headquarters of the group.

The Rosicrucian teachings of Heindel advocate the occult worldview of
Theosophy. Heindel also picked up the astrological emphases of Theosophy
and two of his books *Simplified Scientific Astrology* and *The Message of the
Stars* were major factors in the twentieth-century revival of astrology in
America. The Fellowship also publishes the popular *Ephemeris*, the annual
table of the position of the planets in the astrological signs, a necessary tool
for constructing astrological charts. A monthly astrology column continues
to be an important feature in the Fellowship's monthly *Rays from the Rosy
Cross*.

Heindel was succeeded by his wife, Augusta Foss Heindel, an accomplished occultist in her own right. In 1920 Mt. Ecclesia was dedicated. The Society has established some small groups, but the majority of its efforts are through various mail order courses it offers in astrology and the occult.

Rosicrucian Anthroposophic League

Hearkening back to the influence of Rudolf Steiner on Max Heindel, S. R. Parchment, a former member of the Rosicrucian Fellowship, formed the Rosicrucian Anthroposophic League in San Francisco in the 1930s. Parchment wrote a series of books to expound his version of the Rosicrucian teachings: *The Middle Path, Steps to Self Mastery, Operative Masonry*, and *The Just Law of Compensation*. Parchment offered a variety of correspondence courses using the texts. The League also published a magazine, *Rosicrucian Quarterly*.

The occult basis of the League is spelled out in its objectives:

> To investigate the occult laws of nature and the superphysical powers of man;
>
> To promote the principles which will eventually lead to recognition of the truth of the universal brotherhood of man, without distinction as to sex, creed, race or color;
>
> To acquire, disseminate, and exemplify a knowledge of spiritual truth as given to the world by the Elder Brothers of the White Lodge;
>
> To study and teach ancient religion, philosophy and astrology in the light of modern needs;
>
> To encourage the study of science and art in the hope that religion, art and science—which are a veritable trinity, the equilateral triangle which has always been used as a symbol of the Divine—may again be recognized as portals through which egos must pass in attaining to the mastery of self;
>
> And finally, to attain to self-conscious immortality which is the crowning feat of evolution.

Like Heindel, Parchment had a prime interest in astrology and wrote an astrological classic, *Astrology, Mundane and Spiritual*. Since his death, the book has been kept in print by the American Federation of Astrologers. Recent information about the status of the League had been unavailable.

Lectorium Rosicrucianum

The Lectorium Rosicrucianum was formed in 1971 by former members of the Rosicrucian Fellowship in Holland under the leadership of J. Van Rijckenborgh. The Lectorium sees itself as a new instrument for the Universal Brotherhood, the spiritual hierarchy popularly known as the Great White Brotherhood. Its basic teaching is termed "transfigurism," based upon the idea of two natural orders. The first is of God, the second that in which we normally live, the result of a catastrophe due to man's disobedience to Divine Law. The way to escape this order in which we are bound by the endless cycles of reincarnation is through transfiguration, i.e., giving up our lives in order to participate in God's original order. The transition is exemplified in Jesus Christ's resurrection.

American headquarters of the Lectorium are in Bakersfield, California. English editions of Rijckenborgh's books, including his main work, *Dei Gloria Intacta*, and lesson material, are disseminated from there by mail to students across the United States.

Ausar Auset Society

The Ausar Auset Society was formed by R. A. Straughn, known by his religious name, Ra Un Nefer Amen, a member during the 1970s of the Rosicrucian Anthroposophic League. A black man, Straughn became an occult teacher to the black community and around 1980 established an independent organization which applied the universal occult truths of Rosicrucianism to the Afro-American situation. Straughn has written several occult texts: *The Realization of Neter Nu, Health Teachings of the Ageless Wisdom*, and *Meditation Techniques of the Kabalist, Vedantins and Taoists*. Other books manifest the particular interest in the needs of black Americans: *Black Woman's, Black Man's Guide to Spiritual Union* and *Black Woman, Black Man in a Quandary*.

In 1980 he started a magazine, *The Oracle of Thoth*, and by 1982 offered classes in the Society's occult teachings in New York, Washington, D.C., Chicago, Philadelphia, New Haven, and Norfolk.

R. Swinburne Clymer, *The Rosy Cross, Its Teachings* (Quakertown, PA: Beverly Hall Corporation, 1965).

George Winslow Plummer, *Principles and Practice for Rosicrucians* (New York: Society of Rosicrucians, 1947).

H. Spencer Lewis, *Rosicrucian Questions and Answers with Complete Answers* (San Jose, CA: Supreme Grand Lodge of AMORC, 1969).

Max Heindel, *The Rosicrucian Cosmo-Conception* (Oceanside, CA: Rosicrucian Fellowship, 1909).

S. R. Parchment, *Astrology, Mundane and Spiritual* (San Francisco: Rosicrucian Anthroposophic League, 1937).

The Way of the Rosycross in Our Times (Haarlem: Rozekruis-Pers, 1978).

R. A. Straughn, *The Realization of Neter Nu* (Brooklyn, NY: Maat Publishing Co., 1975).

Harold V. B. Voorhis, *Masonic Rosicrucian Societies* (New York: Press of Henry Emerson, 1958).

Christopher McIntosh, *The Rosy Cross Unveiled* (Wellingsborough: Aquarian Press, 1980).

Paul M. Allen, ed., *A Christian Rosenkreutz Anthology* (Blauvelt, NY: Rudolf Steiner Publications, 1968).

Frances A. Yates, *The Rosicrucian Enlightenment* (London: Routledge and Kegan Paul, 1972).

A. E. Waite, *The Brotherhood of the Rosy Cross* (London: Rider, 1924).

H. SATANISM AND THE CHURCH OF SATAN

Satanism is the worship of Satan, the Christian's devil. Traditionally associated with Satanism are a number of practices including: the black mass, the essence of which is the profaning (usually through parody) of Christian worship (e.g., repeating the Lord's Prayer backwards) and/or the desecration of sacred objects (i.e., trampling a sacramental host underfoot, spitting on a cross, etc.); the ritual slaughter of animals, usually a dog or cat; the murder, mutilation and/or rape of a human victim; and black magic, the invocation of Satan for the purpose of working malevolent sorcery.

Satanism provides the type of material from which novels and motion pictures can easily be constructed, and during the twentieth century, such books and movies have done far more to supply a popular understanding of Satanism than any reference to actual Satanic groups and practitioners. For example, British novelist Dennis Wheatley wrote a series of best-selling novels which developed the theme of an ancient worldwide secret and powerful Satanic society which regularly gathered its conspiratorial forces to attack the structures of order and goodness. While novels such as these, for example, the novel and movie *Rosemary's Baby*, make entertaining stories, there is no evidence that such novels even remotely reflect an existing social phenomenon. An examination of all the evidence shows no large organized Satanic movement or group.

Satanism as it now exists and has existed during the past two centuries has been a most unusual cult. It has produced almost no literature and individual groups have come and gone without connecting with previously existing Satanic groups or leaving behind any progeny. The Satanic tradition has been carried almost totally by the imaginative literature of non-Satanists, primarily conservative Christians, who describe the practices in vivid detail in the process of denouncing them. That is to say, the Satanic tradition has been created by generation after generation of anti-Satan writers. Sporadically, groups and individuals have tried to create groups which more or less conform to the Satanism portrayed in Christian literature.

Such Satanic activity showed a noticeable rise in the early and mid-1970s with police reporting an increase in the manifestations of ritual remains in graveyards, church break-ins and vandalism, and mutilated bodies of animals and humans. By the end of the decade the number of incidents had decreased, but the existence of any Satanic group remains a matter of concern as such groups tend eventually to become involved in illegal activity—from the desecration of graves to more serious crimes of burglary and even murder.

Such groups of traditional Satanists tend to be quite small (3 to 5 individuals) and their existence short (a few weeks or months, rarely a few years).

It should be clearly noted that the small groups of traditional Satanists stand in stark contrast to the second form of Satanism which has recently appeared—that of the Church of Satan. While the former have usually been involved in illegal activities, such is not the case within the Church of Satan. The Church specifically admonishes its members about abiding by all of the laws of the land and doing harm to no other in the pursuit of their otherwise "Satanic" goals. Anton LaVey, the Church's founder, is a former police employee and still works as a consultant on cases that involve the occult.

The Church of Satan

Although it draws on the reputation and images of more traditional Satanism, the Church of Satan has attempted to take classical occult and magical teachings and re-organize them around a Satanic motif. A philosophy of individual pragmatism and hedonism is more important than the worship of Satan. Founder Anton S. LaVey (b. 1930) has institutionalized his movement and given it all the formal trappings of a religion.

The Church of Satan was founded on May Eve (Walpurgis Night) 1966. LaVey shaved his head and announced the year 1 S.A. (anno Satanas). For the previous decade he had become increasingly involved in the occult and had been leading a "magic circle," out of which the Church evolved. The Church received wide publicity during its first years, especially after LaVey performed his first Satanic wedding in January 1967 and a funeral for a sailor (along with full Navy colorguard) in December 1967. Membership grew rapidly though, contrary to many media reports, the active membership was never more than approximately 2,000.

In 1969 LaVey authored the first of three books, *The Satanic Bible*, which became an occult bestseller. It was followed by *The Compleat Witch* (1970) and *The Satanic Rituals* (1972). LaVey also extended his consulting work (which he had done for many years for the police department) to the movie industry. He became the occult advisor on several films and appeared as the Devil in a few, including *Rosemary's Baby*.

The perspective of the Church of Satan is summarized in the 9 Satanic Statements found at the beginning of *The Satanic Bible*:

1. Satan represents indulgence, instead of abstinence!
2. Satan represents vital existence, instead of spiritual pipe dreams!

3. Satan represents undefiled wisdom, instead of hypocritical self-deceit!
4. Satan represents kindness to those who deserve it, instead of love wasted on ingrates!
5. Satan represents vengeance, instead of turning the other cheek!
6. Satan represents responsibility to the responsible, instead of concern for psychic vampires!
7. Satan represents man as just another animal, sometimes better, more often worse than those that walk on all fours, who because of his divine spiritual and intellectual development has become the most vicious animal of all!
8. Satan represents all of the so-called sins, as they lead to physical or mental gratification!
9. Satan has been the best friend the church has ever had, as he has kept it in business all these years!

The Church of Satan promotes the development of strong individuals who seek the greatest gratification out of life and practice selfish virtues as long as they harm no other. An individual's birthday is the single most important religious holiday on the Church's calendar.

Current Status

By the early 1970s, the Church of Satan had established groups around the United States, but in spite of its image as one of the larger occult organizations in America, its active membership was never more than a few hundred (knowledgeable sources estimate between 250 and 500, enough to support a newsletter, *The Cloven Hoof*. Other smaller groups not connected with the Church of Satan could be found in Chicago, Los Angeles, Toledo and New York. However, in the mid-1970s the Church of Satan was rent by a number of withdrawals of grotto leaders and expulsions of others. The several schisms cost the Church of Satan the majority of its membership. Some of the former members founded other Satanic groups, which were, with one exception, even more minute in size. All the groups not originally connected with LaVey had dissolved by the end of the decade due to either the death or loss of interest of the leaders.

Wayne West (Detroit), John DeHaven (Dayton), Ronald E. Lanting and Harry L. Booth (St. Petersburg), all former members of the Church of Satan formed the Church of Satanic Brotherhood in 1973. The Church, with never more than 25 members, mostly in the Detroit and Dayton areas, lasted for only a few years. In a dramatic incident staged for the St. Petersburg area media in 1974, John DeHaven professed his conversion to evangelical Christianity.

Clifford Amos in Louisville and Joseph Daniels of Indianapolis, with few if any additional members, formed the Ordo Templi Satanis. Daniels issued a newsletter, *True Grimoire*, for both the OTS and the Church of Satanic Brotherhood. It, too, folded within a few years.

The Temple of Set

In 1975 the substance of the Church of Satan, led by Michael Aquino, a Magister Templi with the Church and Lilith Sinclair, head of the Lilith Grotto in Spotswood, New Jersey, left the Church of Satan and established the Temple of Set as a religious society dedicated to Set, the ancient Egyptian deity believed to have later become the model for the Christian Satan. Beginning with Church of Satan teachings, especially those never revealed to the public in LaVey's several books, the Temple has developed a more sophisticated form of "Satanism" beyond that taught by LaVey. Teachings are contained in *The Book of Coming Forth by Night*, not available to non-members, and other more common occult texts.

During its first decade, the Temple of Set grew to include over 500 members scattered around the United States. It views itself as elitist and selective in taking in new members for initiation. Group activities are irregular as most magical work is performed in private. Teaching is done either through correspondence or in personal tutoring sessions. A newsletter, *Scroll of Set*, is published from the San Francisco headquarters. The Temple of Set is, as of 1985, the only viable Satanic group in the LaVey tradition operating in America.

Controversy

As the number of Satanic groups decreased in the late 1970s, and LaVey became more reclusive, the public concern with Satanism declined. It reappeared in the 1980s, however, as incidents of reported cattle mutilations were ascribed to Satanic rites. Then around 1984, reports based upon the testimony of children began to surface of a national underground and well-financed Satanic cult which were responsible for many of the disappearances of children. The children claimed to have survived rituals in which they were sexually molested and others had been killed.

Attempts to follow-up numerous reports of the cattle mutilations have led investigators to dismiss most reports as misidentified predator damage, with a few cases of genuine mutilations being associated with copycat killing and mutilation of cattle by "cultists" who have read the cattle mutilation stories.

Attempts to verify the reports of the children have yielded no such hard evidence of cult activity, but have in a number of cases revealed a hoax by the child who had been given the story by a family member. Given the difficulty of maintaining such a secret occult society over a period of time, a skeptical approach must accompany any conclusions drawn from the children's stories until and unless substantial evidence, independently obtained, is made public.

Anton Szandor LaVey, *The Satanic Bible* (New York: Avon, 1969).

Anton Szandor LaVey, *The Satanic Rituals* (Secaucus, NJ: University Books, 1972).

Anton Szandor LaVey, *The Compleat Witch* (New York: Lancer Books, 1970).

Burton H. Wolfe, *The Devil's Avenger* (New York: Pyramid Books, 1974).

Arthur Lyons, *Satan Wants You* (London: Rupert Hart-Davis, 1970).

Gini Graham Scott, *The Magicians* (New York: Irvington Publishers, 1983).

John Fritscher, *Popular Witchcraft* (Secaucus, NJ: Citadel Books, 1973).

Henry Ansgar Kelly, *The Devil, Demonology and Witchcraft* (Garden City, NY: Doubleday, 1974).

I. SPIRITUALISM

Spiritualism is a religion based upon the belief that mediumship, the ability demonstrated by a few select persons to contact the world of spirits, proves that the individual survives bodily death. It arose in mid-nineteenth-century America and has spread around the world.

Origins

During the centuries prior to Spiritualism's emergence, Western society received a massive attack upon its belief in the supernatural world, first from Protestants, who did away with some of the more basic elements in Roman Catholicism's supernaturalism (transubstantiation, relics, indulgences), and then from Deism and Freethought, which decried the very notion of the supernatural itself. Many of these people began to look to the extraordinary paranormal experiences of certain individuals as proof that at least part of what supernatural religion had always affirmed was true. As early as 1684, Increase Mather produced the first of several volumes of accounts of supernatural occurrences out of his observations and reading and that of his son, Cotton Mather.

While the Mathers and, in the next century, such Christians as Methodist founder John Wesley appealed to paranormal experiences to substantiate their faith, others developed new movements that had psychic paranormal experiences at the core of their belief. Among the most prominent were Emmanuel Swedenborg (discussed elsewhere in this volume) and Franz Anton Mesmer, who believed that he had discovered a Universal Fluid, "animal magnetism," the manipulation of which led to hypnotism, spiritual healing, and a trance-like state. The popularity of both Swedenborgian thought and Mesmerism set the stage for Spiritualism.

Spiritualism dates to 1848 and the so-called Hydesville rappings. In that year, two female children in the Fox family of Hydesville, New York, in response to some mysterious noises in their home, discovered that the rapping sounds would intelligently react to their questions and commands. After a system of communication had been established, the girls learned that the rappings were produced by the spirit of a man who had been murdered in the house some years before. The phenomena continued when the girls moved to the home of their sister in Rochester. A public investigation the following year discovered no evidence of fraud.

The publicity given the Fox sisters struck a resonant chord in people across the country and within a short time circles in which similar phenomena were exhibited appeared. The popular movement also encountered a young magnetist, Andrew Jackson Davis (1826–1920), who had been receiving material from the spirit world for several years while in trance. As early as 1844, Davis had been hypnotized and communicated with two spirit entities who called themselves Galen and Emmanuel Swedenborg. He began to do magnetic healing and to receive metaphysical teachings. He published his first book, *The Principles of Nature* in 1847. He followed with his most important book, *The Great Harmonia*, which appeared in five volumes from 1850 to 1855 and went through numerous editions.

Davis gave Spiritualism a coherent system of thought to substantiate the central experience of mediumship. He replaced orthodox Christianity with a belief in an immanent God, who was the active moving principle in nature. Davis also conceived of "Summerland," the land of perpetual summer to which the dead go.

The movement spread as numerous autonomous pockets of people came together to experiment. As mediums were discovered, they traveled the country lecturing and giving demonstrations. Newspapers such as the *Spiritual Messenger, Shikinah* and *The Spiritual Telegraph* appeared. The movement became the subject of great interest and controversy for a decade but suffered in the late 1850s as a result of reports of fraudulent mediums and the general disruption of the Civil War. After the War, state and local associations, such as the Society of Spiritualists and Progressive Lyceum founded in St. Louis by Davis, were formed, and as early as 1864 an attempt to form a national organization was made at the convention in Chicago.

That initial attempt at organization failed and Spiritualism settled into a three-decade period of slow but steady growth and the establishment of several strong state associations, such as the one in New York. Finally in 1893 the National Spiritualist Association (name changed to the National Spiritualist Association of Churches) was formed and, as Spiritualism continued to grow, other national associations formed in its wake.

Beliefs

The beliefs of Spiritualism center upon the phenomena produced by mediums. Mediums are special people who have, for whatever reason, the ability to communicate with and to be used for communication with the spirit world. Mediumship has proven, Spiritualists believe, personal survival after death. Most of the activity of Spiritualists is concerned with developing and demonstrating mediumship.

Most Spiritualists would also agree with the basic statements concerning God, ethics, and the afterlife included in the N.S.A.C. Declaration of Principles:

1. We believe in Infinite Intelligence.
2. We believe that the phenomena of nature, both physical and spiritual, are the expression of Infinite Intelligence.
3. We affirm that a correct understanding of such expression and living in accordance therewith, constitute true religion.
4. We affirm that the existence and personal identity of the individual continue after the change called death.
5. We affirm that communication with the so-called dead is a fact, scientifically proven by the phenomena of Spiritualism.
6. We believe that the highest morality is contained in the Golden Rule: Whatsoever ye would have that others should do unto you, do ye also unto them.
7. We affirm the moral responsibility of the individual, and that he makes his own happiness or unhappiness as he obeys or disobeys Nature's physical and moral laws.
8. We affirm that the doorway to reformation is never closed against any human soul here or hereafter.

Spiritualists depart from orthodox Christianity at many points. They affirm the essential goodness of humanity (as opposed to the idea of original sin and human depravity), deny any need for salvation, and do not believe in hell.

Organization

Spiritualists are organized into numerous autonomous congregations. Individual churches may or may not be affiliated with the several Spiritualist associations. Church property is either owned by the congregation and administered by a board or owned by the medium-minister and totally controlled by her/him.

Mediums are licensed by the several associations, some of which require a modest amount of study and examination. Several organizations, however, have been organized merely to issue and hold ministerial credentials by otherwise independent mediums and require no more for a license than the payment of a small annual fee.

Associations exist primarily for fellowship, the training of mediums, publication of books and other printed matter, and some low-key coordination of the movement. Possibly more important than the associations are the many camps which provide summer employment for many mediums and the training site for new ones. Many spiritualists vacation at these camps, which offer a full round of lectures, public demonstrations, and seances.

Current Status

No recent survey of Spiritualism has been made, and any estimate of its size would be highly speculative. The emergence of other psychic groups has often obscured its continued and vital presence within American religion. A cursory survey of several Spiritualist publications and the phone directories of the larger urban areas indicate that between one and two thousand Spiritualist Churches exist and that they are concentrated in urban centers and those states with the highest percentage of senior citizens—Florida, California, Arizona, etc.

Many of the churches are members of one of the larger associations discussed below.

NATIONAL SPIRITUALIST ASSOCIATION OF CHURCHES (N.S.A.C.)

Oldest of the several Spiritualist bodies, the National Spiritualist Association of Churches was formed in 1893, and most of the other Spiritualist associations derive from it. In 1982 it had 136 congregations plus affiliated churches in Canada. It sponsors the Morris Pratt Institute as its Bureau of Education and several camps, including Lily Dale in New York and Cassadaga in Florida. *The National Spiritualist Summit* is a monthly magazine.

The N.S.A.C. represents the mainstream of Spiritualist thought, and its conservative stance led to the first schisms in the movement. During the early years of the twentieth century it was split by several controversies. First, one group wished to replace the Declaration of Principles with a Confession of Faith based upon the authority of the Bible. Unable to prevail, the group left to found the Progressive Spiritualist Church, which reported 21 churches in 1930 but seems to have disappeared.

Reincarnation, which has steadily gained adherents throughout this century, is an issue that has continually rent the N.S.A.C. The first group to leave because of a belief in reincarnation was the National Spiritual Alliance in 1913. Then in 1930 the N.S.A.C. adopted a strongly worded statement condemning reincarnation as being subversive of Spiritualism. This resolution led to the loss of the New York State Association, which formed the General Assembly of Spiritualists.

Finally, Spiritualism was split by the same issue that affected other American churches, race. As Spiritualism spread among black people, the N.S.A.C. moved to segregate them and curtail their participation in the national conventions. An initial schism of black members occurred in 1925, and those who left formed the National Colored Spiritualist Association of Churches. An anti-black resolution passed at the N.S.A.C. convention in 1930 became a second factor in the loss of New York members to the General Assembly of Spiritualists.

UNIVERSAL CHURCH OF THE MASTER

The Universal Church of the Master was formed in Los Angeles, California in 1908 by West Coast Spiritualists and for many years was a small regional body. However, during the 1960s it began to grow and became national in scope. In 1980 it reported approximately 300 congregations, 1,300 ministers (mediums), and 10,000 members. Headquarters are in San Leandro, California.

UNIVERSAL HARMONY FOUNDATION

The Universal Harmony Foundation was founded in 1942 as the Universal Psychic Science Association by Revs. J. Bertran and Helene Gerling. It combines Spiritualism with both Eastern and New Thought teachings. Headquarters are in Seminole, Florida, where a seminary for training ministers is located. A periodical, *The Spiritual Science Digest*, serves the Association.

Controversy

Spiritualism was from its inception hobbled by continued accusations of fraudulent mediums. Charges of deception date to the very beginning of Spiritualism, as Margaret, one of the Fox sisters, in 1888 confessed that she and her sister Kate had faked the original rappings. By the time she made the confession, which she later recanted, numerous incidents of fake phenomena had been uncovered.

Many of the frauds revolved around attempts to materialize spirits, frequently accomplished by the medium's having accomplices dress in luminous cheesecloth. Mediums kept files on regular and potential clients so they could produce convincing information supposedly derived from the spirit world during seances. Mediums also attempted to produce objects (called "apports") from the spirit realm, which would mysteriously materialize during a seance.

The constant repeated exposure of fraudulent mediumship hindered but by no means stopped Spiritualism's growth or the practice of fake seances. A 1960 exposure of fake materialization seances at Camp Chesterfield in Indiana did not noticeably effect the status of the offending mediums but *The Psychic Observer*, the paper which printed the story, was destroyed as a Spiritualist newspaper by the loss of advertising and subscriptions. The failure of the movement as a whole to rid itself of the openly operating pockets of fraudulent leaders has prevented its acceptance as a legitimate religion in many quarters.

Ollah Eloise Toph, ed., *The Centennial Memorial of Modern Spiritualism, 1848–1948* (St. Louis: Thomas E. Tororovich (for the National Spiritualist Association of U.S.A.), 1948).

Centennial Book of Modern Spiritualism in America (Chicago: National Spiritualist Association of United States of America, 1948).

Grand Souvenir Book, World Centennial Celebration of Modern Spiritualism (San Antonio, TX: Federation of Spiritualist Churches and Associations, 1948).

A New Text of Spiritual Philosophy and Religion (San Jose, CA: Universal Church of the Master, 1972).

E. W. Wallis and M. H. Wallis, *Mediumship Explained* (Summit, NJ: Stow Memorial Foundation, n.d.)

George Lawton, *The Drama of Life After Death* (London: Constable, 1933).

Slater Brown, *The Heyday of Spiritualism* (New York: Hawthorn Books, 1970).

G. L. Nelson, *Spiritualism and Society* (New York: Schocken Books, 1969).

Vieda Skultans, *Intimacy and Ritual* (London: Routledge and Kegan Paul, 1974).

Mariam Buckner Pond, *Time Is Kind* (New York: Centennial Press, 1947).

J. THEOSOPHY

The Theosophical Society was founded in 1875 by Helen Petrovna Blavatsky, Henry Steel Olcott, and William Q. Judge. Blavatsky and Olcott met in 1874 in Chrittenden, Vermont, where each had gone to see the phenomena generated by the Eddy brothers, two famous materialization mediums. Blavatsky joined in and demonstrated her skills as a medium. Olcott, a reporter, attended the seances and wrote several enthusiastic accounts.

Back in New York City, Olcott became the leader of an informal circle of people interested in the psychic and occult which had grown around Blavatsky. Judge, an Irish-born lawyer, was a member of this circle and joined with Blavatsky and Olcott in forming the new organization. Olcott was elected President; Madame Blavatsky, Corresponding Secretary; and Judge, Counsel to the Society.

In 1877 Blavatsky finished her first important book, *Isis Unveiled*, in which she summarized Western occult philosophy as opposed to Spiritualism, the dominant psychic movement in America at that time and the movement out of which Blavatsky had come. The next year Blavatsky and Olcott moved to India, leaving the American work to Judge, though Abner Doubleday, the inventor of baseball, was designated the new president in Olcott's stead.

Blavatsky and Olcott settled in Bombay and in 1879 began a magazine, *The Theosophist*. In 1882 they moved to Madras. Once in India, both began to pay increasing attention to Hinduism and Buddhism. Olcott became an enthusiastic supporter of Buddhism and spent much of the rest of his life in helping Buddhists in Ceylon resist British missionaries; attempting to promote international Buddhist unity; and spreading Buddhism to the West. Blavatsky increasingly absorbed Eastern esoteric ideas into a more comprehensive and unique Theosophical system, which she described in her second major work, *The Secret Doctrine* (1888).

Instead of the spirits of the Spiritualists, Blavatsky drew her authority from a number of masters or mahatmas, highly evolved beings who taught her and demonstrated their powers by various paranormal events, primarily the mysterious materialization of objects and messages. At Adyar, near Madras, where permanent headquarters were established, Blavatsky had a cabinet built into which messages and other gifts from the masters frequently were found.

Blavatsky died in 1891. Her death was followed by a decade of internal dissension within the larger Theosophical movement. In 1888 Annie Besant, an atheist and leader in the British Freethought movement, converted to Theosophy. Blavatsky quickly recognized her capabilities and moved her into a leadership position. She succeeded Blavatsky as head of the Esoteric Section, an inner group within the Society which experimented with magic and occultism, and when Olcott died in 1907 she became the new President.

Meanwhile, in America, Judge had built the American Section of the Society into a large group. He had authored several books and launched two periodicals, The Path (1886) and The Theosophical Forum (1889). After Blavatsky died, a power struggle developed between Besant and Judge. Unable to resolve the conflict, in 1895 the American Section under Judge became independent of the British and Indian branches. Only a few lodges remained affiliated to Besant and Olcott.

In 1896 Judge died. Like Blavatsky, he had a few years before his death met a talented young woman who became his successor—Katherine A. Tingley. She took complete control in 1898 and the Theosophical Society in America experienced further schisms. Members in Syracuse, New York, formed the Temple of the People, and others in New York City formed the Theosophical Society of New York.

Twentieth Century

Tingley brought to Theosophy not only a background in Spiritualism but in social work. Upon taking control of the Theosophical Society in America, she reorganized it as the Universal Brotherhood Organization and Theosophical Society. She purchased land on Point Loma at San Diego, California, and introduced American Theosophy to a community she built there. She invited members to move to Point Loma and created a communal society that included a school, the Isis Temple of Art, Music, and Drama, a Greek theatre, and a hotel-sanatorium.

Tingley moved the Society into social work beginning with the establishment of the War Relief Corps and a hospital on Long Island for soldiers wounded in the Cuban campaign of the Spanish-American War. She brought Cuban children to Point Loma to be educated and set up schools on the island after the war ended.

Tingley died in 1929. Gottfried de Purucker succeeded her. He immediately began to refocus the organization. He sold the property on Point Loma and began to build the chapters, many of which had been lost through Tingley's neglect. Membership, which had declined nationally, rose again. Shortly before his death in 1942, he moved the headquarters to Covina, California.

The early years of the twentieth century were a time of rebuilding for the Theosophical Society under Annie Besant. Soon after the Judge schism and the reorganization of the Society, a major setback occurred when it was revealed that the new head of the American section, Alexander Fullerton, was a homosexual who had seduced a minor. He was arrested and eventually sent to a mental institution, but the Society rebounded and by 1925 could claim 7,333 members in 268 lodges in the United States.

In 1912 A. P. Warrington established the Krotona Institute of Theosophy, a Theosophical community in Hollywood, California, a rival of Point Loma. In 1924 Krotona moved to a 118-acre site at Ojai, California. In 1926 land was purchased in Wheaton, Illinois (a Chicago suburb) and a national headquarters built.

Theosophic Perspectives

The Theosophical Society set three objectives for itself:

1. To form a nucleus of the Universal Brotherhood of Humanity without distinction of race, creed, sex, caste, or color.
2. To encourage the study of comparative religion, philosophy and science.
3. To investigate unexplained laws of nature and the powers latent in man.

Within the context of these objectives, Theosophy sees itself as a body of the truths that form the basis of all true religions; hence, Theosophy is not so much a new religion as a restatement of the essence of religion. This Theosophical perspective was preeminently stated by Blavatsky in The Secret Wisdom, a most difficult book to read without one of the many study guides and summaries published by the several Theosophical organizations.

Theosophy posits one eternal, infinite Reality, the Divine, which underlies everything. From this infinite unknowable Reality, the creative principle is emanated, and from the creative principle, God, many and various spiritual beings—angels, etc.—have emanated. Thus the universe is a manifestation of the life of God.

Each human being is a monad, a spark of the Divine, a microcosm of the macrocosm, which enters into physical embodiment to evolve from a latent divinity into full perfection. To enter physical manifestation, the monad passes through the various planes of existence from the Divine through the Monadic, Atomic and Buddhic down to the Upper and Lower Mental, Astral (Emotional), and Physical. As the monad descends into the lower realms, it acquires a set of sheaths or bodies termed the causal body (Upper Mental), mental body (Lower Mental), astral body, and physical body. These allow the monad to function in various appropriate manners.

The monad develops through a series of embodiments, i.e., reincarnations. Gradually it gains enough knowledge and experience to be free from the need to reincarnate.

The spiritual hierarchy bridges the gap between humans and the Divine. Individuals who have completed their cycle of development through successful incarnations now work for the evolution of the race. At the bottom of the hierarchy are the Masters or Mahatmas who periodically select a few members of the human race to become their messengers for a generation. Blavatsky was such a select messenger. The majority of the disagreements within the Theosophical Movement concern the acceptance and rejection of the claims of people to be messengers of the masters. Claimants include Alice Bailey, William Q. Judge, Guy Ballard, and Francia LaDue, to mention only a few.

The Theosophical perspective has been accepted by many occult organizations, some of which don't realize that the source of these ideas is the Theosophical Society. A number of individuals have claimed contact with one of the Masters first described by Blavatsky and have begun new organizations based upon the individual revelation imparted. Alice Bailey was contacted by the Master Djwhul Khul; Ballard regularly spoke with St. Germain; and LaDue received her messages from Hilarion. Each assumed a basic agreement with Theosophy but found new emphases according to their special revelations. The Theosophical Society in America and the Theosophical Society have been the least open to the claims of new messengers, while those growing out of the work of Guy Ballard ("I AM" Movement, the Church Universal and Triumphant, etc.) have relied upon the leadership of a messenger.

Controversy

During its first two generations, Theosophy was rocked by several major controversies and scandals which greatly hindered its growth, contributed to its splintering, and could have proved fatal to a weaker organization. First, in 1885, Richard Hodgson and the British Society for Psychical Research issued their report of Hodgson's extensive investigations of the paranormal phenomena which had been reported around Madame Blavatsky. Hodgson concluded that most of the phenomena had been fraudulently produced by Blavatsky and several associates. The previous year, one of those associates, Emma Coulomb, had turned over incriminating documents to the *Christian College Magazine* in Madras, which had published the extracts in several exposé articles.

The attacks accused Blavatsky of writing the messages which she claimed came from the masters and placing or dropping them so that they would appear mysteriously. She was also accused of planting objects that would "materialize" to the amazement of the naive and gullible.

Efforts to investigate further and defend Blavatsky only increased the accounts of fraud, which have been kept alive over the years by writers on Theosophy. Because of the marked influence of her books and the Theosophical Society, and the key role that she claimed for the masters in the development of both, the cloud that remains over her life is still a matter of intense interest.

Following Madame Blavatsky's death, when leaders were striving for control of the Society, Judge claimed to have received messages from the masters. His opponents in the Society accused him of forgery. When Besant turned against him, Judge gathered his supporters and led them to assert their autonomy of Europe and India.

After Judge left, the small minority of supporters of the Besant-Olcott position reorganized and elected Alexander Fullerton as its leader. The fighting between the two groups became intense, especially after Katherine Tingley succeeded Judge. Thus when Tingley received word of Fullerton's attempted seduction of a male minor, she released the information to the authorities who arrested him.

Finally, in 1906 Besant's major associate, the Rev. Charles W. Lead-beater became the center of a sex scandal on the very eve of Besant's becoming president of the International Society. He was accused of teaching masturbation to some youths placed in his charge, as a means of controlling their emerging sexual drives. Besant and Leadbeater had been closely identified and had authored a number of books together. Besant was forced to ask for his resignation. He returned a few years later as Besant inaugurated the Order of the Star of the East, an organization to announce the coming of a new World Teacher Saviour. In 1909 Besant announced that the Lord Maitreya, the master most closely associated with Jesus of Nazareth, was returning and would be embodied in a young Indian named Jiddu Krishnamurti. Krishnamurti became head of the Order, traveled on its behalf, and accepted the promotion given him until 1929. That year he dissolved the Order, denied any role as the World Teacher, and became an independent guru.

While the Besant branch of the Society suffered through its travails with Fullerton, Leadbeater and Krishnamurti, the branch under Katherine Tingley also had to survive several attacks on its credibility. In 1902 she won a major lawsuit against the *Los Angeles Times*, which had accused her of permitting gross immoralities among her disciples. She also won a battle with the New York Society for the Prevention of Cruelty to Children, which had tried to block the arrival of the Cuban children she had brought to the United States for education at Point Loma.

After these early tumultuous years, both Societies have been relatively free of major controversies for half a century, though they have not been allowed to forget their past.

Present Status

During his years of leadership, Gottfried de Purucker changed the name of Tingley's Universal Brotherhood Organization and Theosophical Society to, simply, the Theosophical Society. Headquarters moved from San Diego to Covina and eventually to Altadena, California, where they are located today. Associated with the Theosophical Society is the Theosophical University Press, which issues *Sunrise*, a periodical, and operates a large library for the members.

The Theosophical Society in America, the branch of the Society chartered by the International Society in India, is headquartered in Wheaton, Illinois. The large headquarters building houses the Olcott Library for members. The American branch of the Theosophical Publishing House and Quest Books are also located at Wheaton. They publish several periodicals, including the *American Theosophist* and *Discovery*. *The Theosophist*, founded in 1979, is still published in India.

A smaller branch of Theosophy is the United Lodge of Theosophy, formed in 1909 by Robert Crosbie, a former member of the Point Loma community. Headquarters are in Los Angeles, as is the associated Theosophy Company, the publishing arm. *Theosophy* is their monthly periodical.

Quite apart from the several groups which retain the word "Theosophical" in their name, Theosophy has spawned numerous occult bodies in the United States. The main groups, each of which has splintered into several factions, include The Arcane School, the I AM Religious Activity, the Liberal Catholic Church and the Rosicrucian Fellowship (founded by Max Heindel). All are discussed elsewhere in this volume.

Josephine Ransom, *A Short History of the Theosophical Society* (Adyar: Theosophical Publishing House, 1938).

The Theosophical Movement, 1875–1950 (Los Angeles: Cuunningham Press, 1951).

Charles J. Ryan, *H. P. Blavatsky and the Theosophical Movement* (Pasadena: Theosophical University Press, 1975).

Howard Murphet, *When Daylight Comes* (Wheaton, IL: Theosophical Publishing House, 1975).

L. W. Rogers, *Elementary Theosophy* (Wheaton, IL: Theosophical Press, 1956).

Bruce F. Campbell, *Ancient Wisdom Revisited* (Berkeley: University of California Press, 1980).

Emmett A. Greenwalt, *California Utopia: Point Loma: 1897–1942* (San Diego: Point Loma Publications, 1978).

Marion Meade, *Madame Blavatsky, the Woman Behind the Myth* (New York: G. P. Putnam's Sons, 1980).

Arthur H. Nethercot, *The First Five Lives of Annie Besant* (Chicago: University of Chicago Press, 1960).

Arthur H. Nethercot, *The Last Four Lives of Annie Besant* (Chicago: University of Chicago Press, 1963).

K. THE UNIVERSAL PEACE MISSION MOVEMENT OF FATHER DIVINE

No "cult" group aroused more attention in the period between World Wars I and II than the Peace Mission of Father Divine. During this time, when the word "cult" was first adopted by social scientists, the Peace Mission was frequently cited as a typical example of a cult.

Founder

The Peace Mission was founded by the man known to his followers as Father Major Jealous Divine (1880?–1965). The "facts" of his life prior to 1914 remain a matter of disagreement. According to the most popular story (among those outside the Movement), he was born George Baker around 1880 on a rice plantation in Georgia. In 1899 he became the assistant of an itinerant preacher, Samuel Morris, who called himself Father Jehovia. The two split in 1912, and Father Divine began to gather his own following. Members of the Movement project a much earlier date of birth as they cite June 6, 1882, as the date of his first marriage.

In either case, he emerged in Brooklyn in 1914. Five years later, with his followers, he moved to Sayville, New York, where his wife, Sister Penny, bought them a home. He lived quietly. His followers were organized to work in the community. By the mid-1920s there were from 3 to 40 members, all of whom were black. Sometime during this period, however, the first white members joined.

The most famous events in the life of Father Divine, the ones that catapulted him into the public spotlight, began on November 13, 1931. On that day, responding to neighborhood complaints about traffic congestion around his home, police arrested Father Divine for disturbing the peace. Viewing the incident as racially inspired, he refused bail, pleaded not guilty, and was tried and convicted. The jury asked for leniency. The judge ignored them and handed down a sentence of a year in jail and ordered him to pay a $500 fine. Father Divine went to jail. Two days later the judge, apparently a healthy man, died, and Father Divine freely offered his opinion that the death was not the result of natural causes. One follower is said to have remarked on the day of sentencing, "The judge can't live long now. He's offended Almighty God." From his cell, Father Divine remarked simply, "I hated to do it!" (Since that date, the Peace Mission commemorates June 7, the day of the Judge's death, by publishing accounts of disasters that befell people whose activities conflicted with Father Divine's program.)

Father Divine, spurred by the events in Sayville, moved his followers to Harlem in 1932. He had become a hero to the black community, and once in Harlem, he was able to expand the Mission in response to the Depression. He purchased hotels which he turned into Peace Mission "heavens." Members were able, through the Mission's assistance, to have cheap food, shelter, a job, and a reformed life. New members were instructed to pay off their debts, cancel insurance, return any funds they might have stolen, and in the future to pay their own way in cash.

His first wife having died, Father Divine married Edna Rose Ritchings, a white Canadian, in 1946. Their wedding day is a holiday for the Movement. About this time he also moved his headquarters to Philadelphia. In 1954 he was given Woodmont, an estate in suburban Philadelphia. It served as his country home until his death in 1965. His body is enshrined there.

After his death, Mother Divine succeeded to leadership of the Movement and continues to administer its worldwide affairs.

Beliefs and Practices

The structure and practices of the Movement derived from Father Divine's perception of the situation of the downtrodden of society, particularly black Americans. He proposed a total economic and religious program to reform the individual and restructure society.

The Peace Mission affirms that Father Divine fulfilled all the Biblical prophecies for the Second Coming of Christ and the Coming of the Jewish Messiah. God as Father and Mother are personified in Father and Mother Divine and constitute humanity as one brotherhood. Woodmont is the Mount of the House of the Lord (Micah 4:1-2; Isaiah 2:2-3) from which the Law shall go to all nations. The Mission views itself as the fulfillment of specific Biblical prophecies and the essence of all religion: faith in the one God. It accepts both the Ten Commandments and the Sermon on the Mount.

From this religious perspective a social, economic, and political program has developed. Members look for a day when America, as the birthplace of the Kingdom of God, will become the Kingdom, in fact. The Kingdom is equated with the principles of true Americanism, Brotherhood, Democracy, Christianity, Judaism, and all other true religions.

The Mission teaches that each person is equal in the sight of God and, thus, entitled to basic rights (life, liberty, and happiness) and every convenience and comfort of modern society. Each individual also has the responsibility of protecting every other person's rights and privileges. One step in that protection would be the conviction of all members of a mob that commits murder as first-degree murderers.

Members of the Mission live communally. All possessions are owned cooperatively, and all properties are maintained by the members without compensation for their work on this endeavor. The Mission advocates full employment as a right and opposes life insurance, social security and credit and installment buying. The Mission admonishes members to pay cash for all purchases.

On a personal level, all members adopt Father Divine's International Modesty Code: No Smoking. No Drinking. No Obscenity. No Vulgarity. No Profanity. No Undue Mixing of the Sexes. No Receiving of Gifts, Presents, Tips, or Bribes. Within the group men and women live apart. Within their businesses, the principles are enforced. For example, guests at the hotels run by the Movement must adopt the code while staying at the hotel. Men and women stay on separate floors (even married couples). Women cannot wear slacks or short skirts. Men cannot wear short-sleeved shirts. Visitors are not allowed in the guest's room.

On a social level the Mission teaches the equality of the individual and the right to freedom of worship and voting. Education should be free and in English, the universal language. All racial references should be deleted from books.

The Mission believes in the Declaration of Independence and the Constitution, particularly in the Bill of Rights. All people have a right to live safely and securely under the Constitution. Restitution is a basic step toward the ideal life as spelled out in the Constitution. The Mission advocates nations returning territory taken by force, governments restoring losses due to mob violence, and individuals returning all stolen possessions. It advocates mass production as the means of eliminating poverty and social inequality.

In putting his principles into action, Father Divine created a far-flung organization.

Organization

The Universal Peace Mission Movement began as a small group around Father Divine in his home in Sayville, New York. The group functioned as an extended family with Father Divine as patriarch. He took personal responsibility for the members by placing ads for employment opportunities and providing inexpensive food and shelter. During the Depression in Harlem, he became known for the lavish banquets he gave for his followers and guests at little or no cost.

As the organization grew, so did his personal staff. He hired secretaries for correspondence, filing, and typing. As the organization grew, the large secretarial staff became a personal entourage that included a cook and chauffeur.

The growth of the Movement soon required the acquisition of houses of worship, housing for followers, and restaurants. However, once the Sayville property was sold, no property or other assets were placed in Father Divine's name. Rather, groups of believers incorporated independently as a church and affiliated with Father Divine and his principles.

Five separate corporations were formed that now hold all the property. They are held together within the Movement only by their allegiance to Father (and now Mother) Divine. During Father Divine's life, he approved all nominations to the Churches' boards, and the Churches conformed to Father Divine's rules.

Individual members of the Mission also formed businesses that they associated with the Movement. They named the businesses so as to identify them with Father Divine. They were allowed to make that identity if they followed Father Divine's rules: sell only for cash, sell below the price of their competitors, accept no tips or gratuities, refrain from dealing in tobacco or liquor.

Within the Movement, members may also participate in one of three religious orders, which together are estimated to include approximately fifty percent of the group. The younger women (up to middle age) can become Rosebuds. They wear dark red jackets with a white "V" (for virtue) over their hearts. Shirts are navy blue. They assist in conducting worship services, perform in dramatic productions, and participate in the Movement's holiday celebrations. Rosebuds ascribe to an extensive set of special rules aimed at inculcating the virtues of submissiveness, meekness, and sweetness.

Older women may join the Lily-buds. They wear green jackets trimmed in white and lead in music and reading at services. Men may join the Crusaders. Members of the orders must devote all of their free time to the Mission.

The Universal Peace Mission Movement now exists as a number of independent church corporations, businesses and religious orders interrelated by the participants' belief in Father Divine and his teachings.

Growth

The Peace Mission had its greatest growth during Father Divine's life. As of 1982, it had churches meeting in Philadelphia (4), the Bronx, Newark (3), Los Angeles, and Sacramento. One congregation each can be found in Australia and Switzerland. The New Day Publishing Company publishes the bi-weekly newspaper, *The New Day*, which is, for the most part, filled with quotations from and pictures of Father and Mother Divine. Hotels (formerly known as "heavens") conducted by the Movement include the Divine Lorraine and Divine Tracy in Philadelphia, the Divine Riviera in Los Angeles, and the Divine Hotel in Ulster County, New York.

The home in which Father Divine lived from 1919 to 1932 in Sayville, New York is owned by the movement and has become a shrine.

Mother Divine, *The Peace Mission Movement* (Philadelphia: The Imperial Press, 1982).

Robert Weisbrot, *Father Divine and the Struggle for Racial Equality* (Urbana: University of Illinois Press, 1983).

Kenneth E. Burnham, *God Comes to America* (Boston: Lambeth Press, 1979).

Sara Harris, *Father Divine* (New York: Collier Books, 1971).

L. THE WORLDWIDE CHURCH OF GOD

The Worldwide Church of God is the most successful of the several church bodies to grow out of the Seventh Day Church of God Movement. It also incorporated the teaching known as British-Israelism into its theology and thus shares some affinity with the Identity Movement.

Founder and Early History

The Worldwide Church of God was founded by Herbert W. Armstrong, an Iowan who moved to Oregon in 1924. In Salem, Armstrong's wife, Loma, met Ira Runcorn, a sabbatarian Bible student, who convinced Loma that the proper day of worship and rest was Saturday, not Sunday. Angered at his wife's new belief, Armstrong agreed to try to prove her wrong. He also began to study the Bible concerning evolution, the truth of which was being advocated by a neighbor. Six months of study convinced him of seven basic truths: God exists; evolution is a false theory; the Bible is God's inspired, infallible instruction book; the Saturday Sabbath is still binding today; the Jewish holy days and festivals are also binding; death, not eternal punishment, awaits the unsaved; and eternal life is God's Gift to believers.

Being convinced of these truths, in 1927 he sought baptism at the hands of a Baptist minister but joined no church. Rather, he began to seek for the true church and, through Ira Runcorn, was led to the Church of God headquartered in Stanberry, Missouri. This oldest branch of the Seventh Day Church of God, since splintered into numerous independent church bodies, was the Adventist group which accepted Saturday as the Sabbath but rejected the unique teachings and revelations of Ellen G. White, founder of the Seventh Day Adventist Church. It had only about 50 members in Oregon, but Armstrong affiliated with it, frequently preached for several of the small congregations, and wrote articles for the denominational periodical.

Armstrong's entrance into the Church coincided with its period of turmoil. The members in Oregon, suffering during the Depression, did not wish to send money to Missouri. In 1930 Armstrong led the formation of the Oregon Conference of the Church of God, by which he was later ordained. In 1933, the Church of God (Stanberry, MO) split. A group in Salem, West Virginia, headed by A.N. Dugger, wanted a reorganization of the Church along what they felt were Biblical standards. The group rejected congregational church government and chose its leadership, 12 apostles, seventy evangelists, and 7 elders by lot. In the first drawing, Armstrong was selected as one of the seventy. He remained loosely connected with the Salem faction for several years, even after he began his own independent ministry.

Armstrong began that independent ministry in 1933. In April of that year he edited and issued the first copy of *The Bulletin of the Churches of God in Oregon*. That summer he began an evangelistic service in Eugene, Oregon, at the close of which the members decided to start a congregation independent of the Churches of God of Oregon. Then in September, he began a radio broadcast, "The Radio Church of God," over station KORE in Eugene. A second congregation was organized in October. These events are now seen as the beginning of the Worldwide Church of God.

On February 1, 1934, Armstrong issued the first copy of the magazine with which he has subsequently been identified, *The Plain Truth*, to 106 listeners to his radio broadcast. Growth proceeded slowly through the 1930s, but by 1940 *The Plain Truth*, now printed instead of mimeographed, reached a circulation of 3,000, and four radio stations (Eugene, Salem, Portland, and Seattle) carried the broadcast. Armstrong became committed to using the mass media as the major means of reaching people with his teachings.

On a trip to California in 1941, Armstrong arranged to have his program broadcast over KMTR in Hollywood. He had decided to drop any remnants of a worship service and concentrate entirely on Biblical teaching and interpretation. He changed the name of the broadcast to "The World Tomorrow," the name by which it is still heard. The high response from his California audience and the opportunity for daily broadcasts led him to shift his attention to Southern California. The work expanded quickly, and in August 1942, he added the 50,000-watt WHO in Des Moines.

After World War II, the Radio Church of God, the corporate name of Armstrong's organization, bought its first printing facilities. He also went on his first baptizing tour to interview, baptize, and receive new members of the Church from among the listeners to the broadcast. Seeing the expansion of his efforts, he envisioned a college which would offer both a Christian liberal education and training for ministers. He moved to Pasadena, California and opened Ambassador College in the fall of 1947. In December 1952 he ordained the first five ministers of the Church and added two more in January. In 1953 the work took on international proportions with the addition of Radio Luxembourg.

For the next two decades after the initiation of work in Europe, the Church grew impressively and Garner Ted, Armstrong's son, who in 1957 began to speak on most of the broadcasts, became one of the most recognizable figures on both radio and television. "The World Tomorrow" was heard in Spanish, French, and German. *The Plain Truth* became a full-color magazine. Two additional Ambassador College campuses opened (in England and Texas). In 1968 the Radio Church of God changed its name to the Worldwide Church of God.

A Period of Controversy

The two decades of spectacular growth were followed by a decade of intense controversy, beginning in 1972. There was widespread expectation in the Church that 1972 would signal the beginning of God's kingdom in a time of disaster and turmoil and the necessity of God's true church to flee into hiding. That expectation was unfulfilled. Then Garner Ted Armstrong left the air in unexplained circumstances, only to reappear four months later. In 1973 the Church reorganized at the regional level. It announced a new policy of openness and, for the first time, offered *The Good News*, a second periodical formerly issued only to members, to nonmembers for the first time.

Then in 1974 the Church was shaken by a massive scandal. Garner Ted Armstrong was charged with multiple counts of sexual improprieties. Added to the scandal was an intense internal theological conflict over the dating of Pentecost and the marriage of divorced members. A number of ministers resigned and began several independent churches, including the Associated Churches of God, the Twentieth Century Church of God, The Church of God, the Eternal, and the Foundation for Biblical Research. The exodus of the ministers and their supporters did little to decrease the controversy. A group of former members in Pasadena attacked the Church through a new periodical, *The Ambassador Report*, originally *The Ambassador Review*, claiming continued unresolved leadership problems.

Much of the continued controversy within the Church centered upon the person of lawyer Stanley Rader, a non-member who was nevertheless managing much of the Church's business. Eventually, he and Garner Ted, Armstrong's designated successor, openly clashed with the result that in 1978 Garner Ted left the Church and began the Church of God International. In the midst of this conflict, his father announced his marriage to a young divorcee (who he would, in turn, divorce in 1984).

Relative quiet did not return to the Church until 1980. In 1979, a group of former members filed suit against Rader and a number of the Church leaders on behalf of the Church, claiming fiscal mismanagement. The Church, defined by the state's attorney and the court as a "public trust," was placed under a temporary court-ordered receivership, which was only lifted when the California legislature passed a law against the state's movement on an ecclesiastical body in such a manner.

Beliefs and Practices

The Worldwide Church of God grew out of the Seventh Day Church of God and accepts many of its basic teachings. It considers the Bible to be the infallible Word of God. Following commonly accepted Adventist teaching, the church affirms God the Creator and Father and the divinity of Christ but denies the Trinity. The Holy Spirit is God's power, shared by Christ and the Father, i.e., the family of God. Salvation is through faith in God and His son, Jesus Christ, who atoned for humankind's sins upon the cross. Baptism (by immersion) the annual memorial of the Lord's Supper, and footwashing (practiced in connection with the Lord's Supper) are ordinances.

The Worldwide Church of God also accepted the perspective on sabbatarianism held by the Seventh Day Church of God. It teaches that the Ten Commandments are God's eternal law and, as such, the keeping of the sabbath has never been abrogated. At the time of the Church's founding, Armstrong was among several Church of God ministers who felt that the Old Testament festivals should also be observed. It extended that belief into a keeping of all seven feasts (Cf. *Leviticus 23*)—Passover and the Days of Unleavened Bread, Pentecost, Trumpets, Atonement, Tabernacles, the Last Great Day and the First Day of the Sacred Year. In every country where the Church has a significant membership, feast grounds are designated where church members gather to celebrate the Holy Days. Popular holidays such as Christmas, Easter, Valentine's Day and Halloween are denounced as pagan. Evolution is also denounced as opposing Biblical teachings on creation.

Integral to Church beliefs is an understanding of the position and role of the Worldwide Church of God in history. That understanding originated in the second key doctrinal point that led to Armstrong's leaving the fellowship of the Church of God (Salem, WV)—his acceptance of British-Israelism. British-Israelism is the belief that the Anglo-Saxon people of Western Europe (and by extension the United States and the peoples of the British Commonwealth nations) are the literal descendants of the ten Northern (the so-called lost) tribes of ancient Israel. Great Britain and the United States, as the present tribes of Ephraim and Manasseh, respectively, have a special role in the inheritance of God's blessings and promises. Among the first books sent to people who receive *The Plain Truth* is *The United States and British Commonwealth in Prophecy,* a detailed statement of the British-Israel perspective.

The Church has also adopted the dispensational view of the history of the Church of God from the Book of Revelation in which the seven churches of chapters two and three are identified as the seven church ages. The Worldwide Church is identified as the Church at Philadelphia, which was to appear just before the "endtime" events described in the remainder of the Book of Revelation. The work of the Philadelphian Church was supposed to occur in two nineteen-year cycles. The first was dated from the beginning of Armstrong's independent ministry in 1934; the second began in 1953 with the internationalizing of the work through the European radio program. It was widely held that in 1972 the Church would begin the tribulation and would have to flee the country to a place of safety. No significant event or move to refuge occurred in 1972, and the Church has since downplayed the nineteen-year cycles.

Organization

During the split between the Stanberry and Salem factions of the Church of God, Armstrong sided with the Salem group, which denied any basis for democratic elections of Church members, choosing instead to choose leaders by casting lots. Armstrong moved toward an even more autocratic system. He saw himself as the chosen prophet and apostle of the church in the last days, who had absolute authority in all matters, including the appointment and dismissal of ministers, the disfellowshipping of members, and the purchase and disposal of property.

The Church is administered through the national offices in Pasadena, California. Local churches are under a regional minister in the United States or a national director in foreign countries. Pastors are appointed from the national office. The national office also has control of the two colleges, the several periodicals, the secular cultural programs, and the feast sites.

Current Status

The Worldwide Church of God is headquartered in Pasadena, California, adjacent to the Ambassador College complex. By 1985, it had approximately 100,000 members worldwide. Most of the congregations meet in rented facilities and, as a rule, do not advertise locally, hence their presence is almost unknown within the communities in which they operate. Two Ambassador College campuses, one in Pasadena and one in Big Sandy, Texas, serve the membership. A third campus in England was recently sold. Feast sites, such as the ones in the Pocono Mountains of Pennsylvania and the Dells in Wisconsin, are located around the United States.

The church publishes four international periodicals. *The Plain Truth* circulates in the millions and has several foreign-language editions (German, French, and Spanish). It is offered free to listeners of "The World Tomorrow" radio and television shows through ads in national periodicals and through displays at many public and business locations. *The Good News* and *Youth* circulate beyond the Church's membership but to a lesser extent. Readers of these periodicals are asked to renew their free subscriptions annually. *The Worldwide News* is available to members only. Through the College, the Church also offers a free Bible Correspondence Course, which teaches basic church doctrine.

In the late 1970s, Armstrong announced the formation of the Ambassador International Cultural Foundation, which extended the work of the Church into secular areas. A magazine, *Quest*, was launched in 1978. A publishing concern, Everest House, issues nonreligious books of general interest. At the auditorium in Pasadena, the Foundation offers concerts and other nonchurch-related cultural programs to the general public.

Controversy

The Worldwide Church of God became a matter of intense controversy as the Church programs appeared increasingly on radio and then television and as more and more people began to receive *The Plain Truth*. Other Church leaders opposed Armstrong's teaching which denied basic orthodox Christian doctrine (the Trinity), emphasized racial themes (British-Israelism), and in general denounced mainline Christianity. By the late 1960s, substantial analyses of the Church's teachings by Evangelical Christians began to appear.

Since 1972, the Church has moved from one intense controversy to another. The major upheavals of 1974 and 1978 caused many members and ministers to leave the church, and they, in turn, released many confidential documents to the public. They revealed widespread opposition to the emphasis within the Church upon Armstrong's many foreign trips to meet with political leaders, the secular programs of the Foundation, the articles in *Quest* (many of which opposed Church teachings), and the leadership of Stanley Rader. Confusion erupted within the Church when doctrines on the keeping of Pentecost and the remarriage of divorced persons were revised. The large personal following of Garner Ted Armstrong left and joined his new organization.

Several ex-members such as former staff member Marion McNair, prominent minister John Robinson, and layman John Tuit, an active force behind the 1978 lawsuit, wrote books (all privately published) about their experiences within the church denouncing its hypocrisy. Their charges centered upon the misuse of church funds for secular programs and the enrichment of Armstrong, Rader, and other church leaders. Both Tuit and Robinson accused Armstrong of gross sexual improprieties.

The Worldwide Church of God has, of the mid-1980s, outwardly recovered from the controversies of the past decades (including Armstrong's divorce from his second wife) and the loss of many key personnel. Membership lost during the height of the controversies (estimated at between 5,000 and 10,000) has been replaced by new converts, and the circulation of *The Plain Truth*, which had fallen drastically during the 1970s, has resumed its earlier rate of growth. The Church seems to have entered a period of relative tranquility, though those opposed to it, such as the staff of *The Ambassador Report*, continue to press their concerns.

Herbert W. Armstrong, *The Autobiography of Herbert W. Armstrong* (Pasadena, CA: Ambassador College, 1973).

This Is the Worldwide Church of God (Pasadena, CA: Ambassador College Press, 1972).

Herbert W. Armstrong, *The United States and Britain in Prophecy* (Pasadena, CA: Worldwide Church of God, 1980).

Herman L. Hoeh, *A True History of the True Church* (Pasadena, CA: Ambassador College, 1959).

Herbert W. Armstrong, *The Wonderful World of Tomorrow* (New York: Everest House, 1979).

Joseph Hopkins, *The Armstrong Empire* (Grand Rapids, MI: Eerdmans, 1974).

J. L. F. Bucher, *Armstrongism Bibliography* (Sydney, Australia: The Author, 1983).

Marion J. McNair, *Armstrongism: Religion . . . or Rip-off?* (Orlando, FL: Pacific Charters, 1977).

David Robinson, *Herbert Armstrong's Tangled Web* (Tulsa, OK: John Hadden Publishers, 1980).

John Tuit, *The Truth Shall Make You Free* (Freehold Township, NJ: Truth Foundation, 1981).

III.
The New Age
Movement

THE NEW AGE MOVEMENT

During the 1970s, religious observers became aware of a diverse new social and religious movement whose most visible proponents were teachers of Eastern and mystical-occult philosophies. Ira Friedlander, an early sympathetic observer, described it thusly,

> A great spiritual energy has been moved to this country and holy men of the East are following it, and, of course, they bring the Light within them to become our mirrors. They establish centers or ashrams and reconfirm the spiritual centers within ourselves. They plant the seeds of inner peace with their divine grace, which remains and nourishes like a good rain that falls on fertile soil; long after the rain has gone, the seed in the soil continues to grow.

This New Age Movement, as it came to be called, grew on what many had perceived to be a great spiritual hunger in the West. David Vaughn, whose *A Faith for the New Age* (1967) was one of the harbingers of the Movement, saw the unmet religious need and yet reflected, ". . . this widespread spiritual hunger is symptomatic not of a healthy, virile Church, but of conditions of famine accompanying volcanic eruptions and earthquakes in the ecclesiastical domain."

Western society has periodically experienced widespread religious hunger accompanied by denunciations of the Church as dead, formal, and spiritually bankrupt. However, for the first time in many centuries, that spiritual hunger coincided with the presence of a number of Eastern religious teachers and a new wave of sophisticated mystical-occult teachers, many with a strong Eastern flavor to their teaching, prepared to feed the general public. The New Age Movement was and is the attempt to find the social, religious, political, and cultural convergence between the new Eastern and mystical religions and the religious disenchantment of many Westerners. While some who explored the new spiritual systems which emerged in the late 1960s became members of one particular group, others found in the ferment a transformative vision of a new world which transcended the limitations of any particular culture or religion or political system and surpassed the outmoded thought forms of old world theologies and beliefs. That transformative visions ties together the bewildering diversity which constitutes the New Age Movement and gives the Movement its name.

Historic Background and Origin

The New Age Movement can best be dated from 1971. By that year, Eastern teachers had opened ashrams and centers and books had been published representing the various strains of New Age concern, and a self-conscious social movement began to emerge. *East-West Journal*, possibly the first national periodical to focus the issues of the New Age Movement was begun by a Boston macrobiotic community, and the first popular book representative of the Movement appeared: *Be Here Now* by Baba Ram Dass. The first networks, a typical New Age organizational form, were created, and in 1972, the first national New Age directories were published: Ira Friedlander's *Year One Catalog* and the first edition of the *Spiritual Community Guide*. Even prior to the Movement, in the 1960s, small groups in various communities began to call themselves "new age" and adopt some of the elements which would in the 1970s characterize the Movement. For example, as early as 1967 Leland Stewart of Northridge, California, had captured much of the essence of the Movement in his International Cooperation Council and its ideal of a new civilization built on "unity in diversity."

The New Age Movement did not develop *de novo*, however; it had many precursors. Its roots can be clearly seen in previous attempts to find points of convergence between East and West. In the United States, possibly the first movement to synthesize the newly discovered wisdom of the East with Western thought was Transcendentalism. Growing out of the religious dissent in New England, the early Transcendentalists took the recently translated holy books of Hinduism and created a uniquely American form of mysticism. Transcendentalism was the first substantial religious movement in North America with a prominent Asian component. Its emergence signaled the arrival of an alternative religious tradition in America which has grown up and existed beside the more prominent churchly and sectarian Christian bodies. This alternative tradition valued mysticism and Eastern religious wisdom, with which it integrated Western values, particularly individualism and success orientation.

Transcendentalism passed its emphases upon mystical experience and Eastern religion to several popular movements: Spiritualism, Theosophy, New Thought, and Christian Science. Within these popular movements, Transcendentalism became wedded to Western occult thought and the new mental healing movement which had been brought to America by the disciples of Franz Mesmer. By the end of the nineteenth century, the alternative religious tradition had grown and splintered into various factions, each of which possessed its own national organization. During the twentieth century, both Spiritualism and New Thought divided periodically, thus producing numerous new organizations, several of which became national in scope. The membership of these groups supplied the initial support for the New Age vision once it was presented to them.

While Westerners were discovering and appropriating Eastern religious thought, Eastern religion itself was reeling under the impact of an imposed Western government and the Christian missionary movement which came with it. The Hindu Renaissance represented a significant adaptation to the Western critique of Hindu polytheism and village religion. It put forth what might be thought of as a Protestant Hinduism stripped of the deities and the accretions of traditional Indian religion so offensive to Western monotheists. It transformed the ashram, traditionally the small isolated residence of a guru, into a communal structure analogous to a Christian congregation. It sought to appropriate the knowledge of the West and valued the opinion of Western religious leaders. Members of the Brahmo Samaj aligned themselves with the Unitarians. Ramakrishna had visions of the Blessed Virgin Mary. Swamis Vivekananda and Yogananda, two outstanding products of the Renaissance, were the first to plant Hinduism in America.

Emerging as a prime example of the Western alternative religious tradition, Theosophy stepped into the midst of the Hindu Renaissance when its founders, Madame H. P. Blavatsky and Col. Henry S. Olcott, moved to India in 1878. Once settled, the Theosophical Society began a conscious attempt to inform its members and the general public about Eastern wisdom and to integrate Eastern thought into Western life. The first book on Hinduism written in English not merely to inform but to "convert" Westerners to Hinduism, *Nature's Finer Forces* by Rama Prasad, was published in 1890 by the Theosophical Publishing House. Blavatsky and the Society standardized the language concerning what we now call reincarnation and became the major conduit for passing the concept to the West.

The classic theosophical statement of what has come to be an essential component of the New Age perspective is Bhagavan Das' *The Essential Unity of All Religions* (1932). Das argued for the "Truth of essential Unity in superficial Diversity" of religions. He demanded the emphasis on the unity of religions as a means to further world peace. He spent over 500 pages defining the elements of Universal Religion and saw its teaching as an imperative.

Theosophy, as did Spiritualism and New Thought, splintered into a number of factions after the death of Blavatsky. Early in the twentieth century, Alice Bailey left the Society to found the Arcane School, and during the 1930s Guy Ballard founded the "I AM" Activity. Each of these groups has further subdivided, producing scores of new organizations.

While propounding the vision of the essential unity of religion, theosophists also proposed the vision of a coming new world religious teacher who would teach the nations the new truth which was being revealed to theosophical leaders by the spiritual masters. Under the leadership of Annie Besant, Krishnamurti Jeddu was nominated as the embodiment of the teacher. After assuming the role for several years, he disassociated himself from Besant and the Society and became a teacher on his own.

Alice Bailey gave impetus to the vision in her book, the *Reappearance of the Christ* (1948), and like Besant, equated the coming of the world teacher with the several prophesied future religious events, the second coming of Christ, and the return of the Buddhist bodhisattva Maitreya.

Another component of a convergence of Eastern and Western thought was the growth of the study of world religion in Western scholarly circles. Beginning in the nineteenth century, scholars stripped away many of the derogatory stereotypes of Eastern religions. Among the visible results of the scholarly enterprise has been the creation of a number of interfaith organizations and conferences, possibly the first being the World Parliament of Religions sponsored by the League of Liberal Churchmen in Chicago in 1893. This conference introduced most Eastern religions to the United States and led to the establishment of the first Hindu, Buddhist, and Islamic organizations. The convergence of religions has been a continued concern of the interfaith cooperatives.

The Coming of the New Age

When the New Age began to be announced in the early 1970s, there was already in place a large audience for its message, the members and constituencies of the several hundred alternative religions which had grown and spread since the mid-1800s. However, in 1965 a significant new factor, crucial for the emergence of the New Age movement, appeared. In that year, the Asian immigration exclusion acts which had been in effect since the early twentieth century were repealed, and Asian and Middle Eastern countries were put on the same immigration quotas which had always been given to Europe. Annually, tens of thousands of Asians have moved to the United States. Where for decades only a trickle of Asian religious teachers came to America, and those primarily to serve Asian ethnic congregations, since 1965 numerous teachers have either moved to America or taken advantage of generous visa regulations to build followings in the United States. Many of these teachers came not to work within the new Asian-American communities but to spread their teaching among Westerners. *The last days of the 1960s saw the launching of a major missionary thrust by the Eastern religions toward the West.* It has not been centrally coordinated but has grown out of a popular idea within all the religious communities in Asia from Japan to India: the West is ready for and in need of the wisdom which the East possesses.

Once the idea of the New Age was articulated, the early exponents began to build the networks which have become so definitive of New Age organizational priorities. The early directories listed those groups and organizations seen to be aligned at least partially. They included centers of the various occult, Eastern, and mystical religions, health food stores, metaphysical books stores, yoga teachers, parapsychology research organizations, psychic development interest groups, communes, and alternative health care facilities. The early directories showed little discrimination and tended to include names of groups which appeared to offer any alternative spirituality, even traditional Christian groups with unusual names.

Once the national networks were defined and a broad community who accepted the basic vision of the Movement evolved, numerous services facilitated the Movement's development. Most important in any decentralized movement, periodicals tied the diverse groups and individuals across the country together and kept the Movement informed. The most important included *New Age* (created by former staff members from *East-West Journal*); *New Realities; New Directions; Yoga Journal;* and *New Age Journal*. Many periodicals also served particular Eastern and occult groups, and newsletters arose whose circulation was limited to a single metropolitan area or one organization's membership. In the early 1970s in San Francisco, *Common Ground* appeared as a directory of local New Age activities and services. Its format was copied in other cities by periodicals which go under names such as *New Age Chicago, Free Spirit* (New York City), *New Frontier* (Philadelphia), and *New Texas* (Austin). *Whole Life Times,* which has copied *Common Ground's* format but is primarily concerned with alternative health networks, appears in several local editions and has spurred similar periodicals such as *Alternative Health* (Fort Lauderdale, FL) and the *Holistic Learning Quarterly* (Pittsburgh).

As the Movement progressed through the 1970s, leading spokespersons began to appear. Baba Ram Dass was the first recognized national exponent of New Age consciousness. A former professor of psychology at Harvard, the Jewish-born Richard Alpert accompanied his colleague Timothy Leary through a period of experimentation with psychedelic drugs before going to India and finding his guru. He reappeared as Baba Ram Dass, a guru in his own right, just as the New Age was being announced. His excellent Western academic background as transformed by his new found Eastern faith made him the perfect symbol of the New Age. The Movement consumed his popular books: *The Only Dance There Is* (1973); *Grist for the Mill* (1976); *Journey of Awakening* (1978) and *Miracle of Love* (1979). He was joined by other popular figures, some of whom were, like himself, leaders of their own alternative religious movements: Kirpal Singh, Yogi Bhajan, Pir Vilayat Khan, Swami Rama, Reb Zalman Schachter-Shalomi, Swami Kriyananda, Sun Bear, Swami Muktananda, and Rabbi Joseph Gelberman, to mention a few.

The Movement also brought forth teachers who were not just aligned to New Age ideals but who founded or led organizations with a primary commitment to the New Age. Most prominent among these is Marilyn Ferguson of Interface Press, editor of *Brain/Mind Bulletin* and *Leading Edge Bulletin*. Ferguson jumped into prominence with her visionary survey of the Movement, *The Aquarian Conspiracy* (1980), which is the most commonly accepted statement of Movement ideals and goals. David Spangler is the most important spokesperson for the Movement after these two. After three years as co-director of the Scottish community at Findhorn, he returned to the United States and founded the Lorian Association, a New Age community near Madison, Wisconsin. His early volume, *Revelation, the Birth of a New Age* (1976), is a popular statement of

New Age perspectives. The 1975 publication of A *Course in Miracles* by the newly formed Foundation for Inner Peace thrust Judith Skutch, an early New Age advocate in New York City, into the spotlight. The multivolume *Course*, a simple restatement of New Thought metaphysics using the metaphor of "miracles," became a very popular study book throughout New Age circles, and several hundred groups were founded across North America during its first decade in print. Other popular New Age teachers include Patricia Sun, George Leonard, Jean Houston, Norman Shealy, Irving Oyle, and Sam Keen.

Preferring cooperation to competition, New Age exponents tried several social structures to embody their ideals. Communes were a natural option, and some older communes were among the first groups to identify with the New Age perspective. Prominent among these communes are the Lama Foundation (NM), the Renaissance Community (MA) and the Stelle Community (IL). Many of the Eastern teachers promoted communal living among their followers, and some nurtured communes within their organizations. Prominent among these communes are the Abode of the Message, founded by Pir Vilayat Khan of the Sufi Order, the Ananda Cooperative Community of Swami Kriyananda, and New Vrindvan, the community of the International Society of Krishna Consciousness in West Virginia.

The most important elements in the New Age Movement are the many individuals, organizations, and businesses which have arisen to facilitate the process of transformation which is at the heart of the New Age vision. Every metropolitan area has scores of individuals who teach transformational techniques from meditation to the martial arts or who practice the various forms of alternative medicine, body therapies, and psychological processes. Organizations, primarily of a local and frequently ephemeral nature, support the practitioners and provide a point of contact between those seeking and those providing services. Particularly in the field of health, national professional and referral associations have arisen to bring some order to the competition among numerous forms of therapy (some of dubious value) offered by individuals with varying qualifications. Among the most prominent are the American Holistic Medical Association (Washington, D.C.) and the Association for Holistic Health (San Diego). Numerous businesses have also arisen which serve the New Age community through their distribution of a wide range of New Age products from yoga mats and meditation cushions to macrobiotic cookwear, health foods, natural vitamins, Oriental art, and incense. Many of these businesses are also trying to be a model of the New Age for the business community and embody New Age principles in the organization of their business.

The New Age Vision

The New Age Movement is among the most difficult of the recently prominent religious groups to grasp, primarily because it is a movement built much more around a vision and an experience rather than doctrines or a belief system. A decentralized movement, it entertains contradictory ideas and among its more important spokespersons are people who voice opinions completely unacceptable to the Movement as a whole. Thus, it is easier to understand in terms of its ideals and goals rather than the beliefs to which it adheres.

The central vision of the New Age is one of radical mystical transformation on an individual level. It involves an awakening to such new realities as a discovery of psychic abilities, the experience of a physical or psychological healing, the emergence of new potentials within oneself, an intimate experience within a community, or the acceptance of a new picture of the universe. The essence of the New Age is the imposition of that personal vision onto society and the world. Thus, the New Age is ultimately a vision of a world transformed, a heaven on earth, a society in which the problems of today are overcome and a new existence emerges. There is a wide range of opinion about the nature of that New Age and the means of bringing it about, but each individual's personal experience of transformation gives the Movement its vitality and appeal.

The power to bring about the necessary transformation of both individuals and society comes from universal energy. Members of the New Age Movement assume the existence of a basic energy that is different from the more recognized forms of energy (heat, light, etc.) and undergirds and permeates all existence. This energy goes by many names— prana, mana, odic force, orgone energy, holy spirit, the ch'i, the healing force. It is the force believed to cause psychic healing to occur. It is the force released in various forms of meditation and body therapies which energize the individual mentally and physically. It is the force passed between individuals in the expressions of love.

The fact that the Movement is based on the experience of radical transformation and universal energy does not deny the presence of concepts and ideas which members of the Movement affirm. Rather, this fact emphasizes the secondary role such ideas have and the nondoctrinaire approach taken toward the ideological framework of the Movement. Affirmation of particular propositions or beliefs is not a criteria for participation in or acceptance by the Movement, and members in good standing may vocally disagree with popular concepts without fear of chastisement or alienation.

The variety of ideals and goals that exist in the Movement have great appeal for some people. In the New Age, it is believed, people will recognize one universal religion. While that one religion will assume many different forms and draw from all the present religious traditions, the same mystical faith will underlie each no matter what its label (Christian or Buddhist). This faith finds inspiration in nature and the changing seasons and the growth and development of individuals through the common cycles of life. It also places great emphasis upon self-knowledge, inner exploration, and the participation in a continual transformative process begun in that initial transformation that led the individual to first identify him or herself as a New Age person.

The emphasis upon continual transformation will lead New Age persons on a *sadhana*, a spiritual path. For some that will mean commitment for a period or a lifetime to the practices taught by a single spiritual teacher. Others will continually sample transformative practices, picking and choosing from them, and thus develop a very individualized and constantly changing sadhana.

Since few individuals complete their sadhana in one lifetime, the commonly accepted belief of reincarnation and karma provides a long-term framework in which to view individual spiritual progression. Individuals will over a period of successive lifetimes in a physical body (reincarnation) accomplish their moral and spiritual development as they live out the consequences of prior actions from this life and previous ones. The law of karma, the rule by which the universe returns rewards and punishment, provides the authority for moral action. Immoral action produces unpleasant consequences on its perpetrator (i.e., bad karma).

The sadhana will have as its goal a mystical consciousness or awareness (frequently called higher consciousness, self-realization, Christ consciousness, or New Age awareness). To have a higher consciousness is to be aware of the universal energy which undergirds existence and of the metaphysical unity which underlies the appearance of diversity. Most (but not all) New Agers identify God with that Ultimate Unifying Principle which binds the whole together and the Power which gives it a dynamic. Thus some New Agers are pantheists, identifying God and the world as one reality. Using metaphysical speculations derived from Einstein's theory of matter, they will occasionally reduce all reality to energy. Others tend toward a form of dualism which sees spiritual reality as ultimately good and real, and matter as the evil which must be left behind in the spiritual-mystical life.

People participate in God as individualized manifestations of that Ultimate Unifying Principle and as channels of the universal energy to the world. Jesus, and the other significant religious teachers such as Buddha or Krishna, were particularly transparent bearers of the Divine, or Christ Principle. Such teachers appear regularly throughout history to illustrate the aware (fully realized) life, to teach individuals the goal of awareness, and to train them in particular techniques (the elements of the sadhana) to reach the awareness of their own Divinity. Some New Age people see the need to find a living guru who is a fully-realized teacher. When such is found, he or she will be judged upon his or her perceived awareness (enlightenment) rather than on more mundane questions of his or her particular religious tradition, personal behavior (until it becomes scandalous or outrageous), or teaching idiosyncrasies.

Worship within the New Age Movement finds its typical expression in meditation and various transformative practices taught by the different spiritual teachers or gurus (to whom followers and critics will ascribe various levels of self-awareness). On the social level the Movement is most clearly expressed in the Universal Worship of the Sufi Order, which honors all religions while seeking to find the consciousness and understanding of the cosmos which underlie each one, and in the celebrations of those times which all the major religions seem to commemorate. For example, in late December, Christmas, Hanukkah, and Yule converge.

Many people within the New Age Movement, primarily those with a
Theosophical background, see the necessity of a particular person, a
world teacher, a new avatar of the status of Jesus or Gautama Buddha,
who will be a catalyst to bring about the New Age. The students of Alice
Bailey have been energetic advocates of this position and have circulated
uncounted thousands of copies of a prayer, "The Great Invocation,"
which calls for this avatar's appearance. It is frequently heard in New Age
gatherings:

> From the point of Light within the Mind of God
> Let light stream forth into the minds of men.
> Let light descend on Earth.
>
> From the point of Love within the Heart of God
> Let love stream forth into the hearts of men.
> May Christ return to Earth.
>
> From the centre where the will of God is known
> Let purpose guide the little wills of men—
> The purpose which the Masters know and serve.
>
> From the centre which we call the race of men
> Let the Plan of Love and Light work out.
> And may it seal the door where evil dwells.
>
> Let Light and Love and Power restore the Plan to Earth.

Not only will there be one universal religion recognized in the New
Age, but there will be an allegiance to the planet and the human race
which will supercede loyalties to the more limited groupings of clan,
nation, race, or religion. This commitment to One World finds a typical
expression in communes. Just as personal transformation is the symbol of
social transformation, communes are the models of the new planetary
society. They demonstrate the values of cooperation and sharing and the
possibility of individual acceptance within an artificially created community.

Allegiance to the planet undergirds many new concerns (concerns also
shared by many people in no way connected with the Movement): ecology, peace, natural foods and healing processes, humanizing technology,
cooperative models of living, overcoming hunger, and global politics.
While some leaders within the New Age community hold well-known and
definite opinions on these issues, the Movement as a whole can be said
only to share a focus and concern for these issues, which they see as
planetary problems to be overcome during the transformation into the
New Age. The concern with the planet and the development of networks
to engage in social change has become a significant factor separating New
Age people from more traditional occultists who tended to avoid social
activism as irrelevant to spiritual development.

New Age people separate themselves from what is termed "fortune-telling," the trivialization of various occult techniques to catch a glimpse of the mundane future. Some traditional occult practices are accepted and used by many New Age people as tools in the acquisition of greater awareness. Most New Agers do not hesitate to consult astrologers, tarot card readers and professional psychics. They will tend to avoid Spiritualist mediums who consult the dead, though they have little difficulty with mediumistic persons who are in contact with higher spirit teachers (conceived as ascended masters, the great white brotherhood, or the medium's own higher self). Such spiritual teachers do not establish contact with deceased loved ones; they limit themselves to religious-metaphysical teachings.

Current Status

It is difficult to measure the extent of the New Age Movement. There is no central organization whose membership can be counted. It is a large movement but hardly as large as some of the directories of New Age networks would suggest. Such directories typically contain a small number of people and organizations with a primary commitment to the New Age vision; a far larger number who share one or more New Age concerns (personal transformation, ecology, peace, cooperative models for living, etc.), but would otherwise not consider themselves New Agers; and many who as entrepreneurs provide services and products to the New Age community (health services, natural food products, etc.) but may or may not have any personal commitment to the New Age.

However, the Movement has become visible in every major metropolitan complex in the United States and has shown itself capable of supporting several national mass circulation periodicals. Several annual gatherings such as the Human Unity Conference and the Whole Life Expo have been able to draw attendance in the thousands. National support for the New Age vision is estimated to number in the tens of thousands of individuals.

Insofar as the New Age Movement represents an updating of the longstanding occult and metaphysical tradition in American life, it has a bright future. This element in the culture has been present for at least a century and a half, and people have been attracted to it at a heightened rate for the past two decades. The continued influx of Asians into the United States is giving the whole tradition the strong support in the larger culture heretofore denied it. Unlike the older forms of the tradition, the Movement has been able to penetrate and even develop its largest constituency from single young upwardly mobile urban adults. Such upwardly mobile persons are most accepting of processes of transformation, which they know must accompany increasing career success. At such an age, they are the least doubtful of the possibility of actually realizing utopian social visions. The population density in the urban centers allows the freedom to develop their own particular variation of the New Age vision in the company of others of like mind. New Agers are, as an affluent social group, among the most capable of (1) providing firm support for a growing Movement, (2) passing it along to the next generation, as yet unborn, and (3) spreading the Movement among cultural influentials.

Resources for Understanding the New Age Movement

I. *Background and Precursors.* The New Age Movement, while making its appearance in the 1970s, follows a tradition in American thought which can be traced unbroken to the early eighteenth century. Judah's book recounts that history. Bailey, Hall, and Heline are three of a number of twentieth-century occult writers who voiced different New Age themes and whose works contemporary New Agers still read.

Bailey, Alice, *The Reappearance of the Christ.* New York: Lucis Publishing Company, 1948. 191pp.

Brooke, Anthony, *Towards Human Unity.* London: The Mitre Press, 1976. 133pp. Reprint of talks given between 1965 and 1973.

Burr, Harold Saxon, *The Fields of Life.* New York: Ballantine, 1972. 215pp.

A Course in Miracles. New York: Foundation for Inner Peace, 1975. 3 Vols.

Das, Bhagavan, *The Essential Unity of All Religions.* Wheaton, IL: Theosophical Publishing House, 1966. 683pp. Originally published in 1932.

Dowling, Levi, *The Aquarian Gospel of Jesus the Christ.* Los Angeles: The Author, 1907. Reprinted many times.

Hall, Manly Palmer, *Twelve World Teachers.* Los Angeles: The Philosophers' Press, 1937. 237pp.

Heline, Corinne, *Healing and Regeneration Through Color.* Santa Barbara, CA: J. F. Rowney Press, 1943. 69pp.

Judah, J. Stillson, *The History and Philosophy of the Metaphysical Movements in America.* Philadelphia: Westminster Press, 1967. 317pp.

Parker, William R., and Elaine St. John, *Prayer Can Change Your Life.* Englewood Cliffs, NJ: Prentice-Hall, 1957. 224pp.

John R. Sinclair, *The Alice Bailey Inheritance.* Wellingborough: Turnstone Press, 1984.

Vaughn, David, *A Faith for the New Age.* London: Regency Press, 1967. 160pp.

II. *Bibliographies.* The several books by Cris Popenoe reveal both the range of concern and thought of the New Age.

Popenoe, Cris, *Books for Inner Development.* Washington, DC: Yes! Bookshop, 1976. 383pp. Rev. as: *Inner Development.* Washington, DC: Yes! Bookshop, 1979. 654pp.

Wellness. Washington, DC: Yes! Bookshop, 1977. 443pp.

III. *Guides, Networks and Directories.* Networks are the most common form of New Age organization. Directories are the most ubiquitous form of literature, as they allow the average New Ager to quickly locate the particular service or realm of concern in which he or she is interested.

Acheson, Louis K., Jr., ed., *International Cooperation Directory.* Northridge, CA: International Cooperation Council, fourth edition, 1970. 72pp. Revised as: *Directory of the International Cooperation Council.* 1974. 160pp. 1975, 228pp. Rev. as: Leland P. Stewart, ed., *Directory for a New World.* Santa Monica, CA: International Cooperation Council, 1979. 344pp.

Adams, Robert, comp., *The New Times Network.* London: Routledge & Kegan Paul, 1982. 148pp.

Biteaux, Armand, *The New Consciousness.* Willits, CA: Oliver Press, 1975. 168pp.

East West Spiritual Community Supplement. Boston: East West Journal & San Rafael, CA: Spiritual Community Publications, 1972. 112pp.

Freundlich, Paul, Cris Collins, and Mikki Wenig, *A Guide to Cooperative Alternatives.* New Haven: Community Publications Cooperative, 1979. 184pp.

Friedlander, Ira, ed., *Year One Catalog.* New York: Harper & Row, 1972. 152pp.

Henderson, C. William, *Awakening, Ways to Psychospiritual Growth.* Englewood Cliffs, NJ: Prentice-Hall, 1975. 244pp.

Hisey, Lehmann, *Keys to Inner Space*. New York: Avon, 1974. 277pp.

John, Michael, comp., *The Rainbow Nation*. McCall, ID: 1982. 94pp.

Joshua, *Journeys of an Aquarian Age Networker*. Palo Alto, CA: New Life Printing Co., 1982. 333pp.

Khalsa, Parmatma Singh, ed., *A Pilgrim's Guide to Planet Earth*. San Rafael, CA: Spiritual Community, Rev. ed., 1984. 320pp.

Kulvinsjas, Viktoras, *The New Age Directory*. Woodstock Valley, CT: Omangod Press. Rev. ed. 1981. 229pp.

Spiritual Community Guide. San Rafael, CA: The Spiritual Community, 1972. 192pp. Rev. ed. 1973. 208pp. Rev. ed.: 1974. 192pp. Rev. as. *The New Consciousness Sourcebook*. Berkeley, CA: Spiritual Community, Inc., 1982. 256pp.

IV. *Scientific Themes in the Movement*. The New Age Movement views itself as "scientific" and sees its worldview as supported by the findings of science. It makes particular use of the findings of parapsychology and some of the related studies in other fields, such as biological studies of the innate rhythms in animal behavior associated with the movement of the planets. However, there is a strain of thought which equates science with either (1) the mere systematic organization of a body of information or (2) the correlation of the subjective experiences of a person over a period of time (Cf. Gopi Krishna, Kirpalvanand). By these definitions, practitioners often make unwarranted claims of scientific underpinning to the practices of various forms of yoga, particularly kundalini yoga. This questionable "science of meditation and yoga," however, should not be cited in order to disparage all the work done by psychologists and others in areas related to the New Age Movement as reported below in the items by Funderburk, Grad, Tart, and the Academy of Parapsychology and Medicine.

The Dimensions of Healing. Palo Alto, CA: Academy of Parapsychology and Medicine, 1972. 172pp.

Funderburk, James, *Science Studies Yoga*. N.p.: The Himalayan International Institute of Yoga Science and Philosophy, 1977. 257pp.

Grad, Bernard, "Healing by the Laying on of Hands: Review of Experiments and Implications." *Pastoral Psychology* 21, 206 (September 1970) 19–26.

Krishna, Gopi, *The Biological Basis of Religion and Genius*. New York: Harper & Row, 1971. 118pp.

Kirpalvanand, Yogacarya, *Science of Meditation*. Kayavarohan, Gujarat, India: Sri Kayavarohan Tirth Seva Samaj, 1977. 208pp.

Motoyama, Hiroshi, *Theories of the Chakras: Bridge to Higher Consciousness*. Wheaton, IL: Theosophical Publishing House, 1981. 293pp.

Rama, Swami, Rudolph Ballentine, Swami Ajaya (Allen Weinstock), *Yoga and Psychotherapy, the Evolution of Consciousness*. Glenview, IL: Himalayan Institute, 1976. 332pp.

Tart, Charles, ed., *Altered States of Consciousness*. Garden City, NY: Doubleday, 1972. 589pp.

——— , *Transpersonal Psychologies*. New York: Harper & Row, 1975. 504pp.

White, John, ed., *The Highest State of Consciousness*. Garden City, NY: Doubleday, 1972. 484pp.

——— , and Stanley Krippner, eds., *Future Science*. Garden City, NY: Doubleday, 1977. 598pp.

V. *About the Movement—Proponents*. The proponents are numerous. Those books listed below are the most popular items by the most popular spokespersons or books which succinctly present a broad overview of New Age thinking.

Allen, Mark, *Chrysalis*. Berkeley, CA: Pan Publishing, 1978. 180pp.

Bartley, W. W., III, *Werner Erhard*. New York: Clarkson N. Potter, Inc., 1978, 279pp.

Castaneda, Carlos, *The Teachings of Don Juan: A Yaqui Way of Knowledge*. Berkeley, CA: University of California Press, 1968. First of six books.

Clark, Linda, *Help Yourself to Health*. New York: Pyramid House, 1972. 267pp.

Dass, Baba Ram, *Be Here Now*. San Christobal, NM: Lama Foundation, 1971.

——— , *Journey of Awakening*. New York: Bantam Books, 1978. 395pp.

——— , *The Only Dance There Is*. New York: Jason Aronson, 1976. 180pp.

———, *Miracle of Love*. New York: E. P. Dutton, 1979. 414pp.

Dezavalle, Jacques J., *Thoughts for a New Age*. New York: Vantage Press, 1976. 91pp.

Ferguson, Marilyn, *The Aquarian Conspiracy*. Los Angeles: J. P. Tarcher, 1980. 448pp.

Gaskin, Stephen, *Hey Beatnik! This Is the Farm Book*. Summertown, TN: The Book Publishing Co., 1974.

———, *This Season's People*. Summertown, TN: The Book Publishing Co., 1976. 167pp.

Hagler, Louise, *The Farm Vegetarian Cookbook*. Summertown, TN: The Book Publishing Company, 1978. 223pp.

Inglis, Brian, *The Case for Unorthodox Medicine*. New York: Berkeley Publishing Corporation, 1969. 256pp.

Joy, W. Brugh, *Joy's Way*. Los Angeles: J. P. Tarcher, 1978. 290pp.

Keyes, Ken, Jr., *Handbook to Higher Consciousness*. Berkeley, CA: Living Love Center, 1972. Fifth ed. 1975. 212pp.

———, *The Hundredth Monkey*. Coos Bay, OR: Vision Books, 1982. 176pp.

Lande, Nathaniel, *Mindstyles/Lifestyles*. Los Angeles: Price/Stern/Sloan, 1976. 495pp.

Mann, W. Edward, *Orgone, Reich and Eros*. New York: Simon and Schuster, 1973. 382pp.

Meyer, Michael R., *The Astrology of Relationship*. Garden City, NY: Doubleday, 1976. 263pp.

Nofziger, Margaret, *A Cooperative Method of Natural Birth Control*. Summertown, TN: The Book Publishing Co., 1976. 128pp.

Orr, Leonard, and Sondra Ray, *Rebirthing in the New Age*. Millbrae, CA: Celestial Arts, 1977. 223pp.

Oyle, Irving, *Time, Space and the Mind*. Millbrae, CA: Celestial Arts, 1976. 145pp.

Perkins, Lynn F., *The Masters as New Age Mentors*. Lakemont, GA: CSA Press, 1976. 228pp.

Perrone, Ed, *Astrology: A New Age Guide*. Wheaton, IL: Theosophical Publishing House, 1983. 228pp.

Popenoe, Cris, and Oliver Popenoe, *Seeds of Tomorrow*. San Francisco: Harper & Row, 1984. 289pp.

Regush, Nicholas M., ed., *Frontiers of Healing*. New York: Avon, 1977. 309pp.

Rosenblum, Art, *The Natural Birth Control Book*. Philadelphia: Aquarian Research Foundation. Rev. ed. 1976. 156pp.

———, *Unpopular Science*. Philadelphia: Running Press, 1974. 111pp.

Rudhyar, Dane, *Rhythm of Wholeness*. Wheaton, IL: Theosophical Publishing House, 1983. 268pp.

———, *Occult Preparations for the New Age*. Wheaton, IL: Theosophical Publishing House, 1975. 275pp.

Satin, Mark, *New Age Politics: Healing Self and Society*. New York: Dell, 1979.

Spangler, David, *Festivals for the New Age*. Forres, Scotland: Findhorn Foundation, 1975. 92pp.

———, *Revelation, the Birth of a New Age*. San Francisco: The Rainbow Bridge, 1976. 256pp.

———, *Towards a Planetary Vision*. Forres, Scotland: Findhorn Foundation, 1977. 151pp.

Wilbur, Ken, *The Spectrum of Consciousness*. Wheaton, IL: Theosophical Publishing House, 1977. 374pp.

VI. *About the Movement-Critics*. The prime critics of the Movement are Evangelical Christians who see in the Movement a challenge to the Christian faith in a revived gnosticism. Cumbey's volume, while a popular seller in Christian bookstores, has been almost uniformly denounced by other Christian writers otherwise concerned about the New Age. The Spiritual Counterfeits Project has written numerous articles on various phases of the New Age Movement in its *Journal* and *Newsletter*. The articles by Alexander, Burrows, and Halverson are but three.

Alexander, Brooks, "Holistic Health from the Inside." *SCP Journal* 2, 1 (August 1978) 5–17.

Burrows, Robert, "New Age Movement: Self-Deification in a Secular Culture." *SCP Newsletter* 10, 5 (Winter 1984–85) 1, 4–8.

Cumbey, Constance, *The Hidden Dangers of the Rainbow*. Shreveport, LA: Huntington House, 1983. 268pp.

Halverson, Dean C., "Breaking Through Spiritual Autism." *SCP Newsletter* 10, 5 (Winter 1984–85) 12–16.

Hunt, Dave, *Peace, Prosperity and the Coming Holocaust*. Eugene, OR: Harvest House Publishers, 1983. 282pp.

Michaelson, Johanna, *The Beautiful Side of Evil*. Eugene, OR: Harvest House Publishers, 1982. 222pp.

Reiser, Paul C., Teri K. Reisser, and John Weldon, *The Holistic Healers*. Downers Grove, IL: InterVarsity Press, 1983. 171pp.

VII. *About the Movement-Observers*. Sociologists have been interested in movements associated with the New Age from the time of its appearance. These volumes are among the most accessible and of most interest to the nonprofessional reader. Journalists also documented the beginning of the Movement as it emerged out of its roots in the counterculture of the 1960s and the new wave of Eastern religion (Gustaitis and Houriet).

Glock, Charles Y., and Robert N. Bellah, eds., *The New Religious Consciousness*. Berkeley: University of California Press, 1976. 391pp.

Gustaitis, Rasa, *Turning On*. New York: New American Library, 1969. 288pp.

Houriet, Robert, *Getting Back Together*. New York: Avon, 1971. 408pp.

Needleman, Jacob, *The New Religions*. Garden City, NY: Doubleday, 1970. 245pp.

Scott, Gini Graham, *Cult and Countercult*. Westport, CT: Greenwood Press, 1980. 213pp.

Wuthnow, Robert, *The Consciousness Reformation*. Berkeley: University of California Press, 1976. 309pp.

——, *Experimentation in American Religion*. Berkeley: University of California Press, 1978. 221pp.

Some New Age Groups and Teachers

Many Eastern and occult groups and teachers have identified themselves with the New Age Movement through their literature or by their regular attendance and participation in "New Age" events. Books by these teachers and material published by the groups which they lead can generally be considered New Age. Included would be the following:

Group	Spiritual Leader
Hindu	
Transcendental Meditation	Maharishi Mehesh Yogi
Rajneesh Foundation International	Bhagwan Rajneesh
Hanuman Foundation	Baba Ram Dass
Krishnamurti Foundation	Krishnamurti Jeddu
Siddha Yoga Dham of America	Swami Muktananda
Johannine Daist Community	Da (Bubba) Free John
Self Realization Society	Pamahansa Yogananda
Vedanta Society	Ramakrishna
	Vivekananda
Tantric yoga groups	
Buddhist-Taoist	
Zen Buddhism	
Tibetan Buddhism (Naropa Institute)	Trungpa Rinpoche
The Farm	Stephen Gaskin
Sikh	
Sikh Dharma (3HO)	Yogi Bhajan
Divine Light Mission	Guru Maharaj Ji
Ruhani Satsang	Kirpal Singh
Movement for Inner Spiritual Awareness	John-Roger Hinkins

Islamic
- Sufi Order   Pir Vilayet Khan
- Arica Institute   Oscar Ichazo
- Friends of Meher Baba   Meher Baba

Theosophical-Occult
- Arcane School (World Goodwill)   Alice A. Bailey
- Tara Center   Benjamin Creme
- Association for Research and Enlightenment   Edgar Cayce
- Church Universal and Triumphant   Elizabeth Clare Prophet (Guru Ma)

Spiritualist-Psychic Groups
- Emissaries of Divine Light
- Urantia Foundation (Urantia Book)
- Erhard Training Seminars (EST)   Werner Erhard

New Thought Metaphysics
- Unity School of Christianity
- Church of Religious Science (Science of Mind)

Independent Teachers and Personalities
- Patricia Sun
- Marilyn Ferguson
- Carlos Castaneda
- Sun Bear
- Rudolf Steiner
- Michael Harner
- John Lilly
- Jack Swartz
- Jane Roberts (Seth material)
- Robert Anton Wilson

IV.
The Newer Cults

A. CHRISTIAN FOUNDATION

Like the Children of God, the Christian Foundation of Tony and Susan Alamo claims the prime position at the beginning of the Jesus People Movement in the late 1960s. From its modest beginnings in a frame house near Sunset Strip, the Foundation has grown into a large successful Evangelical Christian body.

Founders

The Christian Foundation was incorporated in 1969 by Susan and Tony Alamo. Susan, born Edith Opal Horn in Arkansas, came to California to begin a singing career under the name Susan Fleetwood. Though her musical efforts did not succeed, she married, converted to evangelical Christianity, and began informally to preach and teach. In 1964 she founded the shortlived Susan Lipowitz Foundation (Lipowitz being her married name).

Tony Alamo was born Bernie Lazar Hoffman in a Romanian Jewish family in Missouri. He journeyed to California as a young man, changed his name, and became involved in show business as a singer and promoter. In 1964, he had a most remarkable experience in the midst of a business meeting. He became deaf to his normal surroundings and he heard a voice say to him, "I am the Lord thy God. Stand up on your feet and tell the people in this room that Jesus Christ is coming back to earth, or thou shalt surely die."

Shortly after the experience he sought out Susan who became his Bible teacher. Eventually they were married and in the late 1960s began to evangelize among the street people in Hollywood. They moved into a house six blocks from Sunset Strip and obtained a brightly painted bus. They and their early converts "witnessed" on the street, and the bus carried interested people to the services each evening at the house. Their ministry was formally incorporated in January 1969. In 1970 they purchased a ranch near Saugus, about forty miles from Los Angeles, and soon the bus was carrying people to the ranch, converted into a camp retreat, for evening meetings. Of the many who attended the services, several hundred decided to stay and become full-time members and workers in the Foundation's ministry.

Soon after the move to Saugus, the Foundation became the target of the growing militant anti-cult movement, Susan realized that she had cancer. In 1973 the Alamos moved to Dyer, Arkansas, Susan's childhood home. Several of the Foundation members joined them. In 1974 they opened a small clothing shop in Nashville, Tennessee. The favorable climate in Arkansas combined with the growing hostility of the anti-cultists in California precipitated the movement of the headquarters and most of the members of the Foundation to Arkansas. Several businesses were purchased, and the shop in Nashville expanded and supplied an economic base for the operation.

In 1982 Susan died. She was interred in a mausoleum at Dyer.

Beliefs

The Christian Foundation is conservative evangelical Christian. It teaches

> that Jesus Christ is the Son of the living God, that he died on the cross and shed his blood for our sins, that he rose from the dead, ascended into the heavens, and took his seat beside God the Father, becoming the high priest, and the appropriation (Propitiation ?) for our sins. We believe that Christ is alive. That he lives forevermore and is coming back to earth very soon. We believe, as the Bible says, that you must be born again. It is a commandment of God that we repent of our sins and ask Christ to come into our hearts and make us a new creature, that old things must pass away and all things, all lives, become new in him.

The King James Version of the Bible is preferred to both the Revised Standard Version and the Today's English Version as the latter attack the Virgin Birth, the redemptive blood, and the deity of Christ.

The Foundation is against abortion, and the Foundation has offered to pay for the delivery of any unwanted babies and to feed, clothe, and house them after birth.

Current Status

Headquarters of the Christian Foundation are at the Holiness Tabernacle in Dyer, six miles east of Alma, Arkansas. Many of the members live in houses owned by the Foundation in Dyer and Alma. They operate several businesses including a restaurant, service station, and clothing store. The store in Nashville has grown into a large Western clothing outlet. Tony also promotes country music in both Nashville and western Arkansas.

Members of the Foundation are totally supported by its activities, and money from the businesses is used to support the total program.

Besides the center in Saugus, California, churches are operated in Chicago and Brooklyn. They hold services each evening and twice on Sunday. Members may be found throughout the country doing missionary work. Besides the witnessing directed primarily to young adults and street people, members have developed a program of visitation to nursing and retirement homes.

Controversy

The militant anti-cult movement, which arose in the early 1970s in Southern California, directed its earliest efforts against several of the Jesus People groups. The Christian Foundation was among its first targets. The Foundation attracted attention after the movement of their operations to Saugus. Critics charged that the Alamos would take unsuspecting young people to the isolated ranch and subject them to highpower conversion pressure. The accusations of deceit and brainwashing from the heyday of the Saugus center followed the Foundation to Arkansas where several attempts to deprogram members have occurred. Out of the unsuccessful deprogramming attempts lawsuits were filed charging the Foundation with holding members in "virtual slavery," in that members worked for the Foundation but received no wages and were forced to live in very poor conditions. While the civil suits did not bear direct fruit, the controversy led to the U.S. Department of Labor filing suit in 1977 demanding that the Foundation pay $15,500,000.00 in back wages to members of the group. When the suit was finally settled in 1983, the Foundation was ordered to pay minimum wages to those who work in the various Foundation businesses.

In response to the attacks upon the Foundation, the Alamos strongly defended their work. They attacked the government for harassing them, and Tony claimed that government pressure had hastened Susan's death. They also cited the complete freedom of movement of the Foundation members, the majority of whom are scattered around the country in the various centers.

Tony Alamo and Susan Alamo, *Tricked* (Alma, AK: Christian Foundation, n.d., 4-page tract).

Tony Alamo, *Tony and Susan Alamo* (Alma, AK: Christian Foundation, n.d., 6-page tract).

James Poett, "Do They Have the Right to Be Weird?," *The Village Voice*, October 24, 1977.

Phil Tracy, "The Jesus Freaks," *Commonweal*, October 30, 1970.

Impact of Cults on Today's Youth (Sacramento: State of California, Senate Select Committee on Children and Youth, 1974).

B. THE CHURCH OF SCIENTOLOGY

One of the few genuinely new religions to originate in the United States during the twentieth century, the Church of Scientology has become known for the numerous controversies, particularly the legal battles, in which it has been involved. During the thirty years of its existence, it has been in a continuous battle with the government, particularly with the Internal Revenue Service, and with those whom it claims have libeled and tried to destroy it.

Founder and Early History

The Church of Scientology was founded by L. Ron Hubbard (b. 1911). A man of varied experience, Hubbard grew up in rural Montana but during his teen years traveled internationally before settling briefly in the east. He attended George Washington University for a year (1931–32) and soon afterward began a successful career as a writer. Though he wrote a variety of true adventure and juvenile fiction, he is best remembered as a science fiction writer. He was made a member of the Explorers Club as World War II began and was able to head one expedition before he began his service in the Navy. Wounded in the South Pacific, he spent almost a year in the hospital.

During the years after his recovery, he synthesized the ideas which later became Dianetics and finally developed into Scientology. In 1948 he informally published and circulated copies of *Dianetics: the Original Thesis*, the first statement of his system. The volume brought him the interest and allegiance of John W. Campbell, Jr., editor of the popular *Astounding Science Fiction*, and Dr. J. A. Winter, a general practitioner from Michigan. In 1949 Campbell began to mention Dianetics in his magazine, and in May 1950 he published Hubbard's first article describing the new way to understand and treat mental health. This article, along with Hubbard's general association with the community of fellow science fiction writers, led many people to label Scientology a "science fiction religion."

Even before the article in *Astounding Science Fiction*, Hubbard had formed the Hubbard Dianetic Research Foundation, headquartered in

Elizabeth, New Jersey. By the end of the year, authorized branches were opened in New York, Washington, Chicago, Los Angeles, and Honolulu. Informal and independent dianetics groups sprang up around the country, especially after the publication of *Dianetics, the Modern Science of Mental Health*, which became a national bestseller in 1951.

Following a brief period of growth, problems arose. The medical and psychiatric community rebuffed Winter's attempt to describe Dianetics in professional journals, and individual doctors attacked the practice. A multitude of independent dianetics groups began to mix Hubbard's thought with occult and Eastern ideas and techniques, and Hubbard discovered that he had lost much control of Dianetic practice.

Amid the chaos and confusion, Hubbard also began to pay attention to a phenomenon which emerged during the dianetics counseling practice called "auditing," "exteriorization," and resulting material on past lives. Exteriorization, similar to astral travel, is the separation of the consciousness from the body. Past lives are previous incarnations of the continuing essence of a person (in Scientology terminology, a "Thetan"). In 1952, Hubbard took these additional insights and, moving to Phoenix, Arizona, founded the Hubbard Association of Scientologists (HAS), soon renamed the Hubbard Association of Scientologists International, by which it is known today. He also published his first books on Scientology.

The additional material on past lives and exteriorization led to speculation on metaphysical and spiritual matters, with the further result that in 1953, Hubbard incorporated the Church of Scientology. The first congregations of the new Church were opened in Los Angeles and Auckland, New Zealand, the following year. The Founding Church of Scientology of Washington, D.C., was established in 1955. Once established, the Church spread quickly throughout the English-speaking world and in the late 1960s began to spread through all of Europe. In 1959 the Church purchased the St. Hill Manor as a residence for Hubbard and a headquarters for the growing movement.

1966 proved an important year for the prospering Church. First, in the face of a growing number of attacks upon Scientology, the office of the Guardian was established and assigned the double task of defending Scientology from attacks by outside critics and keeping the teachings and practice correct throughout the Church. Shortly after the office was created, Hubbard resigned all formal positions within the Church and began to devote his life to further development of the system. Finally, a ship, renamed the *Apollo*, was purchased and the Sea Org(anization), a fraternal group made up of the most dedicated Church members, was organized. Hubbard, a former naval officer, moved on board the vessel and made it his research facility.

The Sea Org became the center for the development of the more advanced grades of Scientological work. In 1967, the Advanced Organization was created to run the new advanced courses. In 1970 the Flag Management Bureau was created to oversee the management of the advanced courses. In 1975, the operation aboard the *Apollo* was abandoned, and the Advanced Organization moved into the facilities of the Church at Los Angeles, which had previously had oversight of the Sea Org. Flag was moved into newly purchased facilities at Clearwater, Florida, and designated the Flag Land Base.

Beliefs and Practices

Though the Church published a creedal statement in 1954, the Creed of the Church of Scientology says little about the Church's unique beliefs, emphasizing instead the conditions under which it hopes people can function. It reads much more like a Bill of Rights than a traditional creed. It does, however, affirm the essential goodness of humans and the basic drive for survival.

According to Scientology, human beings are naturally good, but their goodness has been disturbed by an aberrant state. The problem is caused by a part of the mind, the "reactive" mind, a stimulus-response mechanism created by the true self (the Thetan) that records impressions on an unconscious level. The reactive mind provides programmed responses to specific repeated stimuli. The reactive mind carries images of pain, destructive moments, and injuries. The action of the reactive mind, though on an unconscious level, blocks the Thetan from realizing its true potentials and functioning properly. The individual, through ignorance and the automatic acts of the reactive mind, is led to destructive counter-survival actions.

The Church offers members a series of techniques and disciplines that deal with the problems of the reactive mind and train the Thetan to remember its true nature and express itself. The primary discipline involves work with an auditor, a spiritual counselor and teacher, who leads the member through a series of exercises to erase the effects of the reactive mind. The auditing sessions confront individuals with counter-survival aspects of their lives and allow them to be more free and responsible. When the reactive mind is eliminated and no longer exerts involuntary control over life, people are said to be "clear." Further work in Scientology is devoted to exercising the abilities of the operating Thetan, particularly the ability to exteriorize.

The goal of the Thetan is survival. The individual seeks to express the urge to survive in eight sectors, "the eight dynamics." The urge to survive begins as a drive to exist as a self. It is further expressed in a drive to live through sexual activity, through identification with progressively select groups of human beings (tribe or nation), humankind, the larger animal kingdom, and the physical universe. The seventh dynamic finds the self in the purely spiritual realm and includes the urge toward immortality. The eighth dynamic is the urge to exist as infinity or to find expression in the light of the Supreme Being. While individuals can expand their abilities so as to increasingly function in all dynamics, only when the seventh dynamic is reached can the meaning of the eighth be encompassed. For the

Scientologist, God is approached after a lengthy process as the end product of their development as an operating Thetan. The Church has been reluctant to speculate on the nature of God and has concentrated on the spiritual problems of humanity and the necessary metaphysical conclusions of its more practical emphases.

The goal of all Scientology is a clear planet on which the effects of the reactive mind are eliminated. The immediate sign of a clear planet would be freedom from war, pollution, insanity, drugs, and crime. Humans, fully aware of their true nature, could operate along all eight dynamics. The Church's social programs have begun to implement their social goals.

Worship in Scientology takes second place to the daily work of becoming clear and exercising one's life as an operating Thetan. However, weekly worship services are held at all churches and missions following the order prescribed in the book of *Ceremonies*. A number of holidays have been designated, the most prominent being March 13 (Founder's Birthday) and May 9 (May 9 Day), which commemorates the publication of *Dianetics: the Modern Science of Mental Health* in 1950.

Organization

The International Church of Scientology is located in Los Angeles, California. The Guardian's Office is the administrative Bureau of the Church and oversees public relations, finances, and legal and social matters. It is charged with seeing that Scientology practice follows the established strict guidelines and defending the Church from attacks by outside forces. The Guardian's Office charters each Scientology church and mission and assigns to each a representative of the Office. The Guardian's Office also directly oversees the social action programs of the Church: Narconon (anti-drug), the Citizens Commission on Human Rights, the Committee on Public Health and Safety, American Citizens for Honesty in Government, the Committee for a Safe Environment, and the National Commission on Law Enforcement and Social Justice.

The Sea Org, the elite fraternal organization, is headquartered at the Flag Land Bases in Clearwater, Florida. It is assigned the tasks of assisting Hubbard in his continuing research and development, of overseeing the higher levels of the program, and of generally promoting Scientology worldwide. The Advanced Organization runs the final programs leading to the state of clear and the operating Thetan classes and programs. Bridge Publications is the current publishing arm of the Church.

Local churches and missions chartered by the Church of Scientology offer the basic courses. Some churches also currently offer the final work leading to the state of clear. Advanced work, however, must be taken at one of the Advanced Organization centers, in the United States at Los Angeles. Local centers are staffed with trained ministers who oversee the administration of the church and provide the auditing. Those wishing to function as lay ministers may take the volunteer minister's course.

Current Status

Both the national and international headquarters of The Church of Scientology are at the Church of Scientology of California, in Los Angeles. Flag Operations Liaison Offices for the Eastern and Western United States are in New York City and Los Angeles, respectively.

The Church publishes a number of periodicals; many serve primarily to inform members of programs, classes, schedules, and new publications. Among the more substantive national church periodicals are *Source*, published by the Flag Service Organization; *Advance*, published by the Church of Scientology of California, Advanced Organization of Los Angeles; *The Auditor*, published by the Church of Scientology of California, the American Saint Hill Organization; and *Freedom*, a tabloid on religious freedom issues published by the Church of Scientology of California.

In 1985 the Church reported approximately 3,000,000 members worldwide. This is a cumulative figure of the numbers of people who have received a service from the Church during the past several years. Active membership is estimated to be in the tens of thousands.

Controversy

The history of the Church of Scientology has to a large extent been a history of controversy. Since 1958 the Church has been in almost constant litigation with the Internal Revenue Service. It fought a ten-year battle with the Food and Drug Administration, and in Australia it ended over sixteen years of war with the government in 1983. In addition to its problems with various government agencies, the Church became enmeshed in the anti-cult controversies of the 1970s, which led to a number of civil lawsuits. Finally, the Church sent several members incognito to selected government agencies which were collecting data upon the Church. The members involved with this operation were arrested, tried, and convicted of theft of government documents. In 1958 the Internal Revenue Service revoked the tax-exempt status of the Founding Church of Scientology in Washington, D.C., and the Church of Scientology of New York. The Church filed suit to have its tax-exempt status reinstated. Meanwhile, as the tax case was awaiting trial, in 1963 the Food and Drug Administration seized the E-meters used in auditing, claiming that they were unauthorized devices in the diagnosis and treatment of disease. After ten years of litigation, the E-meters were returned to the Church, although much of the literature seized along with the meters was destroyed over the decade. The continuing tax issue reached its most recent juncture in 1984, when a court, in a lengthy 200-page decision, once again denied tax-exempt status to the Church.

Trouble in Australia began in 1967 when the Chairman of the Victoria Mental Health Authority initiated an investigation of Scientology. In 1965, Victoria passed the Psychological Practices Act, popularly called the Scientology Prohibition Bill. Western Australia and Southern Australia did the same in 1968. The Church assumed the name of the Church of the New Faith. Litigation in Australia finally ended in 1983 when the nation's Supreme Court ruled in favor of the Church, thus legitimizing its status as a religious organization.

The controversy in the courts concerning the status of the Church gave way to public controversy, and a number of books attacking the Church were written. Among these, some were considered so libelous and harmful by the Church as to warrant a lawsuit. The most famous of these books, *The Scandal of Scientology*, was published in 1971. Tower Books (the publisher) settled out of court and withdrew the book in 1973, and in 1976 Paulette Cooper signed a lengthy statement with a retraction of over 50 significant erroneous and unsubstantiated accusations. Cooper has remained an active critic of the Church and has since retracted her statement and retraction. In like measure, the Church has continued to monitor and attack Cooper.

The suits against books that attacked the Church were joined by several against deprogrammers who had attempted unsuccessfully to persuade members to leave the Church. However, the most famous case of this type was brought by Julie Christofferson, a member in Oregon, who was successfully deprogrammed and sued the Church. She charged the Church with outrageous conduct leading to severe emotional distress. Awarded $2,000,000 by a jury, the case was reversed on appeal in 1978. Retried in 1985, the case led to a second multi-million dollar award by the jury. However, the judge declared a mistrial and the decision was discarded.

Possibly the most notorious events in the Church's often intense interaction with its critics began in 1977. In July of that year, the FBI conducted a raid on the Washington, D.C., and Los Angeles churches and seized many files of documents. Though the raid was declared illegal, the documents remained in government possession and were open to public scrutiny. They yielded the information that the Church kept files on people it considered actually or potentially unfriendly and that there had been various attempts to infiltrate anti-cult organizations. The designation of the Alliance for the Preservation of Religious Liberty as a front group for the Church largely destroyed that organization's credibility.

Most importantly, after the raid, a number of top officials of the Church, including Guardian Jane Kember and Hubbard's wife Mary Sue, were indicted and convicted for theft of government documents. After their conviction, the Church withdrew support for any appeal. Those convicted were released from their Church offices, and the Church began a thorough reorganization of the Guardian's Office.

The Church has complained throughout the period of its controversies with both public and private critics that it has been unjustly singled out and targeted. It has responded aggressively. Some of its social action has been directed toward correcting abuses in areas of medical practice, particularly in the mental health field. It has responded to government attacks by claiming an anti-Scientology conspiracy and pursuing (and, in part, documenting) the conspiracy with documents obtained through the

Freedom of Information Act. The 1984 tax ruling against the Church was followed by a series of advertisements in the *New York Times* that attacked the IRS and called for present and former employees to supply information about any illegal IRS activities.

Throughout the controversies, the Church has continued to grow and to develop its program. Continued expansion will depend in large measure upon its ability to put the controversies which have diverted so much of its resources behind it. During the mid-1980s, an attempt to change the Church's negative image through a national media campaign using celebrities who are Scientologists, is one move toward a more nonconfrontational stance.

What is Scientology? Los Angeles: Church of Scientology of California, 1978.

L. Ron Hubbard, *Dianetics, the Modern Science of Mental Health*. New York: Hermitage House, 1950.

——, *Ceremonies of the Founding Church of Scientology*. Los Angeles: The American St. Hill Organization, 1971.

——, *Have You Lived Before This Life?* Los Angeles: Publications Organization, 1977.

Trevor Meldal-Johnson and Patrick Lusey, *The Truth About Scientology*. New York: Tempo Books, 1980.

Roy Wallis, *The Road to Total Freedom*. New York: Columbia University Press, 1976.

Omar V. Garrison, *The Hidden Site of Scientology*. New York: Citadel Press, 1974.

C. THE CHURCH UNIVERSAL
AND TRIUMPHANT
(SUMMIT LIGHTHOUSE)

Frequently confused with the "I AM" Religious Activity, and often presented as its modern embodiment, The Church Universal and Triumphant was founded quite apart from the "I AM" Activity. The founders of the Summit Lighthouse (the name under which the Church Universal and Triumphant was organized) were never affiliated with the "I Am" Religious Activity or its corporate manifestation, the Saint Germain Foundation, and its teachings are at considerable variance with the older organization founded by Guy and Edna Ballard.

At the same time, the similarities of the two organizations, at least to the public and the media, has led to their constant confusion. Both organizations were founded by and during their first generation led by individuals designated as Messengers of the Ascended Masters. Both groups focus on the saying of decrees, invocations to the "I Am Presence" and the Ascended Masters. Both groups assign a special importance to the Ascended Masters Saint Germain and Jesus and recognize Guy Ballard, the founder of the "I AM," as an Ascended Master. Finally, the art and iconography are similar. The Church Universal and Triumphant circulates portraits of Saint Germain and Jesus which not only closely resemble those circulated by the "I AM" but were in fact originally used by the Saint Germain Foundation. In like measure both groups use very similar pictorial representations of the "I AM" Presence, though not without important differences.

Founders and Early History

The Church Universal and Triumphant (CUT) was founded in Washington, D.C., by Mark L. Prophet (b. December 24, 1918, Chippewa Falls, Wisconsin). He served in the United States Air Force in World War II, and during the years after the war became familiar with the teachings of the Ascended Masters given through previous Messengers. However, in 1958 the Ascended Master El Morya anointed him as a new Messenger of the Masters, the Great White Brotherhood, and appointed him to begin a new thrust of Ascended Master activity. He began to lecture and to publish dictations (teachings of cosmic law) he received from the Masters in a series of *Ashram Notes*.

In 1961, while delivering the Ascended Masters' teachings in Boston, Prophet met Elizabeth Clare Wulf (b. April 8, 1940, Red Bank, New Jersey), who was studying political science at Boston University. Several years later they were married. In the meantime, Elizabeth became a student of the Ascended Masters and was tutored both by Prophet and directly by El Morya. Eventually she was also anointed as a Messenger.

That same year El Morya announced the formation of the Keepers of the Flame Fraternity through which students could receive systematic and graded instruction in the teaching of the Masters. A religious-teaching center was founded in the Prophets' home in Beacon's Head, Virginia. At the "Holy Tree House," as the center became known, Prophet conducted classes that centered upon the dictations of the Masters who spoke through him. These dictations were published and distributed to students around the country.

In 1966 headquarters of the Summit Lighthouse, as the work was called, moved to Colorado Springs, Colorado. Growth was slow but steady. The Weekly *Pearls of Wisdom* succeeded the *Ashram Notes* and was sent free to all who requested it. During these years, Elizabeth, while continuing to assist the growth of the movement, became the mother of four children.

On February 26, 1973, Mark died suddenly of a stroke, and Elizabeth took on the full responsibility for and leadership of the Summit Lighthouse. According to Church teachings, Mark Prophet ascended immediately and is now known as Ascended Master Lanello, the Ever-Present Guru. From his Ascended Master state, through Elizabeth, he has given a series of dictations later compiled into a book, *Cosmic Consciousness, The Putting on the Garment of the Lord* (1976), later reissued as *Cosmic Consciousness as the Highest Expression of Heart*.

From Summit Lighthouse to the Church Universal and Triumphant

The Summit Lighthouse expanded dramatically during the 1970s. In 1970, Montessori International was founded to offer both secular education and spiritual nurturance for children and youth, nursery through high school. Summit University was established in 1972 to provide a three-month retreat experience with accompanying studies in science, culture, and religion. In 1974 Mrs. Prophet and the Board of Directors incorporated the Church Universal and Triumphant and designated the Summit Lighthouse as the publishing arm of the new Church. It continued to publish *Pearls of Wisdom*, numerous books, and a growing collection of tapes. In 1975, "Summit International," the structure which ties together the various corporations and departments which have grown out of the original Summit Lighthouse, was announced and plans for the establishment of teaching centers around the country were initiated.

Even before Mark's death, efforts had begun to raise funds and build a headquarters complex, including a church and school, in Colorado. However, these plans were revised and Southern California selected as the new site for the complex. In 1976 the former Pasadena College was leased, and the administrative center of the Church moved on campus. Nine regional teaching centers had been chartered by this time, and growth continued at a steady pace. Also, during this same period, the White Lodge, an ascended master group headquartered at Del Mar, California, decided to affiliate with the Church.

The Church stayed in Pasadena only a short time. In 1978 it purchased the 218-acre former campus of Thomas Aquinas College near Malibu and moved all its offices to the new site, renamed Camelot.

Beliefs

The Summit Lighthouse and Church Universal and Triumphant sees itself as a distinctive activity of the Ascended Masters initiated by the Ascended Master El Morya through the Messengers Mark and Elizabeth Prophet. In carrying on the work of the Great White Brotherhood, the Messengers have brought forth new teachings both from those Masters who spoke initially through Madame Blavatsky or Guy Ballard and other Masters from both the East and the West. The Church sees itself as the true church of Jesus Christ *and* Gautama Buddha as well as the hosts of the Lord ascended, referred to in the Bible as "the saints robed in white." It also venerates the Virgin Mary and sees her as an outstanding representation of the Divine Mother. The nature of the Brotherhood and their basic teachings are clearly outlined in two books, *Climb the Highest Mountain* (1972) and *The Great White Brotherhood in the Culture, History and Religion of America* (1983) and summarized in the Church's twelve "Tenets."

The Church affirms belief in God, The Source of Life and Being. From the Great Central Sun, the metaphysical center of the Cosmos, light came forth and was individualized in numerous individual sparks, each a replica of God, a personalized fragment of the Deity. These seeds of light are the "I AM" Presence, the Lord, or godly part of each individual.

Each person was created as a soul, an infinite potential intended to return to the source of its creation, to fully unite with its individualized God-presence. Mediating the process of the soul's return and eventual union with the "I AM" Presence is the universal Christ consciousness, individualized as the Real Self of each child of God. Individuals, souls, may choose to walk the path of initiation that leads to self-mastery, at which time they are wed to their Christ self. Eventually, each soul ascends into the light, at which time they become one with the "I AM" presence. The historical Jesus walked the earth as one whose soul was one with his Christ consciousness. At the end of his earthly existence, he ascended immediately.

In this age, the particular challenge for each individual is to raise up the feminine principle, i.e., to master the energies appropriate to the life of the soul, the feminine aspect of each individual, often spoken of as the inner mastery of the planes of matter, and then to wed the soul to the Universal Christ consciousness in a balancing action of Alpha (Spirit) and Omega (Matter), representative of the fusion of the energies in God who is both Father and Mother.

As a means of assisting individuals in their goal of self-mastery, the church stresses a practical path of discipleship which includes instruction in the lost arts of healing, an understanding of the laws of karma and reincarnation, and the use of the science of the spoken word (which includes prayers, affirmations, decrees, and mantras) to invoke light, to expose evil and to give illumination to God's people. It expects members to tithe ten percent of their income. Strongly patriotic, the church has encouraged members and students to assume an active role on various social issues. It has spoken against abortion, child pornography, nuclear warfare, terrorism, and world communism. It vigorously supports family life, the four sacred freedoms, and a strong defense for America.

Organization

The Church is headed by Elizabeth Clare Prophet, the Messenger of the Ascended Masters. The administration of the Church is in the hands of a Board of Directors, which has responsibility for directing the centers and appointing their leadership. The various departments of the Church are located at Camelot and the Inner Retreat at the Church's 30,000-acre Royal Teton Ranch in Montana, where regular conclaves (conferences), all open to the general public, are held.

The Keepers of the Flame Fraternity remains the heart of the Church. It consists of men and women who have pledged to keep the flame of the inner self, in reality God within the self, nurtured, and who are dedicated to the freedom and enlightenment of humanity. Some weekly services at the various teaching centers are designed especially for and limited to Keepers of the Flame.

The most dedicated members of the Church are the communicants. To become a communicant (i.e., full member) one must be a Keeper of the Flame, subscribe to the "Tenets" of the Church, be formally baptized and tithe his/her income. Individuals must make application to become a communicant member, and periodically ceremonies are held for christening or accepting new members.

At Camelot and through various centers, the Church offers communicants the opportunity to live in a spiritual community. Though only a minority of communicants have chosen such a living arrangement, those who do form a core of highly dedicated people. They accept upon themselves additional duties of devotional service and activity to spread the church's teachings. Each teaching center carries on a daily program of worship and classes, led by the resident members. Members at the center also hold weekly study groups at various locations in the community.

Summit University, also located at Camelot, offers spiritual training for Keepers of the Flame and advanced classes especially for those who plan to become ministers. The publishing arm, Summit Lighthouse, upon moving to Camelot, has greatly expanded. Through it the Church provides hundreds of books, booklets, devotional (decree) materials, and cassette tape albums of all the conferences at which the Ascended Masters have spoken through the Church's Messengers.

Current Status

As a policy, the Church Universal and Triumphant does not release figures on the number of students or members, and only estimates can be given. Church centers were located across the United States from New York and Washington, D.C., to Chicago, Minneapolis, and San Francisco. Each center housed approximately twenty communicant members. Four to five hundred attend the various weekly events at Camelot. A major land development project is underway at the Inner Retreat in Montana.

Controversy

Though the Church Universal and Triumphant has not been attacked to the extent of the more well-known newer religions such as the Unification Church or the Hare Krishnas, it has joined the list of groups labeled "cults" by the anti-cult movement. The adoption of a communal life style by members in-residence at the centers and the exacting requirements on those who live at Camelot have brought the common charges of excessive indoctrination and brainwashing. Such charges have been aired on national and (in California) local television news shows, and in numerous newspaper and magazine articles featuring ex-members.

One major set of attacks on the Church relates to its outward financial success. Critics have cited Elizabeth Prophet's wardrobe and jewelry, the acquisition of property, and the proliferation of publications and audio-visuals. The Church has countered with its observations that the wardrobe was donated, the jewels (the property of the Church, not of Prophet personally) are focuses of spiritual light and healing power, and that the expansion of the Church's program and membership has required a greater amount of property.

More recently, the Church has come under attack by several ex-members, including a few who were asked to leave for violating the Church's standards. Their charges, as well as counter-charges by the Church against them, are being adjudicated in several civil suits yet to be heard.

Mark Prophet and Elizabeth Clare Prophet, Climb the Highest Mountain (Colorado Springs, CO: Summit Lighthouse, 1972).

Mark Prophet and Elizabeth Clare Prophet, My Soul Doth Magnify the Lord! (Colorado Springs, CO: Summit Lighthouse, 1974).

Elizabeth Clare Prophet, *The Great White Brotherhood* (Los Angeles: Summit University Press, 1983).

Elizabeth Clare Prophet, *Prophecy for the 1980s* (Los Angeles: Summit University Press, 1980).

Elizabeth Clare Prophet, *Quietly Comes the Buddha* (Colorado Springs, CO: Summit Lighthouse, 1977).

D. DIVINE LIGHT MISSION

The arrival in the United States in 1971 of a 13-year-old religious leader from India was met with some ridicule but, more importantly, an extraordinary amount of interest from young adults who were willing to seriously examine his claims of being able to impart direct knowledge of God. From that initial support, Guru Maharaj Ji was able to establish a flourishing American branch of the Divine Light Mission.

Founders and Early History

The Divine Light mission was founded by Shri Hans Maharaj Ji (d. 1966), the father of Maharaj Ji. Early in life he encountered Sarupanand Ji, a guru of the Sant Mat tradition by whom he was initiated. Though Sarupanand Ji had told his disciples to follow Hans Maharaj Ji, after the guru's death another disciple, Varaganand, claimed the succession and took control of the guru's property. Hans Maharaj Ji began to spread the teaching independently in Sind and Lahore, and in 1930 he established an informal mission in Delhi. His following grew steadily. In 1950, shortly after Indian independence had been declared, he commissioned the first mahatmas, followers who had the ability to initiate and who devoted themselves full time to the work of propagating the teachings of Shri Hans Maharaj Ji. He also began a monthly magazine, *Hansadesh*. By 1960 followers could be found across northern India from Bombay to Calcutta, and the need to organize them more formally led to the founding of the Divine Light Mission (Divya Sandesh Parishad).

Just six years after the founding of the Mission, Shri Hans Maharaj Ji was succeeded by his youngest son, Prem Pal Singh Rawat (b. 1957), who was but eight when he was recognized as the new Perfect Master and assumed the title, Maharaj Ji. Maharaj Ji had been recognized as spiritually adept, even within the circle of the Holy Family, as Shri Hans Maharaj Ji's family was called. He had been initiated (i.e., given knowledge) at the age of six and soon afterward gave his first *satsang* (spiritual discourse). After his father's death he heard a voice commissioning him as the one to take the knowledge to the world. He assumed the role of Perfect Master at his father's funeral by telling the disciples who had gathered, "Dear Children of God, why are you weeping? Haven't you learned the lesson that your Master taught you? The Perfect Master never dies. Maharaj Ji is here, amongst you now. Recognize Him, obey Him and worship Him." Though officially the autocratic leader of the Mission, because of Maharaj Ji's age, authority was shared by the whole family.

During the 1960s, Americans in India searching for spiritual guidance discovered the Mission and a few became initiates (i.e., "premies," or "lovers of God"). They invited Maharaj Ji to the United States. In 1970 Maharaj Ji announced his plans to carry the knowledge throughout the world and the following year, against his mother's wishes, made his first visit to the West. A large crowd came to Colorado the next year to hear him give his first set of discourses in America. Many were initiated and became the core of the Mission in the United States. Headquarters were established in Denver, and by the end of 1973, tens of thousands had been initiated, and several hundred centers as well as over twenty ashrams, which housed approximately 500 of the most dedicated premies, had emerged. The headquarters staff expanded to 125, and social service facilities, such as a medical clinic in New York City, were opened. Two periodicals, *And It Is Divine*, a magazine, and *Divine Times*, a tabloid, were begun. Enthusiasm ran high.

After a spectacular beginning in North America, the Mission suffered a major setback in November 1973. It rented the Houston Astrodome for "Millennium 73," an event celebrating the birthday of Maharaj Ji's father and designed to announce the beginning of a thousand years of peace and prosperity. The event failed; attendance was miniscule. The Mission was left with a $600,000 debt which required it to cut its staff and programs.

Millennium 73 was but the first of a series of events which gradually led the Mission to withdraw from the public scene. It was staged just as the anti-cult movement reached national proportions and turned its attention upon the Mission. Several deprogrammed ex-members became vocal critics of the Mission. Through his Executive Secretary, Maharaj Ji announced that he was replacing the predominantly Indian image with a Western one. Among other changes, he began to wear business suits instead of his all-white Indian attire. Many of the ashrams were discontinued.

To the problems caused by the debt and the attack of anticultists were added internal problems within Maharaj Ji's family. In December 1973, when Maharaj Ji turned 16, he took administrative control of the Mission's separate American corporation. Then in May 1974, he married his 24-year-old secretary, Marolyn Johnson, and declared her to be the incarnation of the goddess Dulga, usually pictured with ten arms and astride a tiger. Premies purchased an estate in Malibu into which the couple moved. Mataji, Maharaj Ji's mother, disapproved of the marriage and the life style of the now-successful guru. Relations within the Holy Family were strained considerably. Accusing her son of breaking his spiritual disciplines, Mataji took control of the Mission in India and replaced him with his eldest brother. In 1975 Maharaj Ji returned to India and took his family

to court. In a court-decreed settlement, he received control of the movement everywhere except in India, where his brother was recognized as its
head. Publicity about the marriage and the subsequent family quarrels
caused many Western followers to leave the Mission, though a large
membership remained.

By the late 1970s the Mission in the United States had almost disappeared from public view. Maharaj Ji continues to travel the globe speaking
to premies, and the Mission, while growing little in the United States, has
expanded significantly in Southern Asia, the South Pacific and South
America.

Beliefs and Practices

The Divine Light Mission is derived from Sant Mat (literally, the way
of the saints), a variation of the Sikh religion which draws significant
elements from Hinduism. It is based upon a succession of spiritual masters generally believed to begin with Tulsi Sahib, an early nineteenth-
century guru who lived at Hathras, Uttar Pradesh. It is believed that the
person mentioned as Sarupanand Ji in Mission literature is in fact Sawan
Singh, a prominent Sant Mat guru. In any case Hans Maharaj Ji claimed a
Sant Mat succession which he passed to Maharaj Ji. Maharaj Ji, as do
many of the other Sant Mat leaders, claims to be a Perfect Master, an
embodiment of God on earth, a fitting object of worship and veneration.

The Mission has as one of its stated goals the instruction of the world
in "the technique of utilizing the universal primordial Force, that is, the
Holy Name (Word) which is the same as the Divine Light and which
pervades all human beings thus bringing to the fore the eternal principle of
unity in diversity." In the Sant Mat tradition this practice is called *surat
shabd yoga*, the practice of uniting the human spirit with the universal
divine sound current. The particular methods of accomplishing that union
vary from group to group and are one reason for their separation. Within
the Divine Light Mission, initiation into the yoga is by a process known as
giving knowledge. Though premies were instructed not to talk about their
initiation outside of the Mission, details of the process were soon revealed
by ex-members.

At initiation, a mahatma, the personal representative of Maharaj Ji,
introduces new members to four yogic techniques, all of which are quite
common within Sant Mat circles, although equally unknown to the average person, even to the average Indian. These four techniques reveal the
means of experiencing the divine light, sound, word, and nectar. To
experience the divine light, one places the knuckles on the eyeballs, a
process which produces flashes of light inside the head (and also pinches
the optic nerve). To discover the divine sound or music of the spheres,
one plugs the ears with the fingers and concentrates only on internal
sounds. The third technique involves concentration upon the sound of
one's own breathing. Finally, to taste the nectar, the tongue is curled

backward against the roof of the mouth and left there for a period of time. Once learned, these techniques are practiced daily. Frequently, meditation is done under a blanket, both to block outside disturbances and to conceal the techniques.

Unlike many Sant Mat groups, the Divine Light Mission has had a social program from its beginning. Shri Hans Maharaj Ji called for a balance between temporal and spiritual concerns, and the Mission's stated goals include the promotion of human unity, world peace, improved education for all (especially the poor), and relief from the distress caused by ill health and natural calamities. The Mission made provision for the establishment of hospitals, maternity homes, and residences. This emphasis upon social programs was transferred to the United States.

Three holiday festivals which members are expected to attend are held annually. The Holi-festival is in March or April. The Guru Puja (Maharaj Ji's birthday) is in July. Hans Jayanti (Hans Maharaj Ji's birthday) is in November.

Current Status

Since 1974, the Divine Light Mission has increasingly kept a low profile and at present is virtually invisible in the United States. In 1979 the Denver headquarters quietly closed, and both it and Maharaj Ji moved to Miami Beach, Florida. From there, two periodicals are currently published, *Divine Times* and *Elan Vital*.

In 1980, the Mission reported 10,000 to 12,000 active members in the United States. The Mission is headed by Maharaj Ji, its Spiritual Leader and the Board of Directors which supervises the 23 branches. Ministers (mahatmas) lead the Mission centers around the world. Many of them travel from center to center to give initiation and *satsang* (spiritual discourses). Members are required to participate in meditation daily and attend *satsang* each evening.

Controversy

During the first years of the Divine Light Mission in the United States, both it and Maharaj Ji were constantly involved in controversy. The teachings of the Mission, particularly the public discourses of Maharaj Ji, were condemned as lacking in substance. Maharaj Ji, who frequently acted like the teenager that he was in public, was seen as immature and hence unfit to be a religious leader. At one point, a pie was thrown in his face (which led angry followers to assault the perpetrator). Ex-members attacked the group with standard anti-cult charges of brainwashing and mind control.

However, as the group withdrew from the public eye, little controversy followed it except for the accusations of Robert Mishner, the former president of the Mission, who left in 1977. Mishner complained that the ideals of the group had become impossible to fulfill and that money was increasingly diverted to Maharaj Ji's personal use. Mishner's charges, made just after the deaths at Jonestown, Guyana, found little support and have not affected the progress of the Mission.

Shri Hans Ji Maharaj (Delhi: Divine Light Mission, n.d.).

Guru Maharaj Ji, *Reflections on an Indian Sunrise* (Divine Light Mission, 1972).

———, *The Living Master* (Denver: Divine Light Mission, 1978).

Light Reading (Miami Beach, FL: Divine Light Mission, 1980).

Who Is Guru Maharaj Ji? (New York: Bantam Books, 1973).

James V. Downton, Jr., *Sacred Journeys* (New York: Columbia University Press, 1979).

Maeve Price, "The Divine Light Mission as a Social Organization," *Sociological Review* 27, 2 (May 1979), 279–96.

E. ECKANKAR

Though often missing from the surveys of world religion, the Sant Mat tradition of India has had an important role both in broadening the religious options on the Indian subcontinent and increasing the number of religious groups in the United States. Several of the popular new religions of the 1970s sprang directly from the large Sant Mat groups of India. Some such as Ruhani Satsang were openly representative of the tradition, while others, such as the Divine Light Mission were less evidently attached. A few, such as ECKANKAR and M.S.I.A., while relying almost totally on Sant Mat teachings, have attempted to deny their debt to Sant Mat teachers.

Founder and Early History

ECKANKAR was founded by John Paul Twitchell (d. 1971). After World War II, while working as a correspondent in Washington, D.C., Twitchell joined the Self-Revelation Church of Absolute Monism, an independent congregation begun by Swami Premananda who had left Swami Yogananda's Self-Realization Fellowship. For several years he edited *The Mystic Cross*, the group's periodical. Then in 1955 he met Kirpal Singh, founder of the Ruhani Satsang. He left the Self-Revelation Church and was initiated by Singh. At the same time he became a member of the newly founded Church of Scientology and was among the first to attain the level of "clear."

In the early 1960s he moved to Seattle where he met Gail Atkinson, a librarian whom he eventually married. He introduced her to Kirpal Singh and she was initiated in 1963. Before the year was out, however, he had broken relations with Kirpal Singh and the following year he moved to San Francisco and began to teach classes which emphasized techniques for bi-location, the ability of a person's consciousness (soul or spirit) to separate itself from the body. Then in 1965, he declared himself the Living ECK Master. He incorporated ECKANKAR and established headquarters in Las Vegas, Nevada. The organization grew quickly, especially after the publication of popular paperback editions of *The Tiger's Fang* (1967),

Twitchell's account of his visits to the inner world, and *In My Soul I Am Free* (1968), a biography by popular occult author Brad Steiger. A number of other titles by Twitchell quickly appeared, some in paperbacks and some in hardcover from ECKANKAR's Illuminated Way Press.

In his writings Twitchell claimed that he was the 971st ECK Master, the descendant of an unbroken chain of masters in the Order of the Vaiargi. He received his rod of power from ECK Master Rebazar Tarzs, a Tibetan. Twitchell died on September 17, 1971, just six years after ECKANKAR was founded. On October 22, 1971, Darwin Gross received the rod of power and was acknowledged as the 972nd ECK Master.

Gross' tenure as the leader of ECKANKAR began and ended in controversy. A former professional musician and engineer from Oregon, he had been given a copy of *In My Soul I Am Free* in 1969. He immediately recognized the picture of Twitchell on the cover as the person he had encountered on his own inner journeys. He sent for the ECK lessons, the Discourses, attended the Third World Wide Seminar held that year in Portland, Oregon, and before the year was over, helped organize the first *satsang* group in the state. Then, with less than two years as an ECKist, he suddenly became the new ECK Master and was so acknowledged in a ceremony by Twitchell's widow.

In disagreement over the choice of Gross, ECKANKAR Vice President Dr. Louis Bluth and several other organization notables left. Gross married Gail Twitchell, and for the next several years the organization prospered. A new headquarters was built in Menlo Park, California, and membership more than doubled. He expanded the artistic and cultural development, especially in music. However, all was not well. In 1978 he announced his divorce. The next year Twitchell and ECKANKAR were attacked for plagiarizing from Sant Mat materials and creating the lineage of ECK masters. Gross married again, but after a few months, the marriage was annulled. Then on October 22, 1981, he passed the rod of power to a new ECK Master, though he still retained a leadership role, and the organizations still circulated and published his several books: *Your Right to Know* (1979), *Gems of Soul* (1980), *From Heaven to the Prairie* (1980), *Leadership in ECK* (1982) and *Music from Spirit?* (1982, with Paul Twitchell). However, more recently, Gross was officially cut off from the ECKANKAR organization. He is no longer officially recognized as a genuine ECK master, and his books have been withdrawn from circulation.

Gross was succeeded by Harold Klemp, the 973rd Living ECK Master. According to his autobiography, *The Wind of Change* (1980), Klemp had had spontaneous astral travel (bi-location) experiences. He had joined several open membership occult organizations looking for some explanation of the questions raised by these experiences. In 1967 he answered an ad placed by ECKANKAR in *FATE Magazine* and began the Discourses. In 1968 he bought a copy of *In My Soul I Am Free*, and like Gross, recognized Twitchell as someone he had met on his out-of-body trips. The announcement of Klemp's new position occurred at the 1981 ECK World Wide seminar in Los Angeles.

Belief and Practice

ECKANKAR, the Ancient Science of Soul Travel, is, according to official ECK teachings, the most ancient teaching known to humanity. It has been handed down through an unbroken lineage of Masters, the present Living ECK Master being the 973rd.

ECKANKAR beliefs begin with the "Sugmad," defined as the formless, All-embracing, impersonal, and infinite, the Ocean of Love and Mercy, from which flows all of life, the equivalent of God in theistic religions. All life comes from the Sugmad via the ECK current, the Audible Life Current, which can be heard as sound and seen as light.

Humans are an immortal Soul incarnated in a set of bodies. The Soul body resides within the astral, causal, mental-etheric, and physical bodies to protect it from the coarse lower worlds. The ECK Masters teach the precise techniques and spiritual exercises whereby the soul can be released from the limitations of physical life and travel in the higher spiritual realms to the Sugmad. Travel is along the ECK, the Audible Life Current.

The path back to the Sugmad is through a series of twelve invisible planes. They may, in part, be distinguished by the sound typical of each level. According to ECKANKAR, most occult teachings never get beyond the second or astral plane, the realm of ghosts, spirits and psychic phenomena. The fifth plane is the first in which the soul reaches the pure spiritual worlds. The twelve planes and the sound associated with them are:

12.	Sugmad	music of God
11.	Sugmad World	music of universe
10.	Anami Lok	sound of a whirlpool
9.	Agam Lok	music of the woodwinds
8.	Hukikat Lok	thousand violins
7.	Alaya Lok	deep humming
6.	Alakh Lok	heavy wind
5.	Soul	single note of flute

———— Dividing line between psychic and spiritual worlds ————

	Etheric (top of mental plane)	buzzing of bees
4.	Mental	running water
3.	Causal	tinkle of bells
2.	Astral	roar of the sea
1.	Physical	thunder

The Discourses and other material available to "chelas" (students) teach a variety of techniques to contact and travel the ECK Current. The exact techniques are confidential; an examination of ECKANKAR texts reveals that they are identical with those taught by the various Sant Mat teachers. Chelas are also taught to expect to encounter the ECK Master on their inner journeys, especially while asleep, during the dream state. Once contacted, the Master will guide the student through the various planes.

Organization

ECKANKAR is headed by the corporation's Board of Trustees, which operates under the spiritual leadership of the Living ECK Master. Trustees are drawn from different geographical locales and are active leaders at a regional level. The Trustees appoint the Area Madhis who are responsible for the activities in a particular region, and the Universal Madhis who travel wherever they are needed. Some Madhis are appointed to conduct the lower-level initiations. Working directly with the Board are the North American and European Advisory Councils and the Creative Arts Council.

The basic unit of ECKANKAR is the ECK *Satsang* class which is conducted, usually monthly, for chelas by an accredited Area Representative. In many areas, an ECKANKAR center has been opened. Such centers distribute ECK literature, offer seminars and introductory classes, and assist in the spread of ECKANKAR.

The international headquarters of ECKANKAR are in Menlo Park, California. Illuminated Way Press is responsible for the publication of ECKANKAR books. Twitchell left over 60 manuscripts, approximately half of which have been published. Three periodicals, *Mystic World*, *ECK Meta Journal*, and *ECK News* serve the membership. In 1983 the organization reported approximately 3,000,000 members, a cumulative figure of the number who have at some time taken an ECK course or seminar or purchased an ECK book. Recent estimates of active membership range between 20,000 and 50,000 worldwide. Several hundred *satsangs* can be found in the United States with others located on every continent. The organization is strong in Europe.

Annually five major seminars are sponsored by the international office: the ECKANKAR World Wide Seminar (usually the last weekend in October); the International Youth Conference (Easter weekend); the Creative Arts Festival; the European Seminar; and the Annual Campout.

Controversy

ECKANKAR grew steadily and quietly, in spite of the internal controversies which surrounded Darwin Gross, until David Christopher Lane, a student at California State University, Northridge and an initiate of Sant Mat Master Charan Singh, began to look into Twitchell's writings for a term paper. That exercise led to a lengthy investigation of Twitchell's life and has resulted in two books which have questioned the legitimacy of Twitchell's experiences and the truth of many of the claims upon which ECKANKAR is based. While Lane's book circulated informally as a manuscript, the Spiritual Counterfeits Project, an Evangelical Christian counter-cult group in Berkeley, California, used much of his material in a special issue of the *SCP Journal* devoted entirely to ECKANKAR, "A Hard Look at a New Religion." In 1983, Lane's complete work was published as *The Making of a Spiritual Movement*.

Lane charged Twitchell with covering up his relationship with his former teachers—Swami Premananda, Kirpal Singh and L. Ron Hubbard. He produced the original copies of articles Twitchell had written for various periodicals which later became chapters in his ECKANKAR books. They showed that Twitchell had deleted the names of these three teachers and replaced them with the names of ECKANKAR Masters such as Rebazar Tarzs (who no one outside of ECKANKAR has ever met). Lane charges Twitchell with creating Rebazar Tarzs out of the biographies of several Sant Mat teachers, such as Kirpal Singh and Sawan Singh.

Further, Lane has charged Twitchell with largely plagiarizing several of his books from the writings of Sant Mat author, Julian Johnson. He demonstrated, by a detailed comparison of texts, the many passages Twitchell lifted directly out of Johnson's *The Path of the Masters*. While denying the plagiarism in letters to the ECK chelas, ECKANKAR has not attempted to answer the substantive case put forth by Lane. The long-term effect of his criticism is not yet predictable.

THE CHURCH OF THE MOVEMENT OF SPIRITUAL INNER AWARENESS

Closely related to ECKANKAR in its teaching and history is the Movement for Spiritual Inner Awareness (MSIA).

Founder and Early History

John-Roger Hinkins was one of the early students of ECKANKAR and by 1968 was a second initiate and convenor of an ECK meeting in Southern California. That year he left ECKANKAR and founded MSIA. Sri John-Roger, as he is generally called in MSIA publications, claims that in 1963 he had a meeting on the inner planes with Sawan Singh (1858–1948), prominent leader of the Radhasoami Satsang Beas, the largest of the Sant Mat groups. At the time of his association with ECKANKAR, he believed that he had encountered Rebazar Tarzs, the ECK Master. He discovered his mistake and left ECKANKAR. Hinkins claims that Sawan Singh passed to him the role of Mystical Traveler Consciousness.

Beliefs and Practices

Although it employs a different vocabulary, MSIA adheres to the basic teaching which ECKANKAR inherited from the Sant Mat tradition through Kirpal Singh. The Mystical Traveler Consciousness functions almost identically with its ECKANKAR counterpart, the Living ECK Master. The description of the inner planes follows their delineation in the writings of Paul Twitchell, including, as observers have noted, the retention of those peculiarities introduced into the tradition by Twitchell. MSIA has, however, gone beyond ECKANKAR by identifying itself with the larger New Age/Eastern/metaphysical community and adding many of its practices and emphases to their own program.

MSIA contends that every person is involved in a movement of spiritual inner awareness, and the Movement of Spiritual Inner Awareness is an outward reflection of that universal inner movement. The focal point of the Movement is the Consciousness of the Mystical Traveler. The Mystical Traveler (i.e., John-Roger) exists simultaneously on all levels of consciousness in total awareness and can teach individuals who request his assistance how to develop the same total awareness and, thus, free themselves from the necessity of reincarnation. The Mystical Traveler also can read the karmic records of individuals and assist them in understanding and releasing themselves from their karmic responsibilities.

MSIA has taken a primary interest in helping individuals adjust to the rapid changes and resultant stresses so they are not hindered or distracted in their spiritual quest. Very early in the Movement, several New Age healing techniques, each dealing with a different aspect of the self, were offered to students (and the public): "Aura balancing" is a technique to clear the auric (magnetic) field that exists around each individual. "Inner-phasings" reach into the subconscious to bring to consciousness and remove the dysfunctional patterns learned early in life. "Polarity balancing" releases blocks in the physical body. These initial services blossomed into a major emphasis upon holistic healing and the development of the Baraka Holistic Center for Therapy and Research.

Soon after the success of EST (Erhard Seminar Trainings), MSIA developed its own seminars, which provide intense transformation experiences. The Insight Transformational Seminars are catalysts of self-awareness and the ability to move beyond self-imposed limitations.

Organization

During its early years, MSIA developed in a pattern similar to ECK-ANKAR. John-Roger wrote a set of Soul Awareness Discourses to introduce new members to the basic perspective and practices of the Movement. As members increased in one area, students were urged to form seminar groups. These were organized first in southern California from whence they spread along the West Coast, and, then, from an initial group in Miami, Florida, they spread along the East Coast. The first international groups were organized in England and Japan.

In 1972, *The Movement*, the organization newspaper, began publication and is now offered for sale on newsstands. It has featured interviews with different New Age teachers, news of other Eastern mystical groups, and articles on general New Age concerns while presenting the program and services of MSIA to its readers.

During the past decade the programming offered at the national level has expanded to keep pace with the Church of the Movement of Spiritual

Inner Awareness (as the organization is officially known) as a growing national and international concern. The headquarters of the Church is in Los Angeles, but a major complex of facilities can be found in nearby Santa Monica. It is served by two educational facilities: Kor-E-Nor University in Santa Monica, California, is a graduate school which offers a master's degree in Applied Human Relationships as well as a non-degree extension program and counseling training for clergy. Prana Theological Seminary and College of Philosophy, in Los Angeles, offers master's and doctoral programs in theology and ministerial education.

Baraka Holistic Health Center for Therapy and Research, located adjacent to Kor-E-Nor University, is a fully-staffed alternative health center with practitioners in chiropractic, acupuncture, nutrition, and a variety of other therapies.

Insight Transformational Seminars offers training programs throughout the United States to the general public. A variety of advanced and special interest programs have been developed to supplement the week-long introductory seminar.

MSIA offers many tapes by John-Roger for sale. His numerous books have been published by Baraka Books of New York.

In 1984, the Church reported 250 seminar groups in the United States which met regularly, mostly in private homes. Additional groups could be found in 12 countries. Membership is estimated at between 5,000 and 10,000. Members who have studied the Discourses for two years are eligible to apply for ordination as ministers in the Church.

Controversy

MSIA has grown slowly and quietly and remained virtually unknown beyond those people involved in the New Age Movement or one of the other alternative religions similar to MSIA. It has escaped both significant attention and controversy. However, in 1984, David Christopher Lane, himself a Radhasoami initiate, attacked John-Roger and MSIA, in part using information supplied by two prominent ex-members. Lane accused John-Roger of plagiarism and sexual misconduct and of being a charlatan. In response, an organization called the Coalition for Civil and Spiritual Rights came forward to defend MSIA and attack Lane's credibility as a researcher. In the midst of the exchange of correspondence with the Coalition, Lane had his home burglarized and much of his research material and the records of his magazine, *Understanding Cults and Spiritual Movements*, stolen, thus leaving the issues unresolved.

ECKANKAR

Paul Twitchell, *ECKANKAR* (New York: Lancer Books, 1969).
——— , *The Tiger's Fang* (New York: Lancer Books, 1969).
——— , *The Spiritual Notebook* (Menlo Park, CA: Illuminated Way Press, 1971).
Darwin Gross, *Your Right to Know* (Menlo Park, CA: Illuminated Way Press, 1979).
Harold Kemp, *The Wind of Change* (Menlo Park, CA: Illuminated Way Press, 1980).

M.S.I.A.

John-Roger Hinkins, *The Christ Within* (New York: Baraka Press, 1976).
———, *Possessions, Projections and Entities* (New York: Baraka Press, 1976).
———, *The Spiritual Family* (New York: Baraka Press, 1976).
———, *The Spiritual Promise* (Rosemead, CA: Movement for Spiritual Inner Awareness, 1973).

David Christopher Lane, *The Making of a Spiritual Movement* (Del Mar, CA: Del Mar Press, 1983).
Brad Steiger, *In My Soul I Am Free* (New York: Lancer Books, 1968).

F. FAMILY OF LOVE (CHILDREN OF GOD)

When the Jesus People Revival began in the late 1960s on the West Coast, David Berg, the founder of what is today the Family of Love, had already begun to gather the group which would become famous as the Children of God, the name by which it was known until 1979. Berg, with some justification, claims to be the originating force of the revival, even though the Children of God were the first group to be ostracized by the growing Jesus People Movement because of their doctrinal divergences.

Founder and Early History

The Family of Love was founded by David Brandt Berg, a minister in the Christian and Missionary Alliance Church, a conservative holiness denomination. His mother was an evangelist and had on several occasions received prophecies of future events. In 1967 Berg went to work for Fred Jordan who ran an independent pentecostal ministry, the Soul Clinic, in Los Angeles. In December 1967, alerted by his mother to the growing number of street people (hippies) in Huntington Beach, California, he moved there and took over a work previously begun by Teen Challenge, the youth ministry of pentecostal minister Dave Wilkerson. It centered upon the Light Club Mission, a coffee house near the Huntington Beach pier.

Berg had already developed a critical attitude toward many establishment structures, particularly the organized church, and his message of withdrawal from worldliness and total commitment to a Jesus revolution appealed to the street people. Many of them gave up drugs, and a small group began to live communally. They called themselves Teens for Christ.

In 1969 Berg received a revelation that California was threatened by an earthquake and that he and his followers should leave. They moved to Tucson, where over the summer their number grew from 50 to 75. In the fall they divided into four teams to take their message of the Jesus Revolution across America. After several months, some of the Teens for Christ reassembled at a campground near Montreal. Here they formally organized and Berg ordained about fifty of them as bishops, elders, deacons, and deaconnesses, though the highest offices remained in his immediate family.

Berg then called the entire membership together at Vienna, Virginia, to inform them of some secret revelations he had received in Canada. One of these, called "Old Church, New Church," was directly related to an adulterous affair with his secretary. In a lengthy session before the group, rather than repenting and announcing an end to the liaison, he sought to justify it. His wife and his secretary were, he asserted, models of the church. God had abandoned the old denominational church and had taken a new church (the revolutionary Jesus people), just as Berg had abandoned his wife, who, like the old church, had become a hindrance to God's work, for his new love. This theological metaphor of his sexual life led to the development of sex as a major ingredient of the Children's life and thought. Berg began to speak of America as the Great Whore. He began to articulate, first to the inner leadership, an understanding of revolutionary Christian love that involved communal sex. The practice soon spread to the entire membership.

The group departed Vienna for Washington, D.C., where as the capital mourned the death of Senator Everett Dirksen of Illinois, Berg's followers dressed in red sackcloth and ashes and mourned the death of the nation which had forsaken God. Similar demonstrations occurred in other cities. A reporter called them the "Children of God," and the group adopted this name. Also, in a prophecy spoken during this period, one of the members referred to Berg as Moses. Thus by February 1970, when Jordan turned over his Soul Clinic ranch near Thurber, Texas, to the group, they had become "Moses and the Children of God."

During the period at Thurber, William Rambur, a parent whose daughter had joined the Children of God, organized other angry parents into the "Parents Committee to Free Our Sons and Daughters from the Children of God," later popularly called FREECOG. Claiming their children were under drug-induced and hypnotic control, they aligned themselves with Theodore Patrick, who initiated the practice of deprogramming (discussed more fully in the chapter on the Anti-cult Movement), physically kidnapping members of the group and forcing them to renounce their allegiance to it. A few hostile ex-members began to relate vivid accounts of life among the Children which further increased the public opinion against them. Before the year was out Berg left the country and began to live in seclusion, and Jordan evicted the Children from the Thurber property.

Berg had incorporated the Children of God but, partly as a result of the bad publicity, tax-exempt status was denied. Hence, a second corporation, Youth for Truth, Inc., was quietly established to receive any financial assets, and the original corporation was abandoned.

The Children of God dispersed around the nation in some forty colonies. Some followed Berg's example and left the country. By the middle of the decade, spurred in part by Berg's warning of the destructive potential of Comet Kohoutek, most had emigrated. Berg exercised his leadership of the movement through a series of "Mo Letters," which guided the evolving organization and doctrine of the group. Some letters became internal documents, while others were sold on the street and became the means of spreading the group's message. Berg's understanding of himself as a prophet became more central and his prophecies, increasingly seen as coming from disincarnate spirits, assumed the dominant role in molding the group's ideas.

During this period, Berg extended his increasingly radical ideas about sexual freedom to include the most controversial practice of the group, "flirty fishing." In a Mo Letter at the beginning of 1974, Berg ordered the women of the group to use their natural sexual appeal and talents to gain new members, to become fish bait, hookers for Jesus. The practice declined in the late 1970s after venereal disease ravaged the group.

In the face of the increasingly negative image of the Children of God, given a measurable boost following the deaths of Peoples Temple members in Guyana, Berg decided to change the organization of the group using a family model. He told followers to call him "Dad," and gave the Children their present name, the Family of Love.

Beliefs and Practices

Beginning as a conservative holiness Christian group, the Family of Love adopted David Berg's extreme, but by no means unacceptable, ideas about the imminent end of the world, God's abandonment of worldly structures (governments, churches, economic systems), the coming Jesus revolution, and communalism. As they evolved, however, they thoroughly left orthodox Christian belief and practice. That deviation began with Berg's assumption of the role and not just the image of Moses, a prophet of the endtime. Like Moses, Berg declared war on the evil system of things. The present system was so corrupt that reformation was not possible, only a complete revolution could bring in God's world.

In like measure, the Children of God assumed the role of the harbingers of God's New World. They were to be the living example of a totally new loving society. One sign of the Children's role was their new sexual ethic. Spelled out in a number of Mo Letters, love and sex were equated, and the free expression of sexuality, including fornication, adultery, lesbianism (though not male homosexuality), and incest, were not just allowed but encouraged.

As a prophet, Berg increasingly received revelations that were completely divorced from the Bible. He issued Mo Letters concerning various spirit entities with whom he had established contact—especially Abrahim (a gypsy king). He claimed to fulfill specific biblical prophecies, and as the endtime prophet, he claimed authority to teach new truth regardless of its substantiation in the Bible. He discarded the concept of the Trinity and adopted a belief in universal salvation.

Organization

The Children of God were organized into a pyramid of authority with Berg at the top. Under him were apostles, elders, and deacons. By the time of the loss of the colony at Thurber, the Children could count several thousand members. Berg dispersed them into numerous colonies nationally and internationally and created the new position of shepherds. Apostles oversaw the work nationally and internationally; elders were regional leaders; and shepherds led the individual colonies. In 1975, the colonies were broken into even smaller units, and the leadership roles on the lower levels expanded. By this time, the membership, approaching 7,000–10,000 was scattered internationally throughout Europe and Latin America. Berg supplied direction through the Mo Letters. Members lived communally. New members went through an indoctrination period as babes, soon progressing to become a brother or sister.

In 1979 Berg proposed a radical change in structure. He dismissed the entire leadership and reorganized the Children as a family. He disbanded the existing colonies into small family groups and encouraged everyone to call him "Dad." Taking a new name, the Family of Love, the group has tried to leave the negative image of the Children of God behind it.

Current Status

After leaving the United States, Berg settled in London, where he directs the Family of Love from his suburban estate. The Family has largely abandoned the United States and has no official center, headquarters, or even postal box address to make direct contact with the group. The London address is not published, and mail contact is through postal boxes in Geneva, Switzerland, and Hong Kong.

Most publishing is now done by Gold Lion Publishers in Hong Kong, which has recently issued collected editions of the Mo Letters. A one-volume edition, *The Basic Mo Letters*, reprints the basic doctrinal tracts and outlines the Family's perspective on religion, politics, economics, and sex. *New Nation News*, published in several languages and editions, is the major periodical.

No current statistics on the Family are available. There are an estimated several thousand members widely dispersed internationally. The Family claims membership in the millions, but no verification of these figures has been found. Only a few hundred Family members reside in the United States. They are occasionally seen on the street distributing literature.

Controversy

The Children of God was the first of the new "cults" around which organized opposition developed and toward which the first deprogrammings were directed. It has been a central focus of anti-cult activities. It was prominently mentioned in legislative hearings such as that conducted by the Senate of the State of California in August 1974. A month later, New York Attorney General Louis Lefkowitz released the final report (an interim report issued in January 1974 had received wide publicity) of a lengthy investigation he had conducted. The report gave early justification to the theory of cults assaulting the psyche of new members by brainwashing. The report concluded, "Brainwashing techniques are deliberately employed under the rationalization that it is in the service of a good cause." The report emphasized the nonconventional sexual practices spreading through the group, though Lefkowitz was not yet aware of the "flirty fishing" policy. The report accused the leaders of forcing sexual relations upon members and, in one case, of condoning the rape of a 14-year-old runaway. The Children of God issued a lengthy answer to the Lefkowitz Report, but it had little circulation. Also, by that time, most of the members had left the country. All of the criminal charges made in the report concerned cases outside of Lefkowitz's jurisdiction, thus, no action followed its issuance.

The abandonment of the United States lessened, but by no means killed, hostile attitudes toward the group. The parents of members and ex-members remained key figures of the anti-cult movement, and they used the continuing reports of evangelism by prostitution and Berg's own sexual excesses as appalling examples of the degeneration of life within cults in general.

In the investigation conducted by Lefkowitz, Sarah Berg, the wife abandoned in the "Old Church, New Church" revelation, offered her story as witness to the truth of Berg's immorality. In the late 1970s, Deborah Davis, one of Berg's daughters left the group and published a book about her experience. She goes far beyond the account of her mother in detailing her father's personal excesses, including incest, as well as an account of the flirty fishing at the resorts at Tenerife in the Canary Islands. Shortly after the book appeared, Berg wrote a short rebuttal, but did not answer any of the specific charges. He merely labeled her account a lie.

The sexual manipulation in the Children of God has been so thoroughly documented that it is doubtful whether the organization can ever, in spite of whatever future reforms it might initiate, regain any respectable place in the larger religious community.

David Berg (under pen name Moses David), *The Basic Mo Letters* (Hong Kong: Gold Lion Publishers, 1976).

———, *The Mo Letters* (Hong Kong: Gold Lion Publishers and Zurich: World Services, 1977–1981, 8 Vols.).

———, *Thoughts from Mo* (Hong Kong: Gold Lion Publishers, 1976).

Samson Warner, *We Are the Children of God* (Rome, Italy: Children of God, 1977).

Douglas Pritchett, *The Children of God/Family of Love, An Annotated Bibliography* (New York: Garland, 1985).

Deborah (Linda Berg) Davis, *The Children of God* (Grand Rapids: Zondervan, 1984).

Final Report of the Activities of the Children of God to Hon. Louis J. Lefkowitz (New York: Charities Fraud Division, Attorney General's Office, 1974).

Frankie Fonde Brogan, *The Snare of the Fowler* (Lincoln, VA: Chosen Books, 1982).

Una McManus, *Not for a Million Dollars* (Nashville, TN: Impact Books, 1980).

G. THE INTERNATIONAL SOCIETY FOR KRISHNA CONSCIOUSNESS (HARE KRISHNA)

The International Society for Krishna Consciousness became for many people the symbol of the invasion of Asian religion into American life in the 1970s. Of all the groups, they were the most visible, most frequent targets of humor and satire and, for the anti-cultists, tremendous hostility.

Background

During the debates on cults in the 1970s, the International Society for Krishna Consciousness (ISKCON) was frequently used as the example of a "new" religion. But while ISKCON was founded in the United States in 1965, its tradition goes back at the very least to the sixteenth century and the career of a Bengali saint, Chaitanya Mahaprabhu (1486–1534?).

Chaitanya was a promising young scholar without any particular religious inclination. Then, at about the age of twenty-one he went on a pilgrimage that changed his life. He met the ascetic Isvara Puri who introduced him to chanting. Accepting his new acquaintance as his guru, he returned to his home town only to spend all his time chanting the names of Krishna. Some considered him mad; others attracted by his fervency became his disciples. He moved to Puri in Orissa near the Jagannatha Temple. With the support of the king, he was able to build a strong movement among the Vaishnava Hindus who worshiped Jagannatha as a form of Krishna.

Chaitanya combined the ascetic monastic ideal with a life of intense devotional activity focused upon dancing and chanting. A mystic life came easily to him and he frequently would go into a trance while chanting. Some historians believe that his sudden disappearance in 1534 is best accounted for by assuming that he drowned in the sea while in a trance.

After his disappearance the movement declined but experienced revivals in the seventeenth and mid-nineteenth centuries. One of those who led the revival in the nineteenth century, contemporaneously with the national Hindu revival, Swami Bhaktivinode Thakur founded the Gaudiya

Vaishnava Mission in 1886. After his death, his son Sri Srimad Bhakti Siddhanta Goswami, a former professor of mathematics and astronomy, continued his work. He founded the Gaudiya Math Institute and some sixty-four missions. He was also the guru of Abhay Charan De, the founder of the International Society for Krishna Consciousness.

Founder

A.C. Bhaktivedanta Swami Prabhupada was born in Calcutta September 1, 1896 as Abhay Charan De. He graduated from the University of Calcutta in 1920 with majors in English, philosophy and economics and went to work as the manager of a chemical plant. In 1922 he met Bhakti Siddhanta of the Gaudiya Vaishnava Mission and accepted him as his guru. Noting his ability in English, the swami asked the young devotee to write about Krishna Consciousness in English, and he authored a commentary on the *Bhagavad-Gita*. In 1933 he was formally initiated into the Gaudiya Mission, just three years before its leader died. During those years the Swami gave his new initiate a charge to carry Krishna Consciousness to the West.

Abhay Charan De did not at first take the charge seriously. He continued to produce English-language material for the Mission. In 1944 he began an English periodical. His efforts were recognized in 1944 when he was given the name "Bhaktivedanta."

In 1950 Bhaktivedanta retired and began to give some thought to the task his guru had set for him. In 1954 he adopted the *vanaprastha* (retired) order and moved to Vrndavana and the Vamsi-gopalaji Temple. During this period he began to translate the massive Hindu classic, the *Srimad-Bhagavatam*, three volumes of which appeared in the next decade. He also wrote a small work, *Easy Journey to Other Planets*. In 1959 he took *sannyasin*, the renounced life, and separated from his wife and family. Family obligations had prevented him from moving to the West previously.

Then at the age of 70, in 1965, when the Asian Exclusion Act having been rescinded and migration from India opened to the United States, A.C. Bhaktivedanta Swami Prabhupada took up his mission. He began work in New York City on the Lower East Side. He daily went to Tompkins Park to chant and talk with passers-by. A few hippies discovered the Swami and adopted him as their guru. Within a year a center had been opened and a magazine, *Back to Godhead*, begun with a xerox machine. A San Francisco center was opened in 1967, and the movement experienced a steady growth from that point on.

Swami Prabhupada, while leading the movement, continued to write and translate. He pushed the publishing venture with vigor. In 1968 a copy of his translation of the *Bhagavad-Gita, As It Is*, appeared. He continued to work on the *Srimad-Bhagavatum* and began translation of the *Caitanya-Caritamrta*. In 1972 the Bhaktivedanta Book Trust was established and published over 60 400-page volumes of his work.

Prabhupada continued to lead the movement until his death on November 14, 1977.

Belief and Practice

The International Society for Krishna Consciousness is a transplanted conservative form of Hinduism centered upon the practice of bhakti yoga, a path of devotional service. For ISKCON devotees, the prime method of devotional service is the repetition of the Hare Krishna mantra but includes a number of practices which, taken out of their context in India and thrust in the midst of modern American society, seem very strange.

The worldview that underlies the Krishna's bhakti practices is summarized in a statement widely circulated by the movement:

1. By sincerely cultivating a bona fide spiritual science, we can be free from anxiety and come to a state of pure, unending, blissful consciousness in this lifetime.
2. We are not our bodies but eternal spirit souls, parts and parcels of God (Krsna). As such, we are all brothers, and Krsna is ultimately our common father.
3. Krsna is the eternal, all-knowing, omnipresent, all-powerful, and all-attractive Personality of Godhead. He is the seed-giving father of all living beings, and He is the sustaining energy of the entire cosmic creation.
4. The Absolute Truth is contained in all the great scriptures of the world. However, the oldest revealed scriptures in existence are the Vedic literatures, most notably the *Bhagavad-Gita*, which is the literal record of God's actual words.
5. We should learn the Vedic knowledge from a genuine spiritual master—one who has no selfish motives and whose mind is firmly fixed on Krsna.
6. Before we eat, we should offer to the Lord the food that sustains us. The Krsna becomes the offering and purifies us.
7. We should perform all our actions as offerings to Krsna and do nothing for our own sense gratification.
8. The recommended means for achieving the mature stage of love of God in this age of Kali, or quarrel, is to chant the holy names of the Lord. The easiest method for most people is to chant the Hare Krsna Mantra:
   Hare Krsna, Hare Krsna
   Krsna Krsna, Hare Hare
   Hare Rama, Hare Rama
   Rama Rama, Hare Hare

In joining ISKCON a devotee not only accepts a belief structure but an ascetic, semi-monastic life and disciplines. Like Roman Catholic monks, the new devotee takes a new name. Most devotees also don the traditional clothing associated with the religious life in India. The head of a male devotee is shaved except for a tuft called the *sikha*, a sign of surrender to the spiritual master. A set of japa beads are carried to assist in chanting the mantra. Daily, a clay marking called the *tilaka* is applied to the forehead and nose as a sign that the body is a temple of the Supreme Lord.

Diet for a Krishna devotee is strictly vegetarian. Food is prepared for and offered to Krsna before eating. On the eleventh day after the full and new moons, a partial fast in which grains, cereals, and beans are deleted from the diet is observed.

For most devotees the important activity of the day is *sankirtan*, the congregational chanting of the holy names of God. Frequently this occurs in the temple setting, but, following the example of Chaitanya, the public chanting is also a regular feature of devotee life. Public *sankirtan* has become that aspect of ISKCON's life to be most satirized by the media.

The devotees, in accepting a life of devotional service, give up a great deal, most notably the close company of nondevotees as is common with all monastics. This cutting off from people outside the community has caused the greatest tension, especially among family members of devotees.

Organization

During the lifetime of Swami Prabhupada, he headed the organization. At the time of his death, he appointed twenty commissioners to administer ISKCON, twelve of whom were authorized to take disciples as he had done. The twelve were each responsible for a particular area of the world. For example, Ramesvara Swami Maharaja is responsible for the Western United States (including Hawaii) and Japan. As of 1980, eleven of the twelve still functioned. They have full authority and appoint the temple presidents who administratively head individual temples.

Individual members are initiated only after a trial period. They enter either the unmarried (*brachmacari*) or married (*grhasthas*) order. If they remain celibate, they may enter the renounced order, *sannyasin*. Two orders are defined by function. *Brahmins* serve as priests, teachers, and administrators. *Vaisyas* produce foodstuffs. Ultimately all devotees receive the second initiation as *brahmins* and take on responsibilities for worship, instruction, and the spreading of the message of Krsna devotion.

Each temple is organized on a strict schedule that begins before sunrise. Morning activities include bathing, application of the clay markings, worship and chanting, the eating of *prasadam* (the food offered to Krsna), and veneration of the temple deities. During the day, each devotee has an assigned task which may include work at the temple or *sankirtan*. Some spend the day at the local airport distributing Krishna literature and collecting donations from passengers, an activity that has earned them the antagonism of many.

Growth

Although he arrived in the United States with neither income nor following, Swami Prabhupada accumulated both swiftly. The second temple in San Francisco was opened in 1967. By 1970 21 centers in the United States had been created, and the work spread to Japan, Germany, Canada,

England and Australia. By 1982 they reported 50 centers in the United States including several farms, plus a string of vegetarian restaurants. Centers (more than 175) were found throughout Canada, the British Isles, Europe, and on other continents. ISKCON claims 3,000 initiated members and 500,000 lay members who regularly visit a temple at least once a month.

International headquarters of the movement are Sridhama Mayapur, West Bengal, India. United States headquarters, and the Bhaktivedanta Book Trust, are in Los Angeles. *Back to Godhead*, the monthly magazine, is published in Philadelphia. ISKCON also manufactures a line of incense marketed under the label "Spiritual Sky."

Interaction with the Community

Through its public activities—the annual Rathayatra Festival, soliciting money at airports, and the practice of *sankirtan* on city streets—the International Society of Krishna Consciousness has maintained a high profile in American life. While trying to project an image of a bona fide religion following the traditions of ancient India, it has been seen as a foreign and enigmatic group whose ascetic, communal, and separatist lifestyle opposes dominant American values (to which it offers a distinct alternative) and threatens common family patterns (which, in many cases, it does).

The tension between the Society and the culture increased as the anti-cult movement focused attention upon the group. Various anti-cult groups have made members the object of a series of deprogrammings, beginning with Ed Shapiro who was deprogrammed by Ted Patrick in the early 1970s. Deprogrammed Krishnas have received wide media coverage. Anti-cult groups have also attempted to arouse public opinion against the Society and block attempts by ISKCON to carry out its program. They have moved to stop their public soliciting at the airports and, after years of frustration, finally were able to have some restrictions imposed. They have also lobbied to require building permits (for the establishment of Krishna temples) and parade permits (for street-corner solicitation).

The efforts of the anti-cult groups have been aided by some events within the Society. Annually, beginning in the mid-1970s, Krishnas were arrested for soliciting without a permit while dressed in a Santa Claus suit. Since the Krishnas as Hindus do not celebrate Christmas, the public interpreted such solicitation attempts as efforts to deceive.

In the wake of Jonestown, the Krishnas were reported to be stockpiling weapons. They denied the reports but later confirmed that, in spite of their pacifist stance, they had weapons at several of their farms where local citizens had harrassed the residents. Then a leader in the Bay Area in California was discovered to have a car trunk full of guns. Not widely reported was the fact that the individual had refused to follow the Society's orders to rid himself of the weapons and after the incident was severely disciplined by the Society.

The single most famous incident in the Krishnas' interaction with the public concerns David Yanoff. As a child, David had been given to his father by an Illinois court when his parents divorced. However, his mother took him to California and disappeared into the movement and eventually moved to a Krishna community in Europe. David's father and grandfather launched a public crusade to force the Society to locate and return the boy. They organized public opinion which led to the denial of a zoning change for the Temple in Evanston, Illinois, disrupted soliciting at Chicago's O'Hare Airport, and initiated a suit. After over a year of effort David was returned to his father's custody.

While attacks in the media and from anti-cult groups continued, the Society received a more cordial welcome from the scholarly community. Religious scholars praised Swami Prabhupada's translations. Individual scholars who had studied the group—J. Stillson Judah, Harvey Cox, Larry Shinn, and Thomas Hopkins—defended the group against what they saw as a distorted media image and misrepresentations by anti-cultists. Members of the society were welcomed into the academic organizations such as the American Academy of Religion.

The future of the Society will be determined by the continued strength and perseverance of the anti-cult movement, though the increasing familiarity of the public and the support of the religious academicians will hasten the rapprochement between the Krishnas and American society.

The KRSNA Consciousness Handbook (Los Angeles: ISKCON Press, 1970).

Satsvarupa dasa Goswami, Prabhupada (Los Angeles: Bhaktivedanta Book Trust, 1983).

A. C. Bhaktivedanta Swami Prabhupada, KRSNA Consciousness: The Top Most Yoga System (Boston: ISKCON Press, 1970).

———, Teachings of Lord Caitanya (New York: Bhaktivedanta Book Trust, 1974).

———, Bhagavad-Gita As It Is (New York: Bhaktivedanta Book Trust, 1972).

Steven J. Gelberg, ed., Hare Krishna, Hare Krishna (New York: Grove Press, 1983).

J. Stillson Judah, Hare Krishna and the Counterculture (New York: John Wiley & Sons, 1974).

Francine Jeanne Daner, The American Children of KRSNA (New York: Holt Rinehart and Winston, 1974).

Faye Levine, The Strange World of the Hare Krishnas (Greenwich, CT: Fawcett Publications, 1974).

Morris Yanoff, Where Is Joey? (Chicago: Swallow Press, 1981).

H. THE LOCAL CHURCH (WATCHMAN NEE AND WITNESS LEE)

After visiting a congregation of the Local Church in your community, one might easily question its inclusion in a book on alternative religions. It claims, and appearances back its assertion, to be an orthodox evangelical Christian body of believers. However, as members began to interact with leaders of the Jesus People revival that had emerged on the West Coast in the early 1970s, recognizable differences of theological language (if not beliefs) and particular practices unique to the Local Church led to heated polemics and the branding of the group as a cult. Hence it is included in this volume.

Founders and Early History

The group that is variously called the Little Flock or the Local Church was founded in the 1920s in China by Ni Shu-tsu, popularly known by the English translation of his name, Watchman Nee (1903–1972). Nee was born into a Chinese Christian family. His grandfather had been a Congregational minister. His parents were Methodists. He changed his original name Ni Shu-tsu (Henry Nee) to To-Sheng (Watchman), to remind himself that he was a bell-ringer who would raise up a people for God.

Not particularly religious as a youth, he was converted by Dora Yu, a Methodist missionary. Soon after, working with an independent missionary, Margaret E. Barber, he discovered the writings of John Nelson Darby and the exclusive Plymouth Brethren. He adopted the nondenominational approach to church organization espoused by Darby and soon became the leader of a small group of evangelical Christians. By the end of the decade, he had made contact with a branch of the Brethren led by elder James Taylor. At their invitation, he visited England in 1933, but soon broke with the group because of his unauthorized fellowship with a non-Brethren group headed by T. Austin-Sparks.

From its modest beginnings in Foochow, Nee's movement spread through China. He traveled widely, founding congregations based upon his idea that there should be only one local church (i.e., congregation) in each city as the basic expression of the unity of Christianity (in the face of divisive denominationalism). He expressed this position in his most famous book, *The Normal Christian Church Life*. He also authored *The Spiritual Man*, in which he espoused his conception of the tripartite nature of human beings as body, soul, and spirit.

During World War II, to prevent his becoming a financial burden to the Church, Nee took a job at his brother's chemical factory in Shanghai. After the War, he returned to full-time evangelical work and turned over the factory to the Church in Shanghai to own, manage, and, most importantly, collect the profits. Other members soon followed his example. This action became Nee's downfall, as the People's Republic of China, which came to power in 1949, accused Nee and the Churches affiliated with him of imperialism. Exiled from Shanghai, he was arrested in 1952 and spent the rest of his life in prison. To protect itself, the Church excommunicated him and, for the most part, went underground.

During the 1930s, Nee gained a convert, Witness Lee, a former Protestant minister, who became an elder of the church at Chefoo. By the end of the decade he was among Nee's most valuable assistants. After a three-year absence caused by tuberculosis, Lee joined Nee upon his return to full-time church work in 1946. On the eve of the revolution, Nee sent Lee to Taiwan. Under his guidance, the church flourished and spread around the Pacific basin. Members migrating to the United States brought the movement to the West Coast. Lee moved to the United States in 1962 and founded the Living Stream Ministry. Recognized as the leading full-time worker among the local churches, he has provided overall direction for the spread of the Local Church.

Lee has also been a source of innovation within the movement. He has introduced several theological emphases not found in the writings of Watchman Nee and initiated several practices such as pray-reading and "calling upon the name of the Lord," which have become the subject of controversy.

Organization

The local churches affirm the unity of the church, the corporate nature of church life and the direct headship of Christ over the church. Great emphasis is thus placed on church life, meeting together (several times a week), and the function and responsibility of each member in keeping alive a relationship with God and sharing the duties of congregational life. In rejecting the clergy-laity distinction, a pattern for the practical expression of the church's life has been established.

Beginning with the critique of the denominational fracturing of the unity of Christianity found in John Nelson Darby, through his study of Scripture, Watchman Nee developed his own ecclesiology. He saw a pattern in the New Testament of founding a local church in each city and came to believe that that was the proper pattern for church life. Roman Catholicism and Protestant denominations had departed from that pattern, to which they should return. He also saw the local churches under the control of elders rather than an ordained clergy or episcopal hierarchy.

The rejection of denominationalism created a problem of naming the group. As did other nondenominational groups, such as the Plymouth Brethren before them, they took no name. The brethren were simply the believers who were called the Plymouth Brethren by others because an early prominent congregation was located in Plymouth, England. The Local Church sees itself simply as the Church. The term "local church" is a convenient designation but not a name. Thus local congregations are called "The Church in (name of the city)."

Following Nee's idea, the Local Church is organized as a fellowship of autonomous congregations, one to a city. Each congregation is headed by a small group (usually from two to five) elders who are in charge of its teaching, preaching, and administrative responsibilities. Elders are generally appointed from those among the congregation who seem to be most dedicated and capable.

Nee also saw that there was a need for a continuing apostolic function —for men who would travel among the local churches teaching and training the leadership, and initiating new congregations in cities without a local church. Such men are set aside as was the apostle Paul, as workers. Workers organize their efforts, more or less formally, as an independent ministry. In the case of Witness Lee, his work is incorporated at Living Stream Ministry and is at present the most prominent such ministry among Local Church congregations. Workers travel, speak, and publish as they are led and supported and as their work proves fruitful. While such ministries are formally associated with one congregation as a base of operations. For example, Living Stream shares a building with the Church in Anaheim (California).

Throughout its history the Local Church has spread through the evangelical efforts of the co-workers or the happenstance movements of members, whose migration to the United States led to the founding of the first local church congregations in New York and California. However, in recent years, with Lee's encouragement, the Local Church has adopted a process termed the "Jerusalem Principle," by which church members form a group and migrate together to a new locale for the single purpose of seeding a new congregation.

Beliefs

The local churches follow the teachings found in the numerous books and writings of Watchman Nee and Witness Lee. A convenient summary of these teachings has been compiled by a group of co-workers into a booklet, *The Beliefs and Practices of the Local Churches*. The booklet professes a belief in fundamental Christianity, very similar to that of the Plymouth Brethren. The Trinity, the deity of Christ, the Virgin Birth, the substitutionary atonement, the Resurrection, the Second Coming, and the verbal inspiration of the Bible are all affirmed.

Particular attention is given to an emphasis upon the unity of the Church, the Body of Christ. Sectarianism, denominationalism, and inter-denominationalism are rejected, and the oneness of all believers in each locality affirmed.

The local churches place themselves in a history of recovery (or restoration) of the Biblical church, whose full life and unity were lost over the centuries. That restoration process began with Martin Luther and the Protestant Reformation and continued through the pietist recovery of Count Zinzendorf and the Moravians, John Wesley and the Methodists, and the Plymouth Brethren. Through the local churches, the Christian's experience of the riches of Christ (i.e., the enjoyment of Christ as life), and the practice of Church life according to Scripture are being recovered. The newly recovered practices, which have become the focus of criticism, include: pray-reading, calling upon the name of the Lord, burning, and burying.

"Pray-reading" is a devotional practice which uses the words of verses of Scripture as the words of prayer. Individuals or groups when praying will repeat words and phrases of Scripture over and over, frequently interjecting words of praise and thanksgiving, as a means of allowing the Scripture to impart an experience of the presence of God to the person praying. "Calling upon the name of the Lord," as the term implies, is an invoking of God by the repetition of such phrases as, "O Lord Jesus." It is similar to the use of the Jesus prayer in Eastern Orthodoxy.

"Burning" implies a close contact with God. When a person impresses another with the Gospel, that person has been burned. "Burning" is also an occasional practice by which objects representative of a person's pre-Christian life or a time of lesser commitment are destroyed in a fire. Like burning objects from ones past, "burying" is also a sign of a newer level of Christian commitment and is accomplished through a rebaptism. Thus, a member might be baptized several times.

Worship in the local churches is spirited, with much time given to singing, pray-reading, and testimonies. Speaking in tongues is allowed but not encouraged. Emphasis is also placed upon the elders' teaching of scripture. The Lord's supper is observed weekly during Sunday worship. Most women wear a head covering during worship, but it is not required.

Current Status

The local churches, being autonomous congregations in fellowship with each other, have no central headquarters. However, Living Stream Ministry, which publishes most of the literature used by the churches and is the headquarters for its most prominent ministry, has served as an informal center for information. Living Stream publishes all of Witness Lee's work which includes numerous books, pamphlets and study guides to the Bible. Living Stream regularly holds regional and national training sessions for elders and the more dedicated members in both the United States and Taiwan. Many of Lee's books are the transcribed talks of such sessions.

Increasingly, as the local churches have expanded nationally, other ministries have emerged and several local churches have begun publishing literature and issuing their own periodicals. Northwest Christian Publications located in Seattle, Washington, the ministry of William T. Freeman, has published the most substantive material apart from Living Stream. Local church periodicals include *The Firstfruit* (Chicago); *The Harvest* (Chicago), *The High Calling* (Cypress, CA), and *The News of the Churches* (Los Angeles).

In 1983 congregations in fellowship could be found around the globe, although most members could be found in North America (129 churches and 11,889 members) and Taiwan (77 churches and 119 members). Other prominent congregations could be found in the Philippine Islands, Hong Kong, and England. According to the latest information, the movement has survived in China in spite of persecution. There were reported to be 129,042 members worldwide.

Controversy

The last fifteen years have been a time of continual conflict between the Local Church and those in the larger Evangelical Christian community who perceived the theological innovations of Witness Lee as departing from acceptable Evangelical thought and disagreed with the new expressions of piety with the congregations. Much of that controversy began in the early 1970s when the Church in Berkeley (California) was housed in a building across the street from the World Christian Liberation Front, one of the early Jesus People groups. The two groups had several emotionally charged encounters. Eventually, the WCLF split into two groups, one known today as the Evangelical Orthodox Church and the other as the Spiritual Counterfeits Project. Out of each group a harshly critical book about the Local Church emerged (*The Mind Benders* by Jack Sparks and *The God-Men* by Neil T. Duddy and the SCP).

Both books charged Lee with heresy. Using quotes from a number of Lee's books, they suggested that Lee denied the traditional doctrine of the Trinity. They suggested that he did not believe in the essential distinctions between the three Persons of the Trinity, a position known as "monarchianism." They also took strong exception to the use of the metaphor "mingling" to describe the nature of the relationship of God to redeemed humanity. Lee answered that he was both Biblical and orthodox in his doctrine of the Trinity and his use of "mingling." He claimed that he had been misquoted and made to appear heretical. Both authors also associated the Local Church with a variety of cultic practices. Duddy's more extensive volume, devoted entirely to Witness Lee and the Local Church, went much further and accused Lee, among other charges, of mismanagement of church funds, and being the source of psychological damage to members.

Claiming libel and being unable to obtain a retraction and apology from either author or their publishers, Lee and several of the congregations filed suits. In the suit against *The Mind Benders*, an out-of-court settlement brought an apology, the withdrawal of the book, and a financial settlement. In the case against *The God-Men*, an $11,000,000.00 judgment against its author and Spiritual Counterfeits Project was rendered in an uncontested trial (neither Duddy nor SCP appeared in court). Among other results, the publisher of Bob Larson's *Book of Cults*, Tyndale House, announced it was withdrawing the chapter on the Local Church from future printings and apologized for any damage it might have caused.

Watchman Nee, *The Normal Christian Church Life* (Washington, D.C.: International Students Press, 1969).

Witness Lee, *The Practical Expression of the Church* (Los Angeles: Living Stream Publishers, 1970).

Watchman Nee and Witness Lee, *Outlines for Training* (Anaheim, CA: Living Stream Ministry, 1980).

Bill Freeman, *The Testimony of Church History Regarding the Mystery of the Triune God* (Anaheim, CA: Living Stream Publishers, 1976).

Bill Freeman, *The Testimony of Church History Regarding the Mystery of the Mingling of God with Man* (Anaheim, CA: Living Stream Publishers, 1977).

James Chen, *Meet Brother Nee* (Kowloon Hong Kong: Christian Publishers, 1976).

James Mo-oi Cheung, *The Ecclesiology of Watchman Nee and Witness Lee* (Fort Washington, PA: Christian Literature Crusade, 1972).

Neil T. Duddy and the Spiritual Counterfeits Project, *The God-Men* (Downers Grove, IL: Inter-Varsity Press, 1981).

Angus I. Kinnear, *Against the Tide* (Fort Washington, PA: Christian Literature Crusade, 1973).

J. Gordon Melton, *An Open Letter Concerning the Local Church, Witness Lee and The God-Men Controversy* (Santa Barbara, CA: Institute for the Study of American Religion, 1985).

Dana Roberts, *Understanding Watchman Nee* (Plainfield, NJ: Haven Books, 1980).

I. NICHIREN SHOSHU ACADEMY, SOKA GAKKAI

Nichiren Shoshu Academy is the official name of the Nichiren Shoshu religion and its lay organization Soka Gakkai, the most successful of the several groups which have grown out of the work of Buddhist teacher Nichiren Daishonin. Three of the Nichiren groups can be found in the United States, and two are confined to Hawaii.

History

Until after World War II, Nichiren Shoshu was merely one relatively small Buddhist group among many. However, with the coming of religious freedom, through the efforts of its lay organization the Soka Gakkai, it experienced a phenomenal growth.

Nichiren Daishonin (the Great Holy One) (1222–1282) was a Japanese Buddhist reformer who according to his followers fulfilled the prophecy that humanity would be redeemed by a greater Buddha than Sakyamuni. After Nichiren's death, his tomb was left in the care of six senior disciples who rotated responsibility for the upkeep of the tomb. However, one of the priests took permanent control of the tomb. In reaction, Nikko Shonin left Mt. Minobu (where the tomb is located, and established a temple, Taiseki-ji, at the foot of Mt. Fuji. Mikko Shonin is recognized as the founder of Nichiren Shoshu.

Soka Gakkai, the lay organization of Nichiren Shoshu members, was founded in 1930 as the Soka-kyoiku-gakkai (literally, Value-Creating Education Society) by the two men who were to become its first presidents, Tsunesaburo Makiguchi (1871–1944) and Josei Toda (1900–1958).

Makiguchi, an elementary school principal, was converted to Nichiren Shoshu in 1928. An enthusiastic convert, he began writing a series of books on education and values. In 1937 at the ceremony establishing Soka Gakkai in Tokyo, Makiguchi was elected president. Unfortunately, the new society ran counter to the policies of the increasingly militaristic Japanese government. The Nichiren Shoshu refused to unite with other Nichiren sects, and Makiguchi defied government orders to place a Shinto shrine in every home. In 1943 he and Toda were among a group of Nichiren Shoshu leaders arrested. Makiguchi died in prison.

Josei Toda immediately moved to rebuild Soka Gakkai after the War. He shortened the name and broadened the program from the educational field and saw its purpose as bringing peace and happiness to all. In 1951 he assumed the presidency of the revived movement. In his inaugural address he urged an aggressive proselytizing campaign. His announced goal was 750,000 members in seven years. Shortly after that goal was attained, Toda died.

Toda was succeeded in the presidency by Daisaku Ikeda (b. 1928) the executive director of the organization and student of Toda since 1947. Since his becoming president in 1960, the Soka Gakkai and Nichiren Shoshu has spread around the world. Among his first actions was a trip to the United States to rally and organize Nichiren Shoshu members.

The Nichiren Shoshu faith had been brought to the United States after World War II by Japanese immigrants and American servicemen who had been influenced toward the movement while stationed in Japan. Much of the preparation for Ikeda's visit had been made by Masayasu Sadanaga who had migrated to the United States in 1957, organized the Soka Gakkai in Washington, D.C. and began to contact members around the United States. Ikeda appointed him director and the work began to flourish. The Los Angeles *Kaikan* (headquarters), the first outside of Japan, was established in 1963. To further assist in the growth among Caucasian Americans, Sadanaga changed his name to George M. Williams in 1972.

In 1967 the first Nichiren Shoshu priest arrived and completed the structure of the movement, within which the Soka Gakkai is officially but a lay organization. The movement was reorganized around the several temples which were established and the name Soka Gakkai fell into disuse. About this same time the movement was Americanized. Japanese was discontinued except for chanting and repeating the Lotus Sutra.

Beliefs and Practices

Nichiren Shoshu considers itself the True Buddhism. Within Nichiren Shoshu the individual can find Enlightenment (Buddahood), or the fulfillment of life within and involvement to the fullest in society and the world. Enlightenment and the happiness it brings can be achieved by being in harmony with the universal law, *Nam-myoho-renge-kyo*, i.e., reverence to the wonderful law of the Lotus. Nichiren taught that the Lotus Sutra contained the one needful truth and should be given exclusive place as the essential Buddhist teaching. From his study he began to chant *Nam-myoho-renge-kyo*, which captures the essence of the Lotus Sutra.

From the teachings of Nichiren, three essential practices are extolled. First and foremost is the repetition of the chant. Both morning and evening *Nam-myoho-renge-kyo* is repeated many times accompanied by the recitation of portions of the Lotus Sutra (*Gongyo*). Members are encouraged to fill leisure moments with the chant and to use it when in distress, doubt, or need.

Gongyo and chanting are usually done before the *Gohonzon*, a scroll measuring approximately 10″ x 20″, upon which are inscribed the names of the principal enlightened beings mentioned in the Lotus Sutra. It represents the entity of life itself. Each successive high priest delegates the authority to inscribe the *Gohonzon*, and one is given to each member. It must be appropriately enshrined in the member's home in an altar that contains offerings of fruit, evergreen, candles and incense.

During the daily worship before the *Gohonzon* the scroll is unrolled. The worship is done with prayerbeads and a bell. After the worship the *Gohonzon* may be rolled up but kept in a "protected area."

Nichiren Shoshu also believes in the principle of *Kaidan* (literally ordination platform), pilgrimage to the headquarters, since 1972 the Sho-hondo located at the foot of Mt. Fuji. The first pilgrimage by American members of Nichiren Shoshu found 68 people traveling to the Daisekiji in 1961. In 1972, 1,800 traveled to the dedication of the Sho-hondo.

Organization

Nichiren Shoshu is headed by the High Priest who has followed in succession from Nikko Shonin since the thirteenth century. The High Priest appoints the priests and has administrative responsibility for the organization.

The Soka Gakkai also operates under the High Priest of Nichiren Shoshu, who appoints members to the priesthood. In actual fact, the tremendous growth of Nichiren Shoshu has been due to the activity of Soka Gakkai, and it exercises influence and power far beyond its assigned role as merely a lay organization within the larger sect.

Soka Gakkai is headed by the President and the Supreme Council for Guidance, which insure that Soka Gakkai complies with the teaching of the group. Under the President are the General Director and the Vice-presidents and the Board of Executive Directors, the major decision-making body. A Central Council administers policy decisions.

In 1979, the organization was reorganized at the highest level. A new President, Hiroshi Hojo was named, Ikeda became President of the Soka Gakkai International and honorary President and a new group of leaders were elected to fill major posts. Through an "honorary" post, Ikeda now directs his leadership to the development of the organization around the world.

In the United States two corporations control separate Nichiren Shoshu functions. Lay believers are organized through the Nichiren Shoshu Soka Gakkai of America or the Nichiren Shoshu Academy. Most believers in America came to Nichiren Shoshu through the lay organization and affiliate through the numerous community centers it has sponsored.

Once the priesthood arrived, it was incorporated as Nichiren Shoshu Temple. Though officially in charge of Nichiren Shoshu work in America, the size, power, and prior history of Soka Gakkai gave it a position it has been slow to relinquish. Tensions growing out of the scandal in Japan have carried over into the American organizations.

Present Status

World headquarters for Nichiren Shoshu are at the Taisekiji compound near Mt. Fuji. That compound has been built up by the Soka Gakkai, and the Sho-Hondo (main grand temple) completed in 1972 has become a new focus for the faith. Within its 55,660 square meters, the Dai-Gohonzon is now enshrined. The Soka Gakkai is headquartered in Tokyo. It publishes several periodicals including the monthly English-language *Soka Gakkai News*, which is mailed out internationally. From a height of membership in the mid-1970s of 6,000,000 present estimates (1980) indicate no more than 3,500,000 members.

In the United States, the Nichiren Shoshu Academy is headquartered in Santa Monica, California. From its presses come the monthly *Seikyo Times*, an American edition of a periodical published in Japan, and the weekly *World Tribune*. The NSA World Cultural Center is located in California and is the focus for the Soka Gakkai's numerous cultural and musical events and programs. Over 20 NSA centers are found across the United States.

Nichiren Shoshu Temple has six temples under its hegemony—Flushing, New York; Kaneohe, Hawaii; Chicago, Illinois; Silver Spring, Maryland; Rancho Cucamonga, California; and the headquarters temple in Los Angeles.

Estimates of membership vary widely. NSA claims 200-250,000 members as of 1983. More conservative estimates place the number at 30,000 or less (a number more consistent with the number of active temples and centers and the turnout at major events). Membership is counted by counting all of any family in which there is a member.

Soka Gakkai has produced a large number of English-language books, including the writings of Ikeda. George Williams has begun to publish English translations of the *Gosho*, the collected writings of Nichiren Daishinin. The first volume appeared in 1976 as *The Gosho Reference, I.*

Controversy

In Japan, Soka Gakkai has been a controversial organization from the time of its founding, though most Americans would support its attempts to keep its organizational integrity in the face of government pressure prior to World War II.

After World War II, Soka Gakkai broke into the news after the success of its political arm, the *Komeito*, Clean Government Party. Founded in 1964, the Komeito had, by the mid-1970s, become the third largest party in Japan. As the Komeito grew, Ikeda moved into the political arena and launched a campaign for international world peace. Throughout the 1970s Ikeda traveled and met with such world leaders and intellectuals as Arnold Toynbee, Henry Kissinger, and John Kenneth Galbraith.

The success of the Komeito underscored the most controversial practice of the Soka Gakkai, *shakubuku*, literally "to break and subdue" the evil spirits and make straight the true teaching of Buddha. It is a principle of Nichiren Shoshu that it is the true religion and true form of Buddhism, and it is the duty of every believer aggressively to pressure family, friends, and acquaintances into converting. *Shakubuku* includes strong polemic against other faiths, the use of rational argument, and the application of psychological and even physical pressure. In Japan numerous accusations of violence by Nichiren Shoshu members arose during the 1970s, and opponents charged that much of their growth came through strong-arm tactics. In the United States *shakubuku* has primarily manifested as high-pressure evangelism, without the physical pressure noted in the Japanese situation.

In 1979 scandal erupted within Soka Gakkai in Japan. Some individual members accused President Ikeda of misconduct, and their charges were printed in a number of newspapers, beginning with the Japanese equivalents of America's *National Enquirer*. Also some Nichiren priests opposed to Ikeda charged him with distorting Buddhist teachings. In the immediate wake of the scandal which came to America through the circulation of articles from English-language Japanese newspapers, some members resigned and some Japanese priests broke with the movement. Eventually aired in court, the accusations proved false and those who originally perpetrated them were found guilty of libel. The organization quickly recovered without significant loss of support.

The Sokagakkai (Tokyo: Seikyo Press, 1962).

Yasuji Kirimura, *Fundamentals of Buddhism* (Tokyo: Nichiren Shoshu International Center, 1977).

Complete Works of Daisaku Ikeda (Tokyo: Seikyo Press, 1968).

Daisaku Ikeda, *Guidance Memo* (Tokyo: Seikyo Press, 1966).

George M. Williams, *The Gosho Reference* (Los Angeles: World Tribune Press, 1976).

Noah S. Brannen, *Soka Gakkai* (Richmond, VA: John Knox Press, 1968).

Kiyoaki Murata, *Japan's New Buddhism* (New York: Walker/Westherhill, 1969).

Masaharu Anesaki, *Nichiren, the Buddhist Prophet* (Cambridge: Harvard University Press, 1949).

J. RAJNEESH FOUNDATION INTERNATIONAL

The rise and fall of Bhagwan Rajneesh as a major Indian guru in the United States occurred during the initial writing of this volume. He jumped into the spotlight because of the movement of his headquarters onto a large tract of land in rural Oregon. Attempting to create a model community near the town of Antelope, the Rajneeshees, as his followers are popularly termed, met stiff opposition from local residents who saw them as a foreign intrusion disturbing their rural lifestyle and upsetting the balance of political power in local government. They soon gained many supporters around the state. Then by the end of 1985, the town of Rajneeshpuram dissolved as quickly as it appeared.

The Founder

Bhagwan Rajneesh was born Rajneesh Chandra Mohan at Kuchwada, Madhya Pradesh, India, on December 11, 1931 to a family of the Jain faith. He attended the University of Jabalpur where he received his B. A. degree in 1951. He attained his master's degree in philosophy at the University of Saugar in 1957. Concurrently with his graduate work, he began to teach at Raipur's Sanskrit College and later at the University of Jabalpur.

According to Rajneesh, he first experienced *samadhi* (enlightenment) when he was but seven years old. However, on the evening of March 21, 1953, while still a student at the University of Saugar, he attained complete enlightenment. He describes the event:

> That night another reality opened its door, another dimension became available. Suddenly it was there—the other reality, the separate reality, the really real, or whatsoever you want to call it. Call it God, call it truth, call it Dhamma, call it Tao or whatever you will.
>
> That night I became empty and became full. I became nonexistential and became existence. That night I died and was reborn.

While continuing with the boundaries of his academic career, Rajneesh began to travel and speak to people about his experience and the teachings which grew out of it. He was both an eloquent speaker and advocate for controversial religious views. Finally in 1966 he resigned his university post and became a full-time spiritual leader. He traveled throughout India from his home in Jabalpur for several years before moving to Bombay in 1969 with a small group of his most dedicated disciples. Around 1970 the first Westerners discovered him and began to come to his Bombay apartment headquarters. Then in 1974 he purchased a site for an ashram in Poona and founded the Rajneesh Foundation (now the Rajneesh Foundation International).

During the years in Poona, Rajneesh became one of the most famous nonconventional gurus in all of India. Traditional religionists expressed strong disapproval of his reinterpretation of *sannyas*, the renounced life, and of the public displays of affection shown by his disciples both at the ashram and on the streets of Poona. Meanwhile, his following among Westerners was growing, and centers began to appear in North America, Australia and Europe.

In 1981 events which were to heighten the controversy already surrounding this most controversial religious leader began just as he entered a period of silence. In May 1981 he moved to the United States, first to his center in New Jersey. Two months later, Ma Anand Sheela (Silverman), his secretary, announced the purchase of the 64,000-acre former Big Muddy Ranch near Antelope, Oregon. A small group, which grew to over 200 within a year, moved to the ranch and began to construct Rajneeshpuram, a model community expected to house 4,000–6,000 by the end of the century. The cafe in Antelope was purchased, turned into a vegetarian restaurant, and renamed "Zorba the Buddha."

Tension within the community led to a focus of news coverage as followers of Rajneesh struggled to realize their plans. Slowly the Foundation began to overcome the obstacles it had encountered. In July 1982 approximately 7,000 followers gathered for a lengthy summer festival. In November of that year the petition for incorporation of Rajneeshpuram was submitted. In the December election, disciples of Rajneesh won the mayor's office and a majority of the seats in the city council of Antelope. Finally, in February 1984, efforts to deport Rajneesh were thwarted when papers revealed his 1936 adoption by Swami Swarupananda (the father of Ma Anand Sheela), who had become a permanent resident of the United States in 1973.

Teachings

Both his mystical experiences and his philosophical training led Rajneesh beyond the Jainism of his parents. He has attempted to create a new religious synthesis which brings elements of all the major religious traditions together with the new Western techniques of inner transformation and therapy (many borrowed directly from humanistic psychology). This new religion, called Rajneeshism, is centered upon Rajneesh as the Enlightened teacher, who is generally referred to by the honorific title, "Bhagwan," literally a godman. Following a widespread Indian belief,

Rajneesh teaches that it is difficult to grow spiritually without surrender to an enlightened accomplished master.

Rajneesh offers to his followers a number of techniques to move them along a path to enlightenment. Prior to initiation, followers are called *shravakas*, sympathetic listeners, and *shravakas* are encouraged to become *sannyasins*. Rajneesh has rejected the common designation of *sannyas* as the renounced life. *Sannyas* means the right way to live, to live consciously. Thus rather than renouncing the material life, Rajneesh teaches disciples to accept and affirm all of life and to build a synthesis between the spiritual and material.

Those who take initiation as a *sannyasin*, or more properly, a neo-*sannyasin*, agree to do four things: (1) to dress in red or orange, the colors of the sunrise; (2) to wear a *mala* (a necklace of 108 beads and a picture of the guru) outside the clothes in plain sight; (3) to use the new name given at the time of initiation; and (4) to meditate regularly. Rajneesh teaches a variety of techniques of meditation, the five most important being: dynamic meditation, *kundalini* meditation, *nataraj* meditation, *gourishankar* meditation and *nadabrahma* meditation. These various meditation techniques are integrated into a daily program of activity. The day begins and ends with the chanting of the Buddham Sharanam Gatchchhami:

Buddham Sharanam Gatchchhami
Sangham Sharanam Gatchchhami
Dhammam Sharanam Gatchchhami

which translated means:

I go to the feet of the Awakened One
I go to the feet of the commune of the Awakened One
I go to the feet of the Ultimate Truth of the Awakened One

In the morning, either in groups or alone, disciples attend *satsang*, in which they sit in silence spiritually communing with Rajneesh, and listen to music or tapes of him speaking. In the evening, *darshan* is a celebration in which the disciple, through singing and dancing, melts into the essence of the master. While these activities most closely conform to what is traditionally termed worship, Rajneesh teaches that worship is basically day-to-day living performed not for gain but out of the abundance of the inner self transforming mere activity into creativity.

Rajneesh emphasizes individual freedom within the broad guidelines of the initiate's life. However, initiates are encouraged to refrain from the use of narcotics, to imbibe alcohol only in moderation and at mealtime, and to follow a vegetarian diet.

Disciples of Rajneesh celebrate four special days: March 21, Bhagwan Shree Rajneesh's enlightenment Day; July 6, Master's Day; September 8, honoring all who have died; December 11, Rajneesh's birthday. Master's Day, a day set aside to celebrate the existence of Rajneesh, occurs during the six-week-long World Celebration which was held annually since 1982 at Rajneeshpuram.

Organization

The teachings of Rajneesh are disseminated by the Rajneesh Foundation International until early 1986 headquartered at Rajneeshpuram, Oregon. Also located at Rajneeshpuram was the Foundation's press which prints many of Rajneesh's books and two periodicals, *The Rajneesh Foundation International Newsletter* and *Bhagwan*. The Foundation was headed by Rajneesh and administered by its president, Ma Anand Sheela. Since Rajneesh's departure to India and the resignation of Sheela and several close disciples, the administration of the foundation has fallen into the hands of a group of board members who are currently in the process of reorganizing it. Rajneesh meditation centers have been established throughout North America and around the world.

The Foundation recognizes three categories of ministers: *acharyas*, *arihantes*, and *siddhas*. Ministers are characterized by "the particular type of energy he or she possesses: introverted, extroverted, or a synthesis of the two." *Arihantes* are basically extroverted and reach God through service to others. They are designated to perform marriage and birth ceremonies. *Siddhas*, the introverted, concentrate on personal transformation and are designated to perform the death ceremony. *Acharyas* are given authority to perform all the prescribed ceremonies, including the initiation of new neo-*sannyasins*. To be a minister, a person must have been a neo-*sannyasin* for at least two years and go through a program of meditation and training.

Current Status

As this volume goes to press in January 1986, the following information is correct, however, it will change during 1986 as the corporation is reorganized and as the international and national headquarters and the location of various structures are relocated away from the former Rajneeshpuram.

World headquarters of the Rajneesh Foundation International are located at Antelope, Oregon. The community also houses the Academy of Rajneeshism which oversees the training of the ministers. The Foundation has published most of the several hundred books of Rajneesh, the majority of which consist of transcripts of the discourses he has made over the years.

Estimates of the size of Rajneesh's following vary. In 1984, the Foundation claimed 250,000 followers worldwide. Estimates of the number of current active initiates have been considerably lower. At least 10,000–20,000 disciples are located in the United States in over 100 centers. (The events in Oregon in late 1985 should have no immediate appreciable impact on the number of Rajneesh devotees.)

The Rajneesh Community Trust, which operates under the Foundation, developed programs to bring people to live at Rajneeshpuram. "The Buddhafield Experience" recruited individuals to live at Rajneeshpuram and work in restoring the land. In 1984 the Trust became an object of media attention as it began inviting homeless individuals from cities across the United States to make the new city their home. Several thousand migrated to Oregon at the Foundation's expense.

Controversy

Rajneesh has been a controversial figure from the time he began to assume the role of a spiritual leader while still a teacher at Jabalpur. His redefinition of traditional Indian religious concepts and the overt emotional displays which accompanied some of the group's meditational practices offended many. The open approach to and positive acceptance of sex by Rajneesh and his neo-*sannyasins* (in the face of a cultural image of *sannyasins* having renounced all sexual activity) became a particular focus of hostile criticism during the years of the Poona ashram. Shortly before Rajneesh moved to the United States, a fire swept through the ashram, thought by many to have been set by arsonists.

Attacks upon Rajneesh and his followers began soon after the purchase of the Big Muddy Ranch near Antelope, Oregon, and his arrival in the United States. In the fall of 1981, the Portland district office of the U.S. Immigration and Naturalization Service began an investigation of Rajneesh's followers on charges of immigration fraud. Early in 1982 the Rajneeshees voted to incorporate the ranch as a city named Rajneeshpuram. It became the center of the movement and followers began to move there.

Tensions within the community led to a focus of news coverage as followers of Rajneesh struggled to realize their plans and began to overcome the obstacles. In July 1982 approximately 7,000 followers gathered for a lengthy summer festival. In November of that year the petition for incorporation of Rajneeshpuram was submitted. In the December election, disciples of Rajneesh won the mayor's office and a majority of the seats in the city council of Antelope. Finally in February 1984, an initial effort to deport Rajneesh was blocked when papers revealed his 1936 adoption by Swami Swarupananda (the father of Ma Anand Sheela) who had become a permanent resident of the United States in 1973.

Settled in Oregon, Rajneesh was attacked regularly, more for his show of wealth than for his controversial teachings. His followers had given him a large fleet of Rolls-Royces (almost 100 by 1985) in which he took daily rides. Though he did not own the automobiles, they were made available for his use. The Foundation was, however, also involved in the cult controversies due to the unfamiliar nature of Rajneesh's teachings. While no significant charges of brainwashing were leveled, critics held up for ridicule the unfamiliar practices of dynamic meditation. Lying behind the attacks upon Rajneesh was the fear that other nonconventional religious groups would attempt to form similar communities, thus further distorting the social and political fabric at Antelope.

The controversies continued through the summer of 1985 with both sides scoring what each felt were victories. Then suddenly in September 1985, Ma Anand Sheela resigned her position and Rajneesh denounced her, accusing her of crimes against him and the movement. He also denounced "Rajneeshism," which he said was Sheela's creation. However, the only substantive change he made in his teachings was to release followers from the requirements to wear red or orange clothes and to wear the *mala* with his picture. While the book *Rajneeshism* was to be destroyed, all the other elements of "Rajneeshism" remained in place.

Following the break with Sheela, Rajneesh found himself in a serious situation. On October 23, he was indicted for immigration fraud. Four days later, for reasons unknown, he left Oregon. Believing he was attempting to flee the country, federal agents arrested him in North Carolina. In a plea bargain, on November 14, he confessed to two felonies, paid a $40,000.00 fine, and agreed to leave the United States. He returned to India to establish a new center there.

The fall of Rajneesh was followed by an announcement that the ranch would be shut down and the property, including the automobiles, sold. Almost anti-climatic was the announcement several weeks later that a court had ruled the incorporation of Rajneeshpuram violated principles of separation of church and state, as it amounted to religious control of a municipal government.

Rajneesh and his followers thus return to the decentralized state they were in prior to Rajneesh's arrival in the United States. The movement in other countries around the world were only minutely affected by the events of 1985, and followers everywhere have voiced their faith in Rajneesh's innocence of charges brought against him. While the most serious charges against Rajneesh personally have been settled, the charges against movement leaders will be heard in the coming months and years. Fresh revelations of serious illegal activities could do much to invalidate Rajneesh if tied to him as an active participant. Otherwise the movement is likely to continue to grow for the foreseeable future.

Rajneeshism, An Introduction to Bhagwan Shree Rajneesh and His Religion (Rajneeshpuram, OR: Rajneesh Foundation International, 1983).

Bhagwan Shree Rajneesh, *I Am the Gate* (New York: Harper & Row, 1975).

Bhagwan Shree Rajneesh, *The Great Challenge* (New York: Grove Press, 1982).

Ma Satya Bha ti, *Drunk on the Divine* (New York: Grove Press, 1980).

Vasant Joshi, *The Awakened One* (New York: Harper & Row, 1982).

Sally Belfrage, *Flowers of Emptiness* (New York: Dial Press, 1981).

Gita Mehta, *Karma Cola* (New York: Simon & Schuster, 1979).

Vishal Mangalwadi, *The World of Gurus* (New Delhi: Vikas Publishing House, 1977).

Aubrey Menen, *The Mystics* (New York: Dial Press, 1974).

Khushwant Singh, *Gurus, Godmen and Good People* (New Delhi: Orient Longman, 1975).

K. SIKH DHARMA (HEALTHY, HAPPY, HOLY ORGANIZATION)

The first people of the Sikh faith to come to America seem to have been a few East Indians who visited New England in the 1790s. No large-scale migrations took place until the early twentieth century when Canadian railroads brought many Punjabis into British Columbia. Some of these began to move southward into Washington, Oregon, and, eventually, California. A new element was added to this somewhat stable Punjabi Sikh community in 1968 in the person of S. Harbhajan Singh Puri (known by his followers as Siri Sahib Bhai Harbhajan Singh Khalsa Yogiji and popularly called Yogi Bhajan), a Sikh teacher newly arrived from Amritsar prepared to teach the faith to all.

Founder and Early History

Yogi Bhajan (b. 1929), a well-educated Sikh from Delhi, India, moved to Toronto in 1968 and in December of that year settled in Los Angeles. In 1969 he founded an ashram and the Healthy, Happy, Holy Organization (3HO) to teach kundalini yoga and meditation. During his classes he also began to share his Sikh faith and gather an interested group of believers. In 1971, accompanied by a group of 84 young Americans he visited the Golden Temple at Amritsar, the world headquarters of the Sikh faith, and from the Akal Takhat (the Guru's Throne), the highest spiritual authority in the faith, he was given a sword of honor, ordained a minister, and granted authority to ordain others as ministers and initiate individuals into the Khalsa, the Sikh Brotherhood. As the Chief Religious and Administrative Authority for the Sikh Dharma in the Western World, he is the first person outside of India to be granted such recognition. With the formal establishment of the Sikh Dharma in the West, the 3HO became its educational arm.

In 1974, Gurcharan Singh Tohra, President of the Shiromani Gurudwara Parabandokh Committee of Amritsar (the chief administrative body of the Sikh Dharma in India), and Giani Mahinder Singh Ji, Secretary of the S.G.P.C., toured the Western centers of the Sikh Dharma. At the

Akal Takhat in November, Yogi Bhajan received the honorary title, "Bhai
Sahib," in recognition of his work in spreading Sikhism outside of India.
And the Sikh Dharma had grown. Over 100 ashrams had been founded in
the United States, Canada, and Europe.

The Sikh Dharma is a branch of the orthodox Sikh religion, one of the
major faiths of India. While one in belief with Sikhs around the world, it
is organizationally separate from the several older Sikh bodies in the
United States, such as the Sikh Foundation in Stockton, California, and
the International Sikh Federation in Madison Heights, Michigan. These
latter organizations represent most of the Punjabi Sikhs in North America,
while most of the members of the Sikh Dharma are ethnically non-Indian.

Beliefs and Practices

The Sikh religion was founded by Guru Nanak (1439–1538), who sought
to reconcile the religious differences and social conflicts between the
Hindus and Muslims. The new faith drew elements from both religions.
He emphasized that there was One God, the Creator, and that His Name
transcended the barriers of race, caste, and creed. He taught his followers
to earn an honest living by the sweat of their brow but always to share
their possessions with those in need. Guru Nanak was the first of ten
gurus recognized by Sikhs. After the death of Guru Gobind Singh, the *Siri
Guru Granth Sahib*, the writings of Guru Nanak, became the guru for the
movement. Members are encouraged to learn Gurmukhi, the language in
which the *Granth Sahib* was originally written.

For Sikhs, God is self-existent, immortal, immanent, transcendent,
omnipotent, omnipresent, and omniscient. He is experienced through
chanting of the Name of God, which in the original language is "Sat Nam"
(God's name is Truth) or "Wahe Guru" (Experience of Infinite Wisdom). Chanting God's name is frequently done by repeating the mantra,
"Ek Ong Kar Nam Siri Wha Guru" ("There is One Creator and one
creation. Truth is His name. He is all Great. He is all Wisdom.") Members
normally rise before sunrise each day to chant God's name and meditate.

While not required to do so, individuals associated with the Sikh
Dharma are encouraged to seek formal initiation and join the Khalsa, the
Brotherhood of the Pure Ones, a fellowship begun by Guru Gobind
Singh. New members are baptized with sweetened water stirred with a
sword. Members of the Sikh Dharma are then required to keep the
traditional practices introduced by Guru Gobind Singh that became the
distinguishing marks of the Sikh community, known popularly as the five
"k's." All hair, including the beard is kept uncut (*kesh*) and tied on top of
the head in a turban. The hair is kept neat with a comb (*kangha*). Sikhs
wear special underwear (*kachera*) originally designed to allow freedom of
movement in battle; a steel bracelet (*kara*) symbolic of an inseparable
bond with God; and a dagger (*kirpan*) symbolic of a commitment to
defend truth, righteousness, and those who cannot defend themselves.

Ministers in the Sikh Dharma also normally wear a long hemmed knee-length skirt (*kurta*) and special pants which are loose at the waist and tight around the legs (*chudidas*). Both are solid white as is the turban.

Health is of prime concern within the Sikh Dharma. Natural foods are preferred and fish, meat, alcohol, and drugs prohibited. A number of members have opened health food restaurants and groceries. Members also prefer natural methods of healing.

The Sikh Dharma observes the traditional holidays of Sikhism, especially Balsakhi Day, the birthday of the Khalsa (April); the Martyrdom days of Guru Tegh Bhadus (November) and Guru Arjun Dev (May); and the birthdays of the ten gurus.

Beyond what is normally considered orthodox Sikhism, Yogi Bhajan also teaches kundalini, laya and tantric yoga, the techniques of which he had mastered prior to his coming to the United States. Kundalini yoga consists of exercises which stimulate and control the energy within man which expands the capacity of the self. Laya yoga is the technique of altering consciousness by sound and rhythm. Tantric yoga is practiced by couples who share energies and consciousness. It must be done in the presence of a master or Mahan Tantric (Yogi Bhajan).

Organization

The Sikh Dharma is organized into numerous congregations each headed by a minister approved by Yogi Bhajan and appointed by the Khalsa Council. Ministers are entitled "Singh Sahib" (men) or "Sardarni Sahiba" (women). Regional, national, and international oversight and administration of the Sikh Dharma are in the hands of the Khalsa Council. The Regional and Administrative ministers who constitute this council are entitled "Mukhia Singh Sahib" or "Mukhia Sardarni Sahiba." Ultimate authority rests in Yogi Bhajan. Headquarters of the Sikh Dharma is in Los Angeles. In 1984 it reported 400 ministers and 250,000 members in the United States. The membership figures include all Sikhs in the United States, only 10,000 to 20,000 of which are directly associated with the Sikh Dharma.

The Healthy, Happy, Holy Organization is incorporated separately but shares space in the Sikh Dharma headquarters building. As the Sikh Dharma's educational arm, it carries out an extensive program. It operates a number of ashrams, each headed by a spiritual director appointed by Yogi Bhajan. In most cases the ashram director is a Sikh Dharma minister and the local congregations use the ashram for meetings. 3HO sponsors Yogi Bhajan's workshops and seminars on kundalini and tantric yoga, which he periodically gives around the United States as well as a variety of other programs for the general public.

Under the control of 3HO is the Kundalini Research Foundation headquartered in Pomona, California. Founded in 1973, KRI was established to verify, scientifically, the effects of kundalini yoga. It publishes a number of instructional manuals in yoga and meditation and reports of its research.

In 1984 3HO reported approximately 125 ashrams and centers in the United States. Foreign centers were reported in 22 countries. 3HO publishes two magazines, *Beads of Truth*, its own quarterly, and the *Journal of Science and Consciousness*, the journal of KRI.

Each June 3HO holds its annual Summer Soltice Sadhana which includes classes, lectures by Yogi Bhajan, and business meetings. The event is held near Espanola, New Mexico, where Yogi Bhajan resides.

Yogi Bhajan has been one of the most ecumenical of the Eastern teachers in the United States. He has given strong support to the annual Human Unity Conferences originally begun by Kirpal Singh, a Sant Mat master, and aligned himself with the larger community of Eastern and mystical teachers, generally referred to as the New Age Movement. Associated with the Sikh Dharma is Spiritual Community Publications of Berkeley, California. Spiritual Community periodically publishes *The New Consciousness Sourcebook* (formerly the *Spiritual Community Guide*), a guide to New Age groups in North America, and *A Pilgrim's Guide to Planet Earth*, an international New Age directory. For several years it published *New Directions*, a monthly New Age magazine. It published several important books for the Sikh Dharma, *Guru for the Aquarian Age*, a volume on the life and teachings of Guru Nanak, and *Peace Lagoon*, an English translation of selections from the Granth Guru.

Controversy

The Sikh Dharma has received some attention from the anti-cult movement, and there have been a few deprogramming attempts. One ex-member left and accused Yogi Bhajan of sexual involvement with several of his staff members, but there was no verification of the charges. Controversy has primarily been focused in other areas.

Tension developed during the mid-1970s as members of the Sikh Dharma began to interact with the older American Sikh community. Sikh Dharma members complained that the Punjabi Sikhs had become lax in their discipline, especially in their adherence to the five "k's." The tension led to an attack on Yogi Bhajan and his followers by Dr. Narinder Singh Kapany, editor of the influential *Sikh Sangar*, the magazine of the Sikh Foundation. Kapany condemned Bhajan's emphasis upon yoga and his strictures on diet. Kapany's criticisms have been echoed by other Sikh leaders in both the United States and India. The issues have never been resolved, and the two communities have remained separate.

Sikh Dharma members have encountered constant conflict over their turbans. As early as 1971, Thomas C. Costello faced a military court-martial for refusing to either cut his hair or remove his turban. His case led to a change in Army regulations granting permission for Sikhs to wear turbans. As recently as 1984, Karta Kaur Khalsa was threatened with loss of her teaching certificate because she refused to take off her turban during classes. In 1985 the Oregon Supreme Court declared the law under which she was suspended to be unconstitutional.

While these tensions remain, the Sikh Dharma has been praised highly for its drug rehabilitation program, and Akal Security, a security guard business formed by a group of members in New Mexico, created in no small part out of the image of the fierce Sikh warrior, has been highly sought for its services.

Sardarni Premka Kaur, *Guru for the Aquarian Age* (San Rafael, CA: Spiritual Community, 1972).

The Teachings of Yogi Bhajan (New York: Hawthorn Books, 1977).

Yogi Bhajan, *The Experience of Consciousness* (Pomona, CA: KRI Publications, 1977).

Liberation (Los Angeles: "The Source," n.d. [1970s]).

Kundalini Yoga/Sadhana Guidelines (Pomona, CA: Kundalini Research Institute, 1978).

W. Owen Cole and Piara Singh Sambhi, *The Sikhs* (London: Routledge and Kegan Paul, 1978).

L. TRANSCENDENTAL MEDITATION AND THE WORLD PLAN EXECUTIVE COUNCIL

Is the practice of transcendental meditation a religious exercise and is the World Plan Executive Council really a Hindu religious organization? That is an essential question for anyone discussing TM and the related corporate structures. The World Plan Executive Council claims it is not a religion. The court ruled otherwise. TM's inclusion in this volume is based upon a judgment that the court was correct in its decision.

Founder and Early History

Biographical sketches of Maharishi Mehesh Yogi, the teacher of TM to the world and the founder of the World Plan Executive Council, almost always begin with a reflection of the lack of facts about his early life. It is a common practice of Hindu monks, once they have reached a certain stage in their life, to refrain from any mention of their prior life. Maharishi has followed that example. Some who claim to have known him in India say that he was born Mehesh Prasad Varma in Utter Kashi, October 18, 1911 (other sources say "1918"), the son of a local tax official (some sources say "forest ranger"), of the Kshatriyas (warrior) caste. His confirmed biography begins, however, in 1940, when he graduated with a degree in physics from Allahabad University.

Instead of pursuing a career in science, he left everything to go to Joytir Math (monastery) in Badarinath to study with Swami Krishanand Saraswati, popularly known as Guru Dev. A recluse for many years, Guru Dev had become famous and was finally persuaded to become the spiritual leader of the Math. Maharishi became his favored student and stayed with him until his death in 1953. Guru Dev taught a form of meditation which he had rediscovered by reading the various Hindu holy books. Three years after Guru Dev's death, Maharishi emerged from a period of seclusion and began to teach what has become known as transcendental meditation. Beginning in southern India in 1956, he toured India speaking and lecturing. The Council dates the beginning of Maharishi's worldwide movement from 1957. Then in 1958, at a celebration of Guru Dev's eighty-ninth birthday, he announced the launching of a spiritual regeneration movement to spread the teachings of his guru around the world.

He left soon after the celebration, traveling first to Burma, Singapore, and Hong Kong before arriving in Hawaii in the spring of 1959. He traveled on to San Francisco, Los Angeles and London. He also established an international organization from those who accepted his teachings, the International Meditation Society. Returning to India, he decided to concentrate on teacher training. The first class of teachers, who graduated in 1961, included Beulah Smith, the first teacher in America.

Maharishi made a world tour, which included the United States, annually for the next several years. He visited followers and centers throughout the West. Among his significant students was Jerome Jarvis. Jarvis convinced Maharishi to begin speaking on university campuses, out of which the Student International Meditation Society was born, for several years the most successful branch of the work.

Then in 1967, one of the most important events in TM history occurred: the Beatles, the popular rock group, became followers of Maharishi and endorsed TM. George Harrison, one of the Beatles later connected with the Hare Krishna movement, had been taking lessons from Indian musician Ravi Shankar. Harrison learned of Maharishi's presence in London and persuaded the other Beatles to attend. Together they then went on a retreat Maharishi conducted. In January 1968, along with actress Mia Farrow, they went to Maharishi's center in India. They were the first of a number of celebrities from Efrem Zimbalist, Jr. to Joe Namath who became meditators and who helped make Maharishi a celebrity and turn TM into a fad among older teens and young adults. The movement grew dramatically in the United States and Europe during the early 1970s. By the end of the decade, almost a million people had taken the basic TM course.

On January 8, 1972, Maharishi announced the World Plan, the overall strategy that has guided the movement since that time. The goal of the World Plan is to share the Science of Creative Intelligence, the movement's comprehensive understanding of life and knowledge, of which transcendental meditation is the practical aspect, with the whole world. The goal has been to establish 3,600 World Plan centers, one for each million people on earth. Each center is to have 1,000 teachers, thus establishing a constant ratio of one teacher per 1,000 persons in the general population.

The World Plan, which remains dominant in the movement, suffered several major reverses in the mid-1970s. Around 1976 the number of new people taking the basic TM course dropped dramatically. Faced with the decline in new recruits, the Council announced an advanced *siddha* program, which included as its most dramatic claim teaching meditators to levitate. The program was immediately attacked and in the face of insufficient evidence to substantiate the claims, the organization suffered a credibility gap. The major blow came in 1978, however, when a federal court in New Jersey ruled that TM was a religious practice and, hence, could not be taught in the public schools. Throughout the 1970s, the basic

TM course had been taught in a variety of public institutions supported by public funds. The ruling denied access to what had been a major TM market, and progress slowed dramatically in the United States, though growth proceeded in other areas of the world.

Beliefs and Practice

Transcendental meditation is the basic practice taught through the World Plan Executive Council. It was offered as a simple system of meditation, basically consisting of daily meditation using a *mantra*, a word which is repeated over and over again as one sits in silence. Meditation by the use of mantras is an old and honored Hindu technique. Maharishi, however, advocated the use of a single mantra which was given each student at the time of their taking the basic TM course. According to an early introductory flyer,

> The method of meditation is imparted at a short, private ceremony after preparatory lectures and an interview with the teacher. The object of meditation is a sound, specially chosen to suit the nature of the way of life of the particular man or woman. Further, students are told not to divulge the mantra that they are given.

Two observations on the description of the TM method are important. First, the nature of the ceremony has been revealed to be a simple Hindu devotional service, called a *puja*, venerating the lineage of gurus from which Maharishi claimed his authority and an invocation of various Hindu deities. The mantras are given out only at these *puja* ceremonies. Second, the mantra given to any individual is determined by their sex and age at the time of their *puja*. Several former meditators have compiled and published the list of mantras.

The Council has made extraordinary claims for the effects of the practice of TM. Scientists who were among the hundreds of thousands who took the basic TM course were encouraged to test these claims. Their findings have been published in a variety of scientific journals and summarized in several Council publications such as *Fundamentals in Progress* (1975). TM has claimed that its regular practice can produce changes in the body which, in turn, lead to, for example, increased intelligence, improved academic performance, higher job productivity, improved resistance to disease, and better psychological health. TM can totally transform a person's life.

The scientific findings concerning the effects of transcendental meditation, provide the basis for the proposal of a total world view, the Science of Creative Intelligence, defined as including the experience and knowledge of the nature, range, growth, and application of creative intelligence. Creative intelligence is the single and branching flow of energy and directedness in the universe, a concept approaching what others have called the Absolute, in common parlance, the Divine.

The World Plan spreads the knowledge and experience of creative intelligence through attacking problems in the seven basic areas of human life: individual, governmental, educational, social, environmental, economic, and spiritual. In each area it has a specific objective: to develop the full potential of the individual; to improve government achievements; to realize the highest ideal of education; to eliminate the age-old problem of crime and all behavior that brings unhappiness to the family of man; to maximize the intelligent use of the environment; to bring fulfillment to the economic aspirations of individuals and society; and to achieve the spiritual goals of mankind in this generation.

The basic avenue for achieving these goals is the spread of transcendental meditation in the population. However, Maharishi has also taken additional steps in developing the World Plan. For example, he declared the presence of the World Government of the Age of Enlightenment, a government which has sovereignty over the domain of consciousness. In the name of the World Government, in 1978 he inaugurated a world peace campaign by sending over 100 "World Governors" (adept meditators) to each of five sites of major global tension: Iran, Lebanon, Zimbabwe Central America, and Thailand. In 1983 he announced the readiness of the World Government to solve the problems of any existing government and invited government leaders to make contact. From December 17, 1983 to January 6, 1984, he brought 7,000 TM *siddhas* to join the several thousand students at Maharishi International University in Iowa for a two-week period of peace. The collective meditation of the 7,000-plus adepts was to purify world consciousness.

Organization

The original spiritual regeneration movement begun by Maharishi in 1958 is now in the hands of the World Plan Executive Council whose international headquarters are at the World Plan Administrative Center in Seelisberg, Switzerland. The work of the Council in spreading the World Plan and its practical element, transcendental meditation, is carried through five task-oriented structures. The International Meditation Society has the main task of introducing the general public to TM. The Spiritual Regeneration Movement concentrates upon that segment of the population over thirty. The Student International Meditation Society functions with campus populations. The American Foundation for the Science of Creative Intelligence is in charge of applying TM within the business community.

Maharishi International University is a regular four-year liberal arts college which offers both bachelor's and master's degrees. MIU was given a specific role in implementing the World Plan. It offers a special set of courses on the seven objectives, including teacher training courses. MIU is also developing Global Television, a program to make TM available in every country through modern audiovisual technology.

The backbone of the Council, however, remains the numerous World Plan centers found throughout the world.

Current Status

International headquarters of the Council are in Switzerland. American headquarters are in Los Angeles. MIU, established at Santa Barbara, California, moved to the former Parsons College campus in Fairfield, Iowa in 1974. The American Foundation for the Science of Creative Intelligence has headquarters in Pacific Palisades, California, and has centers in Chicago, Atlanta, Boston, Los Angeles, New York City, San Francisco, and Washington, D.C.

There are over 300 World Plan Centers in the United States and over 1,000,000 individuals have taken the basic TM course. Only a small fraction of those who took the course remain meditators or in any way connected to the World Plan Executive Council. The active meditators, however, are estimated to number in the tens of thousands.

Controversy

The success which Maharishi (and TM) enjoyed in the 1970s made his name a household word. It also brought criticism and controversy, which centered on three issues. First, TM's claims to scientific substantiation have been challenged on several levels. Among the early findings of psychologists were those related to the physical effects of TM, particularly those which relax the body. Psychologists studying yoga and meditation noted that similar results could be produced from a wide variety of practices, of which TM was but one. Other scientists have challenged the findings of their colleagues, pointing out that positive results could only be obtained from special samples of meditators. Social works, such as the sending of the World Governors to the several trouble spots, have had no visible results.

Second, critics, primarily those interested in the separation of church and state, boosted by evangelical Christians who opposed TM as a non-Christian religion, challenged the use of state funds to spread the practice. They argued successfully that the World Plan Executive Council was in fact a Hindu religious organization and TM a practice essentially religious in nature. The major elements of their case were the *puja* ceremony, the pattern of Maharishi's life and its essential Hindu religious roots through Guru Dev, the existence of the Spiritual Regeneration Movement (with its obvious religious overtones), and Maharishi's own religious writings which coincide with the World Plan, particularly *The Science of Being and Art of Living*.

Finally, TM critics have charged the movement with an element of deception. They claim (with good evidence) that Maharishi brought TM to America but soon discovered that it did not appeal to the masses he hoped to reach. Therefore, he created a new image, in part based upon the early scientific papers, and began to deny the religious elements. By this method, arguing that the practice of TM led to reduced dependence on drugs, TM spread through the school system and into the U. S. Army.

It should be noted that, in spite of the 1978 court decision, the Council still insists upon its nonreligious nature, though it does acknowledge a primary "spiritual" goal.

Maharishi Mahesh Yogi, *Concordance for the Bhagavad-Gita* (Fairfield, IA): MIU Press, 1971).

Jack Forem, *Transcendental Meditation* (New York: E.P. Dutton, 1974).

Denise Denniston and Peter McWilliams, *The TM Book* (Allen Park, MI: Versemonger Press, 1975).

Fundamentals of Progress (Fairfield, IO: Maharishi International University, 1975).

Alliance for Knowledge (Seelisberg, Switz.: MIU Press, 1973).

Maharishi Mehesh Yogi, *The Science of Being and the Art of Living* (London: International SRM Publications, 1966).

Herbert Benson, *The Relaxation Response* (New York: Avon, 1975).

John White, *Everything You Want to Know about TM—Including How to Do It* (New York: Pocket Books, 1976).

TM in the Court (Berkeley, CA: Spiritual Counterfeits Project, 1978).

A. H. Chapman, *What TM Can and Cannot Do for You* (New York: Berkeley Publishing Corporation, 1976).

Martin Ebon, ed., *Maharishi the Guru* (New York: New American Library, 1968).

John E. Patton, *The Case Against TM in the Schools* (Grand Rapids, MI: Baker Book House, 1976).

Steve Richards, *Levitation* (Wellingborough, Eng: Aquarian Press, 1980).

M. THE UNIFICATION CHURCH

The Founder

The Unification Church was founded by the Rev. Sun Myung Moon, born Young Myung Moon in Pyungan Buk-do, a rural town in what is now North Korea, on January 6, 1920. When he was ten his parents converted to Christianity, and the family joined the Presbyterian Church. On Easter morning 1936, according to his later reports, the sixteen-year-old Moon had a revelation in which Jesus appeared to him and revealed that he had been chosen to complete Jesus' unfulfilled mission. The vision launched a period of inner searching and struggle during which time Moon finished high school and went to Japan to study electrical engineering at Waseda University. He remained in Japan during World War II but returned to Pyongyang in North Korea in 1948 and began a career as an independent preacher.

Shortly before his return to Korea, he had an intense experience which he described as having entered the spirit world and having won a great victory over the Satanic forces. Following this experience, he changed his name to Sun Myung Moon (i.e., Shining Sun and Moon).

His preaching activity led to his arrest in February 1948. He was sent to a prison camp where he remained until October 14, 1959 when United Nations forces liberated the camp. He fled to Pusan where he commenced preaching again and wrote the first draft of the *Divine Principle*, the book which contains the essence of his revelation. It was first published in 1957. In 1954 he organized those who had responded to his preaching into the Holy Spirit Association for the Unification of World Christianity, the official name of the Unification Church. The movement grew slowly but was able to send out its first missionary to Japan in 1958. Eventually a strong branch of the Church would be built there.

In 1960 Moon married Han Ja Han (his second marriage, the first having ended in divorce) and began the task of completing that part of Christ's unfulfilled mission that included marriage and a family. Over the next two decades, culminating in 1981, Mrs. Moon bore twelve children.

Moon made several visits to the United States in the 1960s, including one in 1964 during which Spiritualist medium Arthur Ford conducted a seance that Moon attended. At the seance, Ford's spirit guide Fletcher called Moon a New Age teacher/revealer who bears the endtime message.

In his talks on this trip, Moon also spoke frequently of his own familiarity with the spirit world.

While the Church was growing and spreading in the 1960s, Moon became a successful businessman with concerns in ginseng, titanium, manufacturing, and pharmaceuticals. He also expressed his intense emotional and philosophical rejection of Communism by launching in the mid-1960s a campaign against Communism, an activity that brought him the favorable attention of South Korean President Park Chung Hee.

On New Year's Day 1972 Moon received a revelation to move to the United States. He signaled this move by launching the One World Crusade and conducting a series of "Day of Hope" rallies in major American cities. Having settled in the United States, he directed the development of a multifaceted program for the Unification Church. He also became the center of several controversies, some created by his support of unpopular causes, others revolving around a growing number of accusations by opponents of the Church. Moon supported Nixon during the Watergate crisis, was investigated by a Congressional committee probing South Korean attempts to buy influence on Capitol Hill, and in 1982 was convicted on tax evasion charges brought by the Internal Revenue Service.

Moon has attempted to project his ideas into all areas of American society. He has founded two major daily newspapers in New York City and Washington, D.C. He financed a Hollywood film, *Inchon*. He has courted the scientific and scholarly world and organized conferences, a peace academy, and a Washington think tank.

Upon the completion of his family and the birth of his twelfth child, Moon took the title "Lord of the Second Advent," an appellation already given him by most of his followers. By this title, Moon asserted that he had completed the work left unfinished by Jesus, whose mission had been cut short by the rejection of his people. Within the movement, he is generally called "Father," and he and his wife are seen as the True Parents who will restore the world to God's original purpose.

The Unification Church in the United States

The Unification Church came to the United States in January 1959 in the person of three Korean missionaries—Young Oom Kim, David S. C. Kim, and Colonel Bo Hi Pak. The Kims settled in Eugene, Oregon where Ms. Kim attended school and where the two worked together for several years. In January 1961 Ms. Kim moved to Berkeley, California and established a branch of the Church adjacent to the University of California campus. Col. Pak, a diplomatic aide at the South Korean embassy, settled in Washington, D.C.

In 1962 Ms. Kim sent the members of the Church in Berkeley to other campus locations in California and the next year dispersed them to cities around the United States. During the 1960s the Church grew slowly, operating under the name, the United Family. A periodical, *New Age Frontiers*, was begun in 1964.

The growth of the Church was spurred in 1972 by Rev. Moon's move to the United States. During the years 1972–1976 it grew from a few hundred members to around 6,000. International headquarters were established in New York City and missions initiated around the world. Church centers were opened in most states (though most were quite small), and members began intense fundraising efforts to give the Church a firm financial footing and money to launch its many programs. In 1975 the Unification Theological Seminary was established to train future Church leaders.

Belief and Practice

Within the Unification Church a pluralistic theological atmosphere exists around a core of belief and practice. During the 1970s, under the pressure of unrealized prophetic expectations and the growing theological sophistication spread through the Church from the Seminary, the belief structures changed radically. The apocalyptic hope of great changes, prophesied for 1957, 1976, and 1981, gave way to a longterm perspective in which the work of building the kingdom initiated by the Lord of the Second Advent would be accomplished over many years. The core of beliefs within the Unification Church centers upon the three principles of Creation, Fall and Restoration.

The Principle of Creation is that God created the world and through the visible world the invisible God can be known. The world is divided into two expressions, the Sung Sang (inner, invisible, feminine) and the Hyung Sang (outer, visible, masculine). God created the world out of his inner nature, his heart, his impulse to love, and to be united in love. The purpose of creation was to experience the joy that comes in loving.

The Principle of the Fall is that Adam and Eve did not realize God's purpose. They fell away from God by the misuse of love (adultery) and subsequent failure to constitute a perfect family. They placed Satan in control of this world. History is the story of God's attempts to restore the original creation and overthrow the rule of Satan.

The Principle of Restoration is that in order to accomplish the task of restoring the world, since God cannot override humanity's free nature but must deal with its immersion in sin, a Messiah is required. The Messiah must meet several requirements. He must be born fully human, must conquer sin, and manifest God's masculine nature. He must also marry a woman who will manifest God's feminine nature. Jesus accomplished only half of his Messianic mission, as he failed to marry. Thus Jesus offers his followers only a spiritual salvation. By completing that mission, Rev. Moon now offers a complete physical salvation as well.

Humans participate in the restoration by aligning themselves with the Messiah. They accomplish this alignment through a process of indemnity and preparation for entering the restored kingdom. The period of indemnity and preparation is spent in sacrificial work and absolute celibacy. At the end of the period, members are matched by Rev. Moon with a suitable mate and married in a ceremony conducted by the True Parents. The consummation of the marriage, which involves a ritual in which the process of indemnity and restoration is dramatically re-enacted, gave rise previously in Korea to rumors of sexual improprieties on Rev. Moon's part, a practice that would be diametrically opposed to the Church's stance on sexual purity.

The work of the Unification Church through its members who have been blessed (i.e., married) is the establishment of the Kingdom of God on earth. In the establishment of the Kingdom, the physical salvation initiated by Rev. Moon becomes manifest through the children born to blessed couples and the spread of the Kingdom ideal of one human family transcending race and nationality. (Typically Unification Church members marry across racial and national boundaries.)

Organization

The Unification Church is headed by Rev. Moon who has complete authority. He is assisted in the task of administering the affairs of the Church by a Board of Trustees, most of whom reside in the United States, and all of whom are Korean by birth. Operating under the Board are the many departments and missions which have been created to carry out the work of the Church. As the Church has created institutions and organizations they have primarily been placed under the direct care of three persons: Col. Bo Hi Pak, who is in charge of most cultural and political programs; Chung Hwan Kwak, who oversees evangelical thrusts; and David Kim, president of the Unification Theological Seminary. The Board also appoints the presidents of the Church in each country who has direct oversight of local congregations.

Through the years the Unification Church has created numerous structures which have two principal goals: the evangelization of the world (i.e., the recruitment and training of church members) and the infusion of the world with the ideals of the Kingdom of God (with all its cultural, religious and political implications) as perceived by Moon. The cultural, charitable, religious and political organizations created by the Church bring members and nonmembers together for the promotion of a limited set of shared ideals from religious liberty to the search for a unity of science and religion in the realm of values. The cultural and political organizations usually serve a secondary goal of acquainting nonmember participants with the Church in a favorable context and offering opportunities to learn of its theology, program, and internal life. It is this secondary goal which has led many critics, not without some justification, to call these organizations fronts for the Church. On the other hand, the Church has endeavored to separate its teaching of theology and recruitment of members from its other programs and has continued to invite people who are personally antagonistic to the Church and its ideals but who share a particular concern (be it religious liberty, interfaith dialogue, anti-Communism, or international relations in the Pacific Basin) to its conferences. Among the prominent church-sponsored structures are the following.

Activities aimed at cultural revitalization have recently been reorganized under the International Cultural Foundation, founded in 1982, which seeks to bring people together across national boundaries in activities to promote international understanding, global morality, and civic understanding. Its most famous activity has been the annual International Conference on the Unity of the Sciences, which has brought together scientists and other scholars to discuss the implications of science for moral and religious values. Equally important on the international level has been the Professors World Peace Academy, which deals with issues of world peace. Out of these two organizations in America has come the Washington Institute for Values in Public Policy, a Washington, D.C., think tank. Each of these organizations has been able to attract some of the country's leading scholars. The ICF also became the seedbed for the new scholarly publishing venture, Paragon Press.

Three structures have been among the prominent charitable programs of the Church. Project Volunteer and the National Council for the Church and Social Action have had major impact in the distribution of food and surplus materials to the poor and needy in a number of urban centers. Between 1977 and 1982 over $6,000,000 in food and other needed supplies were given out in Harlem, Washington, D.C., and Philadelphia. The International Relief Friendship Foundation provides emergency and long-term assistance in over 50 countries through the distribution of food, materials, and medical care.

During the 1970s, the leading institution advocating the Church's political goal of defeating world Communism was the Freedom Leadership Foundation. In the 1980s FLF's thrust has largely been taken over by CAUSA, an anti-Communist group which has found its major support among Spanish-speaking peoples, including the leaders of some South American countries.

The Unification Theological Seminary, located at Barrytown, New York, is the major educational arm of the Church. It offers a two-year theological curriculum. Most of the faculty are non-Unification Church members, but many are very active in initiating and building several church-related programs. The New Ecumenical Research Association, which annually sponsors a variety of academic seminars and conferences, was nurtured by the seminary faculty in its early days. More recently its work has been subsumed under a new umbrella, the International Religious Foundation. The Seminary also assisted in the creation of the Global Congress of the World's Religions. The Seminary initiated a scholarly publishing program through Rose of Sharon Press, though most of that endeavor has now been turned over to Paragon.

Evangelistically the Church has made its presence felt through a variety of programs. The mobile fund-raising teams, usually co-ordinated under the International One World Crusade, regularly saturate the United States to both raise operating funds for the Church and recruit new members. The Home Church program, established wherever the Church has a center, divides the surrounding community into districts. Each district is assigned a member whose task is to visit each residence and offer the Church's resources (usually in the form of community services) to each and every person residing in the area. Possibly the most important evangelistic structure is the Collegiate Association for the Research of Principles (CARP). CARP, one of the oldest UC activities, maintains chapters on many university campuses. It has been one of the Church's most controversial organizations, as it has continually been accused of deceptive recruiting and hiding its connection with the Church. A similar but less active organization directs its activities toward high schools. A publications department oversees a large number of periodicals for the various departments, the most important being *Unification News*, *Today's World*, and the *CARP Monthly*. The Church also publishes two publications for members only: *Principle Life* and *Blessing Quarterly*, both concerned with marriage and the married life in the Church.

The national headquarters of the American branch of the Unification Church are in New York City, a few blocks from the mission center which houses most of the international Church's departments discussed above. The national Church oversees the state Churches. Local centers of the Church are headed by a director who is in charge of worship, recruitment, teaching, and training programs of the Church.

Current Status

As the 1980s began, the Unification Church had approximately 5,000 members in the United States with much larger memberships in Japan and Korea, and Church centers and missionaries in 120 countries. Its intercultural and scholarly programs also involve several thousand academicians, pastors (from a wide variety of denominations), businessmen, professionals, and scientists.

The continuing activity of the Church's opponents and accompanying controversy, while hindering the Church in some areas, has kept its programs before the public and continues to attract individuals to investigate the claims of its enemies. Many so attracted stay to participate in its programs.

The Unification Church, like most first-generation religions, is in the midst of a high degree of change. A major transition occurred in 1982 when over half the American Church members were married in the several mass wedding ceremonies. Much of the future of the Church depends upon the role of the new leadership being created at the Seminary, the quality of life of the now predominantly married membership, the persistent opposition to the church, and the acceptance of the Church by the academic and religious community.

Controversy

It almost seems redundant to include a special section on controversy concerning the Unification Church, as it has been the one major focus of the anti-cult movement since the mid-1970s. However, one major controversy peculiar to itself has consumed the life of the Church in the 1980s—

the conviction of Rev. Moon on tax evasion charges. In 1982 Rev. Moon stood trial for not paying income tax on interest earned in the early 1970s in a saving account in his name. The issue was complicated by one Church official who recreated records for transactions during the period under question and did not reveal that they were recreations until that fact was uncovered by Treasury Department investigators. Moon argued that the money was Church money even though in an account in his name. The state argued that it was his personal money. He was convicted and the Supreme Court refused to hear his appeal. He spent 13 months during 1984–85 in jail.

The anti-cult forces welcomed his conviction as a victory. The Church fought unsuccessfully to keep Moon from jail. However, during the period the case was under appeal, and afterward while Moon was in jail, many people heretofore neutral or hostile to the Church rallied behind it on grounds of religious freedom. Political, academic, and church leaders wrote numerous briefs for the case in the Church's support. It is difficult yet to gauge the long-term effect on Moon's perceived martyrdom in this matter.

Of lesser news, but possibly greater long-term significance, has been the Church's continued effort to make a place for itself within the American media. It has initiated newspapers and magazines, paid for a major motion picture which flopped at the box office, and most recently purchased the defunct *Washington Star* which has reappeared as the *Washington Times*, which in turn has given birth to a national news magazine, *Insight*. None of these ventures has as yet been able to become independent financially.

The future of the Church will largely depend upon its ability to quell the hostility toward it in the general culture, a hostility which has waned but little from its peak in the months following Jonestown. By the end of the decade one should be able to judge whether or not the Church's gamble on its work with the academic and religious community through its various programs will slowly lessen the tension it has created in the larger population.

Divine Principle (Washington, DC: Holy Spirit Association for the Unification of World Christianity, 1973).

Outline of the Principle, Level 4 (New York: Holy Spirit Association for the Unification of World Christianity, 1980).

Pail Chull, Lee Hang Nyong, Sheen Doh Sung, and Yoon Se Won, *Sun Myung Moon: the Man and His Ideal* (Seoul, Korea: Future Civilization Press, 1981).

Sun Myung Moon, *The New Future of Christianity* (Washington, DC: Unification Church International, 1974).

Sun Myung Moon, *Science and Absolute Values* (New York: ICF Press, 1982).

Eileen Barker, *The Making of a Moonie* (Oxford: Basil Blackwell, 1984).

John Lofland, *Doomsday Cult* (New York: Irvington Publishers, 1977).

M. Darrol Bryant and Herbert W. Richardson, eds., *A Time for Consideration* (New York: Edwin Mellen Press, 1978).

Frederick Sontag, *Sun Myung Moon* (Nashville: Abingdon, 1977).

J. Isamu Yamamoto, *The Puppet Master* (Downers Grover, IL: InterVarsity Press, 1973).

N. VAJRADHATU, NAROPA INSTITUTE AND THE TIBETAN BUDDHISM OF CHOGYAM TRUNGPA, RINPOCHE

During the 1970s many representatives of the various schools of Tibetan Buddhism established movements in the United States. Only one of these, Chogyam Trungpa, Rinpoche, has built a national organization with local centers (called *Dharmadatus*) across the country. Vajradhatu has spearheaded the growth of Tibetan Buddhism in the United States.

The Kargyupa Sect

Tibetan Buddhism, as is true of most major religious traditions, has split into many sects and subsects. Among these, the Kargyupa was founded in the late eleventh century by Lama Marpa of Lhabrag. Its most famous teacher is Milarapa, Marpa's successor, whose 100,000 songs are classics of Tibetan literature. During the 12th century the Kargyupa sect split into several subsects, the largest of which was the Karmapa.

Among the centers of the Karmapa Kargyupa was the Surmang monastery complex. The abbot of the monastery was believed to be a *tulku*, an emanation of a Bodhisattva who decides to work on earth for others and who takes birth over a period of time in a series of bodies. Upon the death of a *tulku*, those around him would begin a search for the child in whose body he had taken fresh incarnation. The story of Vajradhatu begins with the death of the tenth Trungpa *tulku* in 1938.

Guided by two visions of the head of the Margyupas, the monks set out in search of the *tulku* in his new infant's body. They soon located the child. He was tested and he was able to pick out the former possessions of the tenth Trungpa *tulku*. Accepted, he was enthroned by His Holiness Gyalwa Karmapa, the head of the sect. Today this baby is known as Chogyam Trungpa, Rinpoche.

The Founder

Chogyam Trungpa, Rinpoche, the founder of Vajradhatu, was born in February 1939 in the village of Geje in northeast Tibet. After being identified as the tenth Trungpa *tulku,* he was taken to Düdtsi-til Monastery to be trained. While still in his teens he received his degrees (equivalent to a doctoratea and masters) but had no time to use either. In 1959 the Chinese invaded Tibet, and the newly ordained monk fled with a small group of his supporters to India. While in India he learned English and was allowed to go to the West. In 1963 he went to Oxford to study art, psychology, and comparative religion.

While at Oxford he discovered Johnstone House, a Buddhist contemplative center in Scotland and in 1967 it was turned over to Trungpa and became Samye-ling Monastery. In 1969 he was severely injured in an automobile accident. While recuperating, he decided to take off his monk's robes and become a layman in order to better communicate with the Western people among whom he had decided to work. His stay with the new monastery was short lived. After a disagreement with some of the other leaders, he abandoned Scotland and immigrated to the United States where a group of his students had purchased some land in Vermont to be named the Tail of the Tiger Monastery. Just before arriving in America, in January 1970 he married Diana Judith Pybus.

During the next few years Trungpa traveled around the country lecturing and teaching and establishing the local centers (*Dharmadatus*). In 1971 he opened the Rocky Mountain Dharma Center at Ft. Collins, Colorado, and the next year organized the Karma Dzong at Boulder. Then in 1973 his national organization, Vajradhatu was created and all of his work placed under it. From that point the work began to expand. Seeing the need for a more systematic and advanced training opportunity for his more dedicated students, he held the first seminary class which led to the formation of Naropa Institute in 1974.

1974 became a spiritual landmark for Trungpa and Vajradhatu as Gyalwa Karmapa, the international leader of the Kargrudpa Buddhists, made his first pilgrimage to America. He visited the Tail of the Tiger which he renamed Karme-Choling and for the first time in the Western Hemisphere performed the famous black hat ceremony. He recognized Trungpa as a Vajracarya, a spiritual master. Since this initial visit, he has returned on several occasions.

Manifesting the maturity of the American work, in 1976 Trungpa named a Dharma successor. Thomas Rich, a disciple of Integral Yoga teacher Swami Satchidananda known as Narayana, met Trungpa in 1971 and became his close disciple. He took the name Osel Tendzen and currently serves as Vakra Regent. He will become head of Vajradhatu upon Trungpa's death or retirement.

Organization

The work built around Trungpa has been organized into two separate corporations. Vajradhatu, the more inwardly directed of the two, recruits, trains, and nurtures the disciples of Trungpa and Tibetan Buddhism. Through the Nalanda Foundation, Trungpa reaches out to the world and demonstrates the value of Buddhism in various otherwise secular realms.

Vajradhatu, literally "the realm of the indestructible," coordinates all the other activities and is headquartered in Boulder, Colorado, in a facility named Dorje Dzong. Under Vajradhatu are: Karme-Choling, the original community located near Barnet, Vermont on a 530-acre farm. Resident members follow a year-round program of meditation and study and sponsor seminars, retreats, and training sessions led by Trungpa and other staff persons. Karma Dzong, founded in 1972, was modeled on Karme-Choling and for most of the 1970s Trungpa moved regularly between the two. Associated with Karma Dzong is the Rocky Mountain Dharma Center, a small facility high in the mountains used primarily for meditative retreats and short-term programs. Dorje Khyung Dzong is an isolated center in the mountains of southern Colorado used only for private individual retreats.

Varjadhatu Seminary is not a place so much as an event. Each fall for eighty days Trungpa and his senior staff offer an advanced course in Tibetan Buddhism including its esoteric aspects. This course is a must for all serious students of Trungpa.

Vajradhatu also has an editorial and recording department. Most of Trungpa's books have been published by Shambhala Publications, a firm that existed prior to Trungpa's coming to America but, while remaining an independent company, has become closely associated with his movement and moved its facilities from Berkeley, California, to Boulder after Trungpa established his headquarters there. Vajradhatu's editorial department oversees the several periodicals of the organization, *Garuda* and *Vajradhatu Sun*. The recording department has begun issuing tapes of Trungpa's lectures and seminars.

The *Dharmadatus*, the local centers established across the United States by Trungpa, are also under Vajradhatu and their directors are appointed from the Boulder headquarters.

Nalanda Foundation was established by Trungpa as a channel for the permeation of society with Buddhism. The main structure under Nalanda is the Naropa Institute, an alternative school grounded in Buddhism. The Institute attempts to create an environment within which Eastern and Western traditions can interact and the standard approach to educational attainment can be complemented by an intuitive approach that grows out of a spiritual discipline. College-level courses at Naropa concentrate upon Buddhist studies, exploration of the self and the world, and the arts.

There are still other aspects of Nalanda. The Maitri Therapeutic Community uses Buddhist practices to confront the issues of personal neurosis. The Mudra Theater Group is a dramatic group whose main presentation is a play by Trungpa, *Prajna*, based upon Trungpa's interpretation of the *Heart-Sutra*, a famous Buddhist work. Alaya Preschool is a preschool educational unit.

The newest addition to the Nalanda program is Shambhala Training, a Buddhist version of the weekend growth seminars made popular by Erhard Seminars Training (EST) and now conducted by a variety of alternative religious and New Age groups.

Beliefs and Practice

Trungpa brought the teachings of the Kargyupa sect of Buddhism from Tibet. However, after his decision to become a teacher in the West, he developed a modern Western vocabulary, primarily that of humanistic and growth-centered psychology, to express the complicated and sophisticated Tibetan tradition. As is characteristic of the Kargyupa tradition, a secret esoteric aspect of the teachings is taught only to advanced students via oral presentation by Trungpa.

Trungpa emphasizes Buddhism as a practice to awaken the mind. The path to the awakened state has three aspects or "wheels": meditation, study, and work. Meditation is the state of being in the present moment and consists of training the mind to exist in the here and now. Study sharpens the understanding of the experience of meditation and the communication of the experience to others. Work allows the meditator to share what has been learned with others.

A major theme of Trungpa's teaching in the Western context is *Cutting Through Spiritual Materialism*, an early book. He believes that the major error of Westerners who follow a spiritual discipline was their conversion of what they had learned to egotistical uses, thus negating its value.

In his role as guru, Trungpa presents a mixed (some would say contradictory) image. He carries many of the trappings of a Buddhist lama, who is not only a religious but a political ruler in a royal priesthood. On the other hand he has divested himself of many Tibetan manners and dresses in Western clothes. He has been heavily criticized for his personal habits, which include eating meat and using both alcohol and tobacco. He describes his role as providing a context within which individuals can find enlightenment. His job is to prod and keep the seeker honest.

Current Status

Vajradhatu has grown slowly but consistently since its formation. By 1980 there were 37 centers including the major communities in Vermont and Colorado. In 1981 the administration and supervision of these centers was transferred to the Vajra Regent Osel Tendzin. Approximately 2,000 students of Trungpa have membership in these centers.

Naropa Institute has grown steadily and received the support of Buddhist leaders and scholars throughout North America. It offers both B.A. and M.A. degrees and has applied for full accreditation as an institution of higher learning. Vajradhatu plans to build Naropa into a full university.

Vajradhatu publishes a bi-monthly newspaper *Vajradhatu Sun* (which replaced the *Sangha Newsletter*). *Geruda* continues to appear on a non-scheduled basis.

Vajradhatu has made substantive improvements in its program and developed new programs each year during the first decade of its existence. There is little reason to doubt that this growth will continue for some years into the future.

Controversy

The only hint of controversy experienced by Vajradhatu in its growth toward legitimacy as a major center of Buddhism in the West occurred in the fall of 1975. One outstanding poet who had participated in the summer poetry school sponsored by Naropa Institute was allowed to attend the classes for advanced students to follow. Being a pacifist, the poet had been disturbed by the bloody images in some of the Tibetan material covered during the sessions. However, the crucial incident occurred during a Halloween party which he and a friend had left early in the evening. During the course of the evening, Trungpa ordered them to return. An argument ensued and the two were stripped of their clothes. The incident sent shock waves through America's poetry community and became the subject of an article in a national magazine and a book.

Chogyam Trungpa, Born in Tibet (Boulder: Shambhala, 1977).

Chogyam Trungpa, Cutting Through Spiritual Materialism (Berkeley, CA: Shambhala, 1973).

Chogyam Trungpa, The Myth of Freedom (Berkeley, CA: Shambhala, 1976).

Herbert V. Guenther and Chogyam Trungpa, The Dawn of Tantra (Berkeley, CA: Shambhala, 1975).

Detlef Ingo Lauf, Secret Doctrines of the Tibetan Books of the Dead (Boulder, CO: Shambhala, 1977).

Rick Fields, How the Swans Came to the Lake (Boulder, CO: Shambhala, 1981).

Shashi Bhushan Dasgupta, An Introduction to Tibetan Buddhism (Berkeley, CA: Shambhala, 1974).

Helmut Hoffman, The Religions of Tibet (New York: Macmillan, 1961).

L. A. Waddell, The Buddhism of Tibet or Lamaism (Cambridge: W. Heffer and Sons, 1971).

R. P. Anuruddha, An Introduction into Lamaism (Hoshiarpur, India: Vishveshvaranand Vedic Research Institute, 1959).

Tom Clark, The Great Naropa Poetry Wars (Santa Barbara: Cadmus Editions, 1980).

O. THE WAY INTERNATIONAL, INC.

The Way International, Inc., was founded in 1942 as "Vesper Chimes," a radio ministry initiated by Victor Paul Wierwille, then pastor of the Evangelical and Reformed Church of Paine, Ohio. Its name was changed to the Chimes Hour in 1944 and incorporated as the Chimes Hour Youth Caravan in 1947. In 1955 the name The Way, Inc. was adopted and finally in 1974, the present name was assumed.

The Founder

Victor Paul Wierwille (1916–1985) decided to enter the ministry while a student at Mission House College (now Lakeland College of Sheboygan, Wisconsin). He attended Mission House Seminary (now United Theological Seminary, Minneapolis, Minnesota) where he earned his B.D. He did graduate work at the University of Chicago and Princeton Theological Seminary which awarded him a M.Th. in 1941. In 1942 he was ordained and became the pastor of the Church at Paine. Two years later he moved to Van Wert, Ohio as pastor of St. Peter's E. & R. (now United Church of Christ) Church.

During the years at Van Wert, Wierwille began the intense personal reading and research on the Bible that would lead to the present teachings of The Way International. He concentrated upon the doctrine of the Holy Spirit, and in 1951 he spoke in tongues for the first time. The results of his research led to his being awarded a Ph.D. in 1948 by the Pikes Peak Bible College and Seminary, an unaccredited correspondence school headquartered in Manitou Springs, Colorado, that is no longer in existence.

The initial results of his research were incorporated into the first Power for Abundant Living class given in 1953. However, Wierwille had not stopped his research. The next year he began to study Aramaic and made the acquaintance of George Lamsa, who had attained some notoriety for his translation of the Aramaic Biblical Texts. Wierwille's research led to his accepting a view of Biblical doctrine increasingly distinct from that of his Church and in 1957 he resigned his ministry in Van Wert and left the Evangelical and Reformed Church. He led The Way until his retirement in 1983.

The Development of The Way

The Way began as a radio ministry but grew during the 1950s by the initiation of the PFAL classes (1953) and *The Way Magazine* (1954). In 1957 Wierwille took control of the family farm outside of New Knoxville, Ohio and deeded it to The Way. There he established his headquarters and for a decade watched the work grow. The steady growth was interrupted in the late 1960s when the ministry burgeoned at the time of the national Jesus People revival. In the wake of the expansion, Wierwille established The Way Corps, a four-year leadership training program. In 1974 The Way purchased the former Emporia College in Emporia, Kansas. It became The Way College, the home of the Corps.

In 1971 Wierwille initiated the Word Over the World Ambassador program which sent young people affiliated with The Way around the United States for a year of witnessing activity. The first Ambassadors were commissioned at the Rock of Ages Festival, an annual gathering of Way members, the first of which was also held in 1971.

Beliefs

The Way International may be characterized as a Pentecostal Ultra-dispensational Christian group. Its beliefs are summarized in an eleven-point statement:

1. We believe the scriptures of the Old and New Testaments were *Theopneustos*, "God Breathed," and perfect as originally given; that the Scriptures or the Word of God is of supreme, absolute and final authority for believing, for all life and godliness.

2. We believe in one God, the creator of the heavens and earth; in Jesus Christ, God's only begotten Son and our lord and savior, whom God raised from the dead; and we believe in the working of the Holy Spirit.

3. We believe that the Virgin Mary conceived by the Holy Spirit, that God was in Christ, and that the one mediator between God and men is the man Christ Jesus.

4. We believe that man was created in the image of God, spiritually, that he sinned and thereby brought upon himself immediate spiritual death, which is separation from God and physical death also which is the consequence of sin, and that all human beings are born with a sinful nature.

5. We believe that Jesus Christ died for our sins according to the Scriptures, as a representative and substitute for us; and that all who believe that God raised him from the dead are justified and made righteous, born again by the Spirit of God, receiving eternal life on the grounds of his eternal redemption, and thereby are the sons of God.

6. We believe in the resurrection of the crucified body of our Lord Jesus Christ, his ascension into heaven and his seating at the right hand of God.
7. We believe in the blessed hope of Christ's return, the personal return of our living lord and savior Jesus Christ and our gathering unto him.
8. We believe in the bodily resurrection of the just and unjust.
9. We believe in the receiving of the fullness of the holy spirit, the power from on high, plus the corresponding nine manifestations of the holy spirit, for all born again believers.
10. We believe it is available to receive all that God promises us in His Word according to our believing faith. We believe we are free in Christ Jesus to receive all that he accomplished for us by his substitution.
11. We believe the early Church flourished rapidly because they operated within a Root, Trunk, Limb, Branch, and Twig set up (decently and in order).

The Way International departs from traditional orthodox Christianity at a number of points. Wierwille denies the doctrine of the Trinity and the divinity of Jesus Christ, a point emphasized in one of his books, *Jesus Christ Is Not God* (1975). He also denies the personality of the Holy Spirit, which he believes to be power of God. This view, generally termed Arianism, was popularized by Arius, a second-century presbyter of the Church in Alexandria. Arianism was condemned at the Council of Nisea in 325 A.D.

Wierwille also teaches Ultra-Dispensationalism, an approach to Scripture which views the Bible books as products of progressive dispensations or periods of different administrations of God's relationship to humanity. Popular dispensationalism, which recognizes seven dispensations (Innocence, Conscience, Government, Promise, Law, Grace, and the Personal Reign of Christ) rose to prominence among the Plymouth Brethren in the nineteenth century, but through its adoption by leaders such as evangelist Dwight L. Moody and teacher C. I. Scofield, editor of the *Scofield Reference Bible* (1909), it spread throughout Evangelical Protestants. Dispensationalists believe the Church presently exists in the dispensation of grace which began at Easter and will continue until Christ's Second Coming.

Ultra-Dispensationalism teaches that there was another dispensation, or a period of transition between Easter and the New Testament Church as seen in Paul's later epistles. This period of transition is characterized by John's water baptism and its story is told primarily in the Book of Acts. This view was first expressed by Brethren leader Richard Holden in 1870 but became well known after its adoption by Anglican Biblical scholar Ethelbert Bullinger, editor of *The Companion Bible*. Ultra-Dispensationalism sees Paul's later epistles (Ephesians, Colosians, Phillipians and Galatians, and especially Ephesians) as the prime documents of the dispensation or administration of grace. Following Ephesians 4:5-6, they believe in one baptism, that of the holy spirit, and hence reject water baptism.

Wierwille has also stressed the role of Aramaic as the language spoken by Jesus and believes that the New Testament was written originally in Aramaic (most scholars believe it was written in Greek). The Way emphasizes the work of George M. Lamsa and uses his *The Holy Bible from Ancient Eastern Manuscripts* (1959) and has reprinted the books of independent Indian bishop K.C. Pillai, *The Orientalisms of the Bible* and *Light through an Eastern Window.*

Organization

The Way International's structure follows the Biblical mandate for decency and order and is modelled on the pattern of a tree. Five educational and administrative centers that serve the organization internationally are termed the "root" locations. They are the International Headquarters at New Knoxville, Ohio; The Way College of Emporia at Emporia, Kansas; The Way College of Biblical Research, Indiana Campus, at Rome, Indiana; Camp Gunnison—The Way Family Ranch at Gunnison, Colorado; and Lead Outdoor Academy at Tinnie, New Mexico.

Countries are termed "trunk" areas. States are called "limbs" and counties and large cities "branches." The basic units of The Way are the numerous local community fellowships, called "twigs." The Way has not moved to purchase church buildings and organize congregations in the traditional sense, hence their membership, which regularly gathered in the home of a member, tends to be largely invisible in the various communities in which it operates.

Administratively, a three-person board of trustees made up of a president, vice-president, and secretary-treasurer head The Way International and make all policy decisions. The trustees appoint a Trustee's Cabinet that oversees the various departments at the International Headquarters and the staff of the other root locations. Each trunk, limb, branch, and twig is led by a resident coordinator.

Individuals usually begin their affiliation with The Way by taking its basic course, called "Power for Abundant Living." It presents the basic Biblical perspective developed by Wierwille and is presented through 33 hours of tape or film presentation. After completion of the course, for which pupils pay a tuition, they are encouraged to take a variety of advanced courses, to become involved in such various programs as The Way Corps, or to become a Word over the World Ambassador.

Current Status

In 1983 The Way International reported 2,657 twigs in the United States with an average of ten members per twig. Over 17,000 attended the 1983 Rock of Ages Festival. Foreign work has been initiated in Zaire, Chile, Argentina, Venezuela, and Colombia. Approximately 14,000 took the basic PFAL course during the year. Advanced courses were offered as

Intermediate PFAL, Christian Family and Sex, Renewed Mind, Witnessing and Undershepherding, Spiritual Contest, and Rise and Expansion.

The American Christian Press, located within the International Headquarters complex at New Knoxville, publishes bi-monthly *The Way Magazine*. It also publishes the many books of Wierwille including *The New,
Dynamic Church* (1971), *Receiving the Holy Spirit Today* (1972), *God's Magni-
fied Word* (1977), and *Jesus Christ Our Promised Seed* (1982).

The basic programs of the Way International are built around The
Way Corps, The Way Family Corps, and the Sunset Corps through which
members are given a thorough training in the Bible and its application to
daily life. The Way Corps is headquarted at the Way College of Emporia, and the Way Family Corps and Sunset Corps (for older members) are
headquartered at the Way College of Biblical Research, Indiana Campus.
Those programs are designed for people (such as entire families) who
cannot take a full four-year curriculum.

Way Productions, based at The Way International's Cultural Center
at New Bremen, Ohio, provides leadership in developing the arts along
Biblical principles. Out of its work have come several musical groups
including "Take a Stand Caravan" and "Branded" (a country and Western group). The Way International Fine Arts and Historical Center at
Sidney, Ohio, houses the historical records of the organization.

Controversy

The Way International, one of the largest of the groups which have
been labeled "cult," has also been the target of deprogramming. During
the early 1980s it replaced the Unification Church as the group reporting
the most deprogramming attempts among its members.

In addition to the standard anti-cult accusations of brainwashing and
mind control, opponents of The Way have leveled two serious charges.
First, anticultists have continually accused The Way of training members
in the use of deadly weapons for possible future use against The Way's
enemies. This charge derived from the adoption at the College at Emporia
of a State of Kansas program in gun safety (primarily for hunters). All the
students at the College were allowed, but not required, to enroll. To date
no violent activity has arisen to substantiate the charge.

Christian anti-cultists have attacked The Way for its radical departure
from orthodox Christianity and its adoption of Arianism. Wierwille's
denial of the divinity of Jesus and the Trinity has been a constant barrier
to The Way's ability to align itself with other Christian bodies.

Elena S. Whiteside, *The Way, Living in Love* (New Knoxville, OH: American Christian Press,
1972).

Victor Paul Wierwille, *Power for Abundant Living* (New Knoxville, OH: American Christian
Press, 1971).

Victor Paul Wierwille, *Jesus Christ, Our Promised Seed* (New Knoxville, OH: American
Christian Press, 1982).

Victor Paul Wierwille, *Receiving the Holy Spirit Today* (New Knoxville, OH: American
Christian Press, 1972).

Victor Paul Wierwille, *The Word's Way* (New Knoxville, OH: American Christian Press, 1971).

J. L. Williams, *Victor Paul Wierwille and The Way International* (Chicago: Moody Press, 1979).

John P. Juedes and Douglas V. Morton, *From "Vesper Chimes" to "The Way International"* (Milwaukee: C.A.R.I.S., n.d.).

Douglas V. Morton and John P. Juedes, *The Integrity and Accuracy of The Way's Word* (St. Louis: Personal Freedom Outreach, 1980).

P. WITCHCRAFT (WICCA), NEOPAGANISM AND MAGICK

Magic (often spelled "magick" to distinguish it from stage illusionism) experienced a revival during the twentieth century. Of the several groups which include magic as an important aspect of their structures, Witchcraft claimed the most adherents and emerged as a popular movement, far outstripping most other groups labeled as a "cult."

Definition

The term "witchcraft" is used to describe a wide variety of phenomena, and very distinct groups can be easily confused. In the Bible, the Hebrew word *ob* is sometimes translated witch, as the famous *ob* of Endor (I Samuel 28). We do not know exactly what the ancient *obs* did, but we do know that they specialized in herbs, poisons, and mediumship. The shamans and priests in many pre-industrial societies are popularly called "witch doctors" and their practice "witchcraft." The medieval Church equated witchcraft with Satanism, the worship of the Devil (Satanism is discussed elsewhere in this volume). Finally, Witchcraft is synonymous with malevolent sorcery, the attempt to do evil by occult or supernatural means. In this context, voodoo (also discussed elsewhere in this volume) is also equated with Witchcraft.

While North America is home to a growing voodoo community, a few Satanists, and even several witch doctor–shamans, the great majority of people who call themselves witches fit none of the categories described above. Rather most modern witches are followers of a nature-oriented polytheistic faith centered upon the worship of the Great Mother Goddess, usually called Diana, Isis, or Demeter, though many different names are used. When a contemporary Westerner describes herself or himself as a witch, it is this form of witchcraft to which they refer.

Founder

Contemporary Witchcraft was founded by Gerald B. Gardner (1884–1964), British civil servant and amateur archeologist. Gardner spent most of his working years in Southern Asia where he absorbed a knowledge of magic. He wrote the definitive book on the Malaysian magical knife, *Kris and Other Mayay Weapons* (1936), joined the Masons, and was introduced to nudity. He returned to England in 1939 and quickly involved himself in the occult scene.

According to Gardner's own account, he joined a Theosophical group, the Fellowship of Crotona. At one of the group's meetings, he met some witches who eventually introduced him to their priestess, a woman known only as "Old Dorothy." After Old Dorothy's death, Gardner was allowed to publish a novel about Witchcraft, *High Magic's Aid* (1949) under his Wiccan name 'Scire,' and *Witchcraft Today* (1954), which he wrote after the repeal of the British Witchcraft Laws in 1951. *Witchcraft Today* maintained that Witchcraft was a dying religion and that Gardner wanted to record what witches actually did for posterity.

Research suggests that Gardner did not discover a pre-existing Witchcraft group. A paper by Gardner published by *Ripley's Believe It or Not* disclosed that Gardner took the magical resources he acquired in Asia and a selection of Western magical texts and created a new religion centered upon the worship of the Mother Goddess. During the 1940s the initial rituals were constructed and went through several revisions. Gardner developed a "coven," a group with which he worked and several others begun by his initiates emerged. Eventually initiates such as Alexander Sanders and Sybil Leek broke with Gardner and began independent covens.

After the publication of *Witchcraft Today*, Gardner's Witchcraft spread throughout England, and the first American Gardnerians, Raymond and Rosemary Buckland traveled to England for initiation. During the 1960s Gardnerian Witchcraft and the Alexandrian (named after Alexander Sanders) revision spread across North America.

Witchcraft in America

During the 1960s both Gardnerian and Alexandrian Witches established covens across the United States and Canada. However, independent variations of Wiccan groups began to appear before the end of the decade. Sybil Leek came to the United States in 1966 and established covens in Ohio and Massachusetts. Other initiates, rejecting the emphasis upon nudity and the lineage of priestesses of Gardnerian covens, created various hereditary traditions. Such independent covens, while often claiming pre-Gardnerian roots, usually took Gardner's rituals and wrote variations upon them which emphasized a particular ancient tradition (Welsh, Celtic, Strege, etc.). During the 1970s, some female witches, who had a strong emphasis upon feminism, developed a militant feminist witchcraft which spoke of it as "Wimmin's Religion."

Soon after Gardnerian Witchcraft established itself in America, people emerged who wished to worship the Goddess but who did not accept the designation "witch." They called themselves "Pagans" and several— Fred Adams, Donna Cole, and Ed Fitch—wrote new rituals that followed broad Gardnerian patterns but introduced a new degree of variety into Goddess-worshipping and, by example, encouraged the development of many new ritual formats. Tim Zell, founder of the Church of All Worlds, dubbed the non-Wiccan Goddess worshippers, "Neo-pagans."

By 1980 most Witchcraft and Neo-Pagan groups were eclectic in that they followed some basic ritual guidelines developed by Gardner while drawing upon a variety of materials and newly written rituals for their group work and training procedures. While the Gardnerians have survived as a recognizable body of covens tied together by a common ritual and the lineage of priestesses, other Wiccan and Neo-Pagan organizations are associations of independent covens that allow an extreme latitude in ritual and practice.

Among Neo-Pagans, the diversity of practice has been limited somewhat by the relatively small number of individuals who have produced sets of rituals for distribution throughout the community. The original set of Neo-Pagan rituals written by Donna Cole and Ed Fitch, published as *A Book of Pagan Rituals* (1974, 1975) remains the most popular. Some Neo-Pagan groups have adopted a particular cultural heritage such as Norse, Egyptian, or Druidic and have subsequently limited their work to that single tradition.

Belief and Practice

Witches and Neo-Pagans worship the Great Mother Goddess, usually seen in her triple aspect as maiden (Kore), Mother (Diana), and crone (Hecate), thus representing the basic stages of life. Beside her is the Horned God (Pan), her consort, and together they represent the male and female principle basic to life. They also acknowledge a pantheon of deities who come to the fore at the various seasonal festivals. Many witches see these deities as merely projected aspirations of the individual or Jungian archetypes.

Witches and Neo-Pagans practice magic, the art of change using the cosmic power that underlies the universe. Magic is of two kinds. Low magic seeks change in the mundane world and is most frequently employed for healing or improvement (a new job, love, or relationship). High magic is worked for the transformation of the individual. Meetings of witches combine the worship of the deities with the invocation of magic.

Ethically, Witches value freedom and harmlessness as expressed in the Wiccan Rede, "Lest ye harm none, do what you will." They also believe that the effects of magic will be returned threefold upon the person working it, a belief that severely limits the pronouncing of curses. A basic love of nature and natural things pervades the Pagan community and leads many to espouse ecology, natural foods, and love of animals.

Witchcraft is organized in small autonomous groups called "covens" (variously, "groves," "nests," and "circles"). Covens will have from four to twenty-six people (ideally, thirteen). They meet semi-monthly at the new and full moons for regular meetings called "esbats." There are eight

major solar festivals, "sabbats," beginning with Samhain or Halloween
(October 31) and continuing with Yule (December 21), Oimelc or Candle-
mas (February 2), Spring Equinox (March 21), Beltane (April 30),
Summer Solstice (June 21), Lammas (August 1), and Fall Equinox (September 21). Sabbats are frequently occasions for several covens to come
together.

Individuals generally pass through three degrees of initiation in a Pagan
or Wiccan group (though some traditions recognize more). Once a neophyte has passed through the first degree, he or she becomes a full
member of the coven. Once the member has mastered a set of basic
knowledge, he or she is given the second degree as an accomplished witch.
The third degree admits one to the priesthood. Admission to the third
degree usually involves the Great Rite (ritual sexual intercourse) between
the new priest/ess and the officiating priest/ess of the opposite sex. The
Great Rite is usually performed symbolically by the plunging of the ritual
knife (the athame) into a chalice of wine. It should also be noted that there
are many solitary witches who practice apart from a coven though they
may join in major festivals.

Current Status

There are, by best estimates, over 30,000 Witches and Neo-Pagans in
North America, a slight majority of whom are female. Most are found in
totally independent covens and keep a very low profile as a means of
protection from what they perceive as a hostile public. A number of
covens (though a minority) have attached themselves to one of the major
national Witchcraft or Neo-Pagan organizations which are discussed
below.

Circle, Inc.

By far the largest Witchcraft-Pagan organization is the Church of
Circle Wicca, headquartered in Mt. Horeb, Wisconsin. It was founded
around 1975 by Selena Fox and Jim Alan who have spent many years
building a national network of Goddess-worshippers. Circle publishes
Circle Network News, the largest circulating Pagan periodical (15,000 in
1983) and holds annually a series of public Pagan festivals, the largest of
which is the Pagan Spirit Gathering every summer. They also publish the
annual *Circle Guide to Wicca and Pagan Resources*, a national directory of
Pagans and Pagan organizations.

Gardnerian Wicca

Oldest of the several Witchcraft groups in the United States, Gardnerian Wicca was brought to North America by Rosemary and Raymond
Buckland who established a Witchcraft Museum on Long Island. They

built a series of covens across the United States. Gardnerian Wicca is distinguished by its worshipping "skyclad" (in the nude) and its lineage of priestesses. New Gardnerian covens are formed by a priestess leaving the coven in which she was initiated and beginning a new group. She acknowledges her initiating priestess as a Witch Queen. While a Gardnerian coven can meet without a priest, it cannot operate without a priestess present.

After the divorce of the Bucklands, leadership of the Gardnerians fell to Theos and Phoenix, a couple who live on Long Island. The major Gardnerian periodical, *The Hidden Path*, is published in Wheeling, Illinois.

Saxon Witchcraft

After leaving the Gardnerians, Raymond Buckland developed a new branch of Wicca which he termed Saxon Witchcraft and which is based upon the worship of the ancient Saxon deities Woden and Freya, as the prime embodiment of the God and Goddess. He published a full exposition of the new system in his book, *The Tree* (1974).

Headquarters of Saxon Witchcraft is in Charlottesville, Virginia where Buckland heads the Seax-Wica Seminary which offers a correspondence course in Saxon Witchcraft and edits the group's periodical, *Seax-Wica Voys*.

Covenant of the Goddess

Second in size only to Circle, the Covenant of the Goddess was formed in 1975 as an association of autonomous covens on the West Coast. It has since expanded into a national organization. Unlike Circle, membership in the Covenant of the Goddess is open only to Witches, but member covens represent the wide variety of Wiccan tradition and diversity.

The Covenant of the Goddess holds an annual festival at which a Grand Council (consisting of all the member covens) conducts Covenant business and elects officers. Each coven is allowed one vote. The Covenant also grants ministerial credentials. Headquarters of the Covenant are in Berkeley, California, from which the *Covenant of the Goddess Newsletter* is published eight times annually.

Feminist Wicca

During the mid-1970s within the Witchcraft movement, a number of women combined Witchcraft with a strong feminist position. They included not only lesbian separatists such as Zsuanna Budapest of the Susan B. Anthony Coven #1 in Venice, California, who saw Witchcraft as "Wimmin's religion" and advocated all-female covens but more moderate voices who saw in Witchcraft a religion that recognized the equality of women and the need for social justice.

Many of the most vocal feminists have become active in the Covenant of the Goddess (Zsuanna Budapest, Margot Adler, Starhawk, Allison Harlow, Deborah Bender), but others continue to lead independent associations of covens. Prominent among the latter is Ann Forfreedom, priestess of the Temple of the Goddess Within of Sacramento, California, and editor of a quarterly, *The Wise Woman*. Ann Forfreedom was the coordinator of the 1982 Goddess Rising Conference, one of the largest Witchcraft-Pagan events ever held.

The Georgian Church

The Georgian Church was founded in the mid-1970s by George Patterson of Bakersfield, California. Known originally as the Church of Wicca of Bakersfield, it underwent a reorganization and name change in 1980. The Georgians follow a modified Gardnerian ritual but allow and encourage creativity and new rituals. Patterson edited the monthly *Georgian Newsletter* until his death in 1984. Member covens are found around the United States.

Neo-Pagan Organizations

Prior to 1976, the largest Pagan organization was the Church of All Worlds, a Neo-Pagan group headed by Tim Zell, who also published and edited *The Green Egg*, which for many years was the prime periodical linking Pagan groups together. However, in 1976, Zell moved from St. Louis to California and dropped his role as editor of *The Green Egg* and leader of the Church. The magazine soon ceased publication and within a few years the national organization disappeared, though several "nests" (as local groups were called) remain.

Once in California, Zell, who changed his name to Otter G'Zell, spent much of his time experimenting with goats in the hopes of producing a unicorn. The result of his work has been the appearance of several Unicorns which have been seen widely around the United States at various exhibitions and circuses.

Neo-Pagans generally adopt a single national-ethnic tradition, the Norse, Druidic, and Egyptian being the most popular. The principal Norse group is the Asatru Free Assembly (formerly known as the Viking Brotherhood). Its headquarters are in Breckenridge, Texas. It publishes a quarterly journal, *The Runestone*.

Egyptian Pagans are represented by the Church of the Eternal Source, in Burbank, California. Druids are tied together by *The Druid Missal-any*, a periodical published by the Live Oak Grove of Orinda, California.

In addition to the particular groups and periodicals mentioned above, the Witchcraft and Pagan community is served by over 100 newsletters and periodicals published by various individuals and groups.

Witchcraft and Paganism

Gerald B. Gardner, *Witchcraft Today* (London: Rider, 1954).

Janet Farrar and Stewart Farrar, *The Witches' Way* (London: Robert Hale, 1984).

Leo Louis Martello, *Witchcraft, the Old Religion* (Secaucus, NJ: University Books, 1973).

Sybil Leek, *The Complete Art of Witchcraft* (New York: World Publishing Company, 1971).

Starhawk, *The Spiral Dance* (New York: Harper & Row, 1979).

J. Gordon Melton, *Magic, Witchcraft and Paganism in America, A Bibliography* (New York: Garland, 1982).

Margot Adler, *Drawing Down the Moon* (New York: Viking, 1979).

David L. Miller, *The New Polytheism* (New York: Harper & Row, 1974).

Jeffrey B. Russell, *A History of Witchcraft* (London: Thames and Hudson, 1980).

V.
Counter-cult Groups

A. EVANGELICAL CHRISTIANITY AND THE CULTS

Evangelical Christianity has been the mainstream of religion in America. In its attempts to be true to traditional Protestant Christian affirmations, it has been among the most conservative of religious forces and has commanded the largest segment of the religious public. It has also been the most attentive to the increasing number of religious options vying for acceptance in America's religious marketplace. Evangelical leaders were the first to recognize that the Christian Church faced a growing number of challenges to its religious hegemony of America and the West.

In 1917, William C. Irvine published his *Timely Warnings*, the first of the modern countercult books. Irvine warned Christians of groups and philosophies that denied the essential doctrines of Christianity. The denial of these key doctrines—incarnation, atonement, the divinity of Jesus, the Trinity, the authority of the Bible—cut the heart out of the Gospel message and turned Christianity into a shadow of itself. Under its new title, *Heresies Exposed*, Irvine's book went through twenty-nine printings by 1955 and remains in print in the 1980s.

Irvine's survey of the heresies faced by orthodoxy stood alone for two decades though specialized studies of single groups such as the Jehovah's Witnesses or Spiritualism appeared. Then, in 1938, Jan Karel Van Baalen's *Chaos of the Cults* set the tone for much future Evangelical interpretation of the cult question. Van Baalen singled out approximately a dozen alternative religions and analyzed them in terms of their denial of central Christian truths but explained their appeal in their central focus upon a single Christian truth which had been largely forgotten in the modern church. For example, he concludes his critical analysis of Spiritualism (which he calls "Spiritism") by noting, "that Spiritism has again called attention to the existence of a spiritual world, to a life hereafter, to future retribution in a time of gross materialism, we can appreciate." He then concludes that in spite of Spiritualism's accomplishment, it is incompatible with Christianity.

Only after World War II did the initial work done by Irvine and Van Baalen call widespread attention to the threat to the Church posed by the growing number of cults, and during the 1950s numerous items of counter-cult literature were published. Louis T. Talbot and Walter R. Martin emerged as prominent Christian apologists on cult issues. Talbot (like Irvine) a member of the Plymouth Brethren and a teacher at the Bible Institute of Los Angeles, published a series of popular booklets on the major cults: the Unity School of Christianity, Christian Science, Seventh-Day Adventism, and Anglo-Israelism. Martin, one of the most-read Evangelical voices on cults, authored three important counter-cult books in the 1950s—*Jehovah of the Watchtower* (1955, co-authored with Norman Klann), *The Rise of the Cults* (1955) and *The Christian Science Myth* (1956, co-authored with Norman Klann). More recently he has written or edited a number of books, including *The Kingdom of the Cults* (1965) and *The New Cults* (1980).

During the 1970s, the amount of Christian counter-cult literature proliferated exponentially. James Bjornstad, Harold L. Bussell, Edmond C. Gruss, Dave Hunt, Bob Larson, Gordon R. Lewis, William J. Petersen, Jack Sparks, M. Thomas Stakes, and J. Stafford Wright are among the most prominent writers. Special mention belongs to Ronald Enroth who became in the early 1980s the single most important Evangelical Christian counter-cult writer. A professor of sociology (that in itself, is unusual as most Christian counter-cultists tend to specialize in either the Bible or theology), Enroth has authored two significant books, *Youth, Brainwashing and the Extremist Cults* (1977) and *The Lure of the Cults* (1979), numerous articles in Christian periodicals, and the lead chapter in Inter-Varsity Press's *A Guide to the Cults* (1983).

With the proliferation of counter-cult literature in the 1970s came a parallel multiplication of the number of independent organizations formed primarily to engage in counter-cult apologetics. A few such groups, specializing in ministries to a particular group, had been formed by converts, for example, Judaism and Mormonism in the nineteenth century. After World War I, efforts directed toward Jehovah's Witnesses were begun. After World War II, a few organizations, such as the Religious Analysis Service, founded in 1946, which dealt with the broad spectrum of cults, emerged. Among the more prominent of the Christian counter-cult organizations which appeared in the 1970s are: the Spiritual Counterfeits Project, which grew out of the Jesus People revival in Berkeley, California; the Christian Research Institute, headed by Walter Martin; the Institute of Contemporary Christianity, headed by James Bjornstad; and Christian Apologetics: Research and Information Service (popularly known as C.A.R.I.S.), headed by Michael Van Buskirk and Robert Passantino.

Beyond the hundred or more independent counter-cult organizations, several evangelical denominations have created counter-cult offices, most important being the Lutheran Church-Missouri Synod and the Southern Baptist Convention. While most denominations have had little to say concerning the cults, these two churches have published an impressive array of material that has steadily improved in quality.

Evangelical Understandings of Cult Phenomena

In general, though the line dividing them is by no means clear, the Christian counter-cult ministries can and should be distinguished from the secular militant anti-cult movement discussed in the next chapter. While like the anti-cult movement, the Christian counter-cult ministries seek to convince people to leave the cults, they also tend to view a person's leaving a cult as merely a step along the way. The ultimate goal is the commitment of the former cultist to an orthodox faith in Jesus Christ.

What is a "cult" to Evangelical counter-cultists? In general, Evangelicals define a cult as a *heretical* group. Josh McDowell and Don Stewart began their best-selling volume, *Understanding the Cults*, by asserting, "A cult is a perversion, a distortion of biblical Christianity, and as such, rejects the historic teachings of the Christian Church." Walter Martin succinctly defines his field, "By cultism we mean the adherence to doctrines which are pointedly contradictory to orthodox Christianity and which yet claim the distinction of either tracing their origin to orthodox sources or of being in essential harmony with those sources."

Most recently, some writers have tried to face the contradiction inherent in the traditional definition of cult: most of the groups generally described as cults are Eastern religions which claim no relationship to traditional Christianity. By Martin's definition, many of the groups considered in his books—Transcendental Meditation, the International Society for Krishna Consciousness, and the Divine Light Mission—would not be cults. Thus many counter-cultists are beginning to distinguish between the Eastern, occult, and metaphysical religions on the one hand and the Christian groups which dissent from traditional doctrinal orthodoxy on the other hand. Enroth and most of the writers for the Spiritual Counterfeits Project, upon whose board he sits, reserve the term cult exclusively for the Eastern and occult groups, while speaking of "aberrant" Christian groups when describing Christian groups which deny an essential doctrine of orthodox Christianity. Gordon R. Lewis, counter-cult writer and professor at Denver Conservative Baptist Seminary, assumes the exact opposite stance, keeping the term cult for deviating Christian groups (Jehovah's Witnesses, Christian Science, the Unification Church) while viewing Eastern religions as a distinctly different category.

However, whatever the definition, Evangelicals have followed a basic format in their consideration of the nonconventional religions. Each group is examined and judged according to its allegiance to doctrines and practices which deviate from those of orthodox Christian faith. The orthodox Christian tradition is expressed in the ancient creeds of the church (such as the Apostles and Nicean) and explicated in the writings of the early church fathers who defined and rejected the classic heresies, and in more recent statements such as the early twentieth century definition of *The Fundamentals*. Using this variety of documents, to which Christians have traditionally looked for the correct presentation of faith, Evangelicals examine any questionable Christian group on its position on key doctrines such as the Trinity, the person and work of Christ, the authority of the Bible, the nature of sin and salvation, to name a few.

With groups which are, in fact, variations on Christianity and which accept the basic ideas and structure of Western orthodoxy while denying one or more traditionally important beliefs, the doctrinal approach can be extremely illuminating. Evangelicals have specialized in criticism of those cults which see themselves as Biblically-based Christians but have either (1) reached different conclusions on basic doctrinal issues or (2) have received an additional revelation which adds to (and thus changes) the Biblical message. With such groups, a doctrine-by-doctrine comparison quickly highlights the areas in which differences are manifest. More complex problems are caused by those groups which not only have taken a variant approach to several key Christian doctrines but which have adopted a radically different metaphysical approach to the world. Both the Church of Christ Scientist and the Unification Church, although they use Biblical language and Christian symbols, give such distinct meanings to certain words and symbols as to raise significant questions as to how they fit into Christian tradition, if in fact they do.

When considering those groups which fall completely outside of the Christian tradition, the counter-cult approach has been not so much the comparison of beliefs, doctrine by doctrine (though a few have tried such a methodology), but a comparison of the total belief system of, for example, Zen Buddhism or Transcendental Meditation with the Christian gospel in an attempt to show the superiority of the latter. Such efforts vary considerably in quality. Many Eastern and occult systems place great emphasis upon experience and the mastering of techniques for spiritual growth, and, hence, do not yield easily to doctrinal analysis (if in fact a coherent doctrinal system can be identified). An approach which emphasizes ideas frequently misses the essence and appeal of a group.

Underlying all Christian counter-cult literature is a strong belief that cults are Satanic, not that they worship Satan, but that, as Dave Hunt affirms, "Satan is the author of every cult and false religion, and his imprint is clearly seen on them all." The rise of cults constitutes a direct sign of Satan's activity in the world, for Satan himself has, in his opposition to God, established rival faiths, and lured Christians into false doctrinal positions. The efforts made to counter cults are for the Christian much more than natural competition against a rival. This is a cosmic battle, a war against the principalities and powers (Eph. 6:12). This opposition to Satanic activity largely guides and motivates the Christian cult ministries.

The Work of the Ministry

Christian cult ministries have, in practice, two major thrusts. The ministries devote the major part of their time, energy, and, especially, literature to the Church. Overwhelmingly, the material produced by the various ministries is purchased and read by Church members. Such materials inform church members of the heretical and false ideas and unChristian practices of cults in hopes of strengthening members in the true faith and preventing them from being attracted to a cult.

A small portion of the counter-cult church literature engages members and leaders in a process of self reflection. The success of different cult groups often highlights the areas in which churches have failed to provide adequate programming. Some cults have succeeded because of their particular attention to evangelism, spiritual nurture and growth, lay leadership, vital worship, or their youth program. Harold L. Bussell of Gordon College suggests that Evangelical churches and cults have much in common and that additional material for reflection will arise from looking at that commonality. (Militant anticultists have also recognized that commonality and have on occasion treated Evangelical churches like a cult and targeted them for deprogrammings along with those groups that both they and the Christian counter-cultists would agree are cults.)

Evangelical ministries also witness directly to members of cult groups. To assist their witnessing work, they regularly produce literature, primarily tracts and booklets, that delineates errors in a particular cult, to which is added an invitation to accept Jesus as Lord and Savior. The literature is distributed to members of the alternative religious groups in a variety of means though most effectively as an aspect of a direct witnessing program. Witnessing activity varies from distribution of literature in spots cult members might pick it up and read it, to low-key long-term contact, to confrontation on the street, to more controversial attempts to invade a group's home territory with an exposé message which questions the integrity of the group, its teachings, or its leadership. Some counter-cultists have made it a practice to visit worship centers (for example, Mormon temples) and pass out anti-Mormon literature to all who would take it.

The Future of Cult Ministries

Cult ministries arose in the nineteenth century as the recognition slowly dawned that the Church was being forced to compete with an ever-growing variety of religious alternatives in the free environment of the modern world. As the number and appeal of these alternatives have increased, so have the number and work of the cult ministries. They have defined a long-term task of witnessing and apologetics, the importance of which to the Evangelical church community can only grow.

Though a few Christian counter-cult ministries have been around for several generations, their expansion and development occurred concurrently with the flowering of Asian religion after 1965. In large measure, the ministries remain in their first generation and are still undergoing a period of experimentation and change as they adjust along with the churches to the new pluralism. Their future seems dependent upon their ability to mature in their knowledge and appreciation of other religious systems. Many contemporary writers of counter-cult literature show their lack of training in comparative religions by their inability to enter into the world of a Buddhist or a theosophist and learn the dynamics and appeal of a foreign faith. This inability leads to the constant misunderstanding of the different alternative religions discussed in Christian literature, and is the source of the many complaints that Christian literature slanders different cult groups by substantively misrepresenting their teachings.

The basic distortion of the teachings of various cult groups, especially the Eastern and occult ones, derives in large measure from the subservience of the cult ministries to the evangelistic task and their rejection of the experience gained in interreligious dialogue. The failure to engage members of other religions in dialogue almost guarantees that errors in comprehension of the targeted faith community will occur, be passed along in the literature, and never be corrected. Such dialogue is imperative when the object of concern is a first-generation religion such as Scientology or the Unification Church, which typically undergoes a process of rapid change during its first decades as it develops and institutionalizes its original vision. The accelerated changes in the newer religions over the past decade have rendered obsolete most of the descriptive literature produced in the 1970s.

Like the cults, the counter-cult ministries have changed dramatically during the last decade. Their ability to be of service in a pluralistic world will greatly depend upon their ability to handle the increasingly complex situation of American religion.

This list is a small sample of the most prominent books on cults representative of the Evangelical Christian perspective as described above.

1. Burrell, Maurice C., *The Challenge of the Cults*. Grand Rapids, MI: Baker Book House, 160pp. 1981.

2. Enroth, Ron, *The Lure of the Cults*. Chappaqua, NY: Christian Herald Books, 1979. 139pp.

3. ———— , *Youth, Brainwashing and the Extremist Cults*. Grand Rapids, MI: Zondervan Publishing House, 1977. 221pp.

4. *A Guide to Cults and New Religions*. Downers Grove, IL: Inter-Varsity Press, 1983. 216pp.

5. Hunt, Dave, *The Cult Explosion*. Irvine, CA: Harvest House Publishers, 1980. 270pp.

6. Larson, Bob, *Larson's Book of Cults*. Wheaton, IL: Tyndale House Publishers, 1982. 428pp.

7. McDowell, Josh, and Don Stewart, *Understanding the Cults*. San Bernadino, CA: Here's Life Publishers, 1982. 199pp.

8. Martin, Walter, *The Kingdom of the Cults*. Minneapolis: Bethany Fellowship, 1968. 443pp.

9. ———— , *The New Cults*. Santa Ana, CA: Vision House, 1980. 419pp.

10. Sparks, Jack, *The Mind Benders*. Nashville: Thomas Nelson, 1977. 283pp.

11. Van Baalen, Jan Karel, *The Chaos of Cults*. Grand Rapids, MI: Wm. B. Eerdmanns Publishing Company, 1960. 444pp.

B. THE ANTI-CULT MOVEMENT

The Problem of Religion

During the 1970s several trends in American religion came together. Since the American Revolution, this country has been shaken by periods of social protest followed by national religious revivals in which the entire population, regardless of religious affiliation, gave a heightened attention to religious concerns. During such periods, new and alternative religions have been born or given surges of growth while the more traditional churches reaped the bulk of the harvest. Such a national revival occurred in the early 1970s on the heels of the social protests of the 1960s.

This most recent revival, however, met a changed condition. Throughout the twentieth century, church membership increased dramatically as an ever-larger percentage of the growing population found an organized religious affiliation. At the same time, the number of denominations also steadily increased. By 1975, at least 800 different denominations competed for the allegiance of the Christian public. Also growing, both in number of organizations and in number of people involved, were the many different varieties of unorthodox and nonconventional religious and spiritual groups—occult, metaphysical, mystical, and Eastern. While most Americans flocked to a Christian church, a smaller, but nevertheless significant number, became Spiritualists, Theosophists, Rosicrucians, Buddhists, and Hindus. These alternative religious perspectives had received a boost in 1965 by the rescission of the Asian Exclusion Acts. Over the next decade, Oriental teachers migrated to America to launch new movements and to pump new life into those previously founded by pioneering bands of disciples. When the revival of the 1970s began, the Asian groups were ready to receive their share of the newly religious.

Observers first noticed the revival on the West Coast where evangelical Christians began work among the hippies and the multitude of street people. By 1970 the "Jesus people" revival was visibly shaking the hippie community from San Diego to Seattle. In California, the Children of God, the Christian Foundation (headed by Tony and Susan Alamo), the Jews for Jesus, the World Christian Liberation Front, and Jesus People International were organized.

As the Jesus People revival gained momentum, other groups also sought an audience. Rev. Sun Myung Moon made his first visit to the United States in 1965 and took up permanent residence in 1972. Swami Bhaktivedanta founded the International Society for Krishna Consciousness in New York in 1965. Yogi Bhajan brought the Sikh Dharma to Los Angeles in 1968. Kirpal Singh, a leader of one branch of the Sant Mat tradition, made the first of several visits in 1965. Maharaj Ji, the teenage guru, made his first visit in 1971, a prelude to his eventual movement to America in 1973. In the beginning, however, these movements were less important than the Jesus People groups.

As this revival spread, it, too, reaped its converts primarily from the young adult population, those individuals prepared to make their first adult religious commitment and most willing to change from the religion in which they had been raised. Also, as in previous revivals, the majority of the newly religious eventually joined mainline evangelical Christian (primarily Baptist and Pentecostal) churches. But enough joined some of the other groups to attract attention and raise more than passing concern.

A few parents of the new converts became disturbed. Their sons and daughters, young people from well-to-do, educated, and mainline religious backgrounds had dropped out of schools and left jobs only to reappear as members of a heretofore-unheard-of group which made a high demand upon their time, boasted unusual ideas, and vocalized a very low opinion of many established societal structures. The changes in their child's behavior—adoption of strange religious apparel, vegetarian diets, chanting and meditation, the rejection of any career orientation, and the assumption of an austere lifestyle—upset the parents even more. Converts of these new religions had, it seemed, moved quickly from the nominal attention to religion so characteristic of Western society to a position in which religion was the dominant reality of their life, infusing every moment and demanding almost all of their time.

Too often, membership in a new religion coincided with an outward break in family relations. Parents blamed the religions for alienating their sons and daughters. All they saw was the radical change in their offspring who rejected all their parents saw as good and right—a college degree, marriage, a career, and a home in the suburbs—all that they as parents had worked to provide. Among the first to express his concern, William Rambur of Chula Vista, California, learned that his twenty-two-year-old daughter, who had just begun her career as a nurse, had left her job and her fiance to join the Children of God. After a frantic search, he located her on the ranch at Thurber, Texas. Through his middle-class suburban eyes, the ranch seemed primitive, appalling. Unable to convince his daughter to leave, he denounced the group to the press and began a personal campaign to warn other parents of what he had discovered. After he returned to California, he met Theodore Patrick, Jr., an employee of the State of California, who had also had a negative encounter with the Children of God through his son and nephew. Together with several other likeminded parents, they formed the first anticult association, The Parents' Committee to Free Our Children from the Children of God (later shortened to "Free the Children of God," and popularly called "FREE-COG."

The Spread of the Anti-cult Movement

As FREECOG became known, parents whose children had joined other demanding and unconventional religions contacted Rambur and Patrick. Although it initially resisted the temptation to diversify, FREE-COG eventually acceded to requests and reorganized as the Volunteer Parents of America. It accepted membership from parents of all cult members though it remained largely a southern California organization.

VPA grew and similar groups appeared in other parts of the country and in Canada. By 1974 Rambur and other leaders of the burgeoning movement, seeing the need of a national organization, formed the Citizen's Freedom Foundation. By 1975 membership reached 1,500 though it was merely the largest of several parent's associations then in existence.

1976 was a crucial year for the movement. By that time the Unification Church had become the major symbol of all that was considered evil in cult life, and the anti-cult movement increasingly targeted its efforts to it. A major sign of the shift was that the leaders of the movement convinced Senator Robert Dole to hold hearings in Washington, D.C., as a forum for parental and other complaints against the cults in general and the Unification Church, in particular. CFF published the proceedings.

The hearings became the catalyst for the formation of what many hoped would be a successful national umbrella organization. The National Ad Hoc Committee Engaged in Freeing Minds was headquartered in the home of George M. Slaughter, III, of Grand Prairie, Texas. Slaughter's daughter Cynthia, recently deprogrammed from the Unification Church, appeared as a star witness at the hearings. The CEFM, however, soon ran into problems and was unable to obtain a tax-exempt status. It was replaced by the Pennsylvania-based Individual Freedom Foundation Educational Trust (IFFET). However, IFFET succeeded in holding the diverse movement together only for a matter of months before it, too, fell apart as a result of various internal disputes. The failure of IFFET returned the focus of the movement to the numerous local groups, only a few of which reached beyond a single metropolitan area. Typically, these organizations published a newsletter (which allowed them to keep in touch nationally), sponsored regular programs for the public, and facilitated parents' efforts to contact deprogrammers.

The failure of IFFET seemed to portend the decline and demise of the whole anti-cult movement. Then the events of November 1978 in Jonestown, Guyana, gave it a fresh start. Seizing the occasion, the movement's leaders mobilized new support, and Senator Dole responded by creating a new anti-cult forum in the form of hearings on the Guyana tragedy. The rebirth of interest in the cult problem served as a catalyst to the formation of another national organization (which did not replace the many local

ones), the American Family Foundation. AFF became important immediately as its leaders included several psychological professionals, most
notably psychiatrist Dr. John R. Clark, an adjunct professor at Harvard
University. It began publishing the most substantive periodical produced
by the movement to date and later began a scholarly quarterly.

The Anti-cult Action Program

From its beginning, the anticult movement focused upon a single
problem, the distress of parents whose young adult sons and daughters (to
whom the literature typically refers as "children" regardless of age) had
abandoned home, career, college, and a "normal" future for membership
in a demanding nonconventional religion (i.e., a cult). This single concern
determines the shape of the movement's program and most of the organizations within the movement exist solely to serve parents who want their
son or daughter removed from a particular religious group. In their effort
to provide more than just personal support for parents grieving over the
loss of a child to a cult, the movement developed an action program. The
program had three main components: deprogramming, legislative procedures, and lawsuits.

Deprogramming. Deprogramming, as developed by Ted Patrick in the
early 1970s, was a coercive technique designed to force cult members to
break their ties to the group which they had joined. It included the forced
detention of the cultist and the application of a variety of intense psychological pressures (interrogation, loss of privacy, profanation of the sacred,
and parental and peer group pressure), with the goal of having the
member renounce his or her religious affiliation and adopt a life and faith
more acceptable to the parents. Deprogramming had only a 50 percent
success rate, primarily among cultists who had been with the group less
than two years. However, the successes were important in giving hope to
those parents who could afford the deprogrammers' services. Successfully
deprogrammed former cultists became important spokespersons for the
movement, adding the authority of their experience in the cult to the
charges of the movement. Once deprogrammed, many ex-cultists became
deprogrammers themselves.

Deprogramming came under attack by civil libertarians almost immediately. As early as 1974, church leaders passed a strong resolution against
it, through the National Council of Churches. Several organizations, such
as the Alliance for the Preservation of Religious Liberties, largely backed
by the Church of Scientology, brought together church leaders, religious
liberty activists, and cult leaders to defend the rights of those groups
whose members were being subjected to deprogramming. Such groups
publicized the accounts of people who had experienced deprogramming
but had remained members of the cult. They placed emphasis upon the
incidents of violence and the personal abuse they suffered. While unable
to stop the practice, opposition did inhibit the legitimization of deprogramming in law and in the courts.

During the 1980s, additional criticism of deprogramming emerged. First, ex-cultists who had been deprogrammed began to speak out against unnecessary coercion and manipulation involved in the practice. Secondly, and possibly more important, led by Ronald Enroth, Christian counter-cultists who had informally supported the anticult groups began to speak out against deprogramming. As Walter Martin, possibly the most prolific Christian writer on the subject of cults, wrote in 1980, "I cannot stand behind such practices. It is true that cultists have been blinded by the 'god of this age,' but it is also true that they have the right to make up their own minds, and we should not stoop to unChristian tactics to accomplish God's ends."

The added attack from former allies forced some anti-cult groups to revise their stance. In 1981 the Citizen's Freedom Foundation issued a new statement on deprogramming in which it abandoned support for the practice as it existed in the 1970s: "CFF does not support, condone, or recommend kidnaping or holding a person against his will." It gave its support to what has since become generally known as "exit counseling," a directed counseling procedure aimed at encouraging a cult member to leave the cult. Other anticult groups as well as individual members of CFF continue to promote and facilitate deprogrammings, though the practice declined markedly during the mid-1980s.

Influencing Legislation. As soon as the anticult movement widened its initial focus upon the Children of God to include all of the new cults, it sought assistance from legislators. As early as 1974, concerned parents were able to convince State Senator Mervyn M. Dymally, Chairman of the California Senate's Subcommittee on Children and Youth to convene a hearing on the "Impact of Cults on Today's Youth." As with the later Dole hearings, no legislative action followed, but during the 1970s and early 1980s legislators, persuaded by the arguments of anti-cult constituents, introduced numerous bills to curb cult activities. Some bills would have granted parents and families of cult members a conservatorship during which time a deprogramming could proceed. Others sought to regulate "non-traditional" religions by forcing them to give prospective members a full disclosure of practices and beliefs before allowing anyone to join. Still others wanted to place cults (as opposed to genuine religions) under the regulations guiding public trusts and non-religious charities.

A decade of attempts to legislate against cults proved both expensive and unproductive. The various bills were overwhelmingly defeated, most never being reported out of committee. Only one, the Lasher Bill (which would have granted conservatorships) passed a legislative vote and was placed on a governor's desk for approval. It was vetoed on two occasions by the governor of New York.

In the Courts. The courts were a final place of redress of parental grievances against cults. Parents explored the possibility of obtaining court-ordered conservatorships over their children who had joined cults. While a few of these were granted, most courts refused such requests as outside the intent of conservatorship laws (designed to protect incapacitated or elderly people). The courts' refusal to act led directly to the legislative attempts to broaden the conservatorship laws. However, even as the anti-cult movement sought remedies in court, so did the cults. Cult members who had gone through a deprogramming attempt filed criminal charges against their abductors. Generally, they too, found the court unwilling to take sides in what was considered a family dispute.

Initially rebuffed, both sides turned to the civil courts. Cult members have had some success. Synanon, for example, won a major libel suit against the Hearst newspapers. In 1977, a class action suit closed the deprogramming center in Tucson, Arizona, and forced the retirement of several deprogrammers. In several lesser suits, brought by individuals against their deprogrammers, courts have awarded damages, though most have ended without any substantial settlement.

The anti-cult movement has had little success in the civil court suits it has brought. In most cases where a lower court did grant damages, the decision was reversed on appeal. Such was the fate of the highly publicized award of $2,000,000.00 to a former member of the church of Scientology. (As this volume goes to press, a multimillion dollar judgment against the International Society for Krishna Consciousness is on appeal.) In the final analysis, the drain of time and financial resources in so many legal actions may prove fatal to the movement's attempts to vindicate its cause in the courts. Legal fees have drained the treasuries of the movement and increased the price of deprogramming beyond the reach of most parents. Without a substantive victory in court, this thrust of anti-cult activity may soon be abandoned.

Dissemination of Information. While its action programs initiated in the 1970s have flagged, the anti-cult movement can point to one clear success. In its first decade of activity it has impressed upon the popular consciousness a negative image of cults, the full effect of which only history will be able to discern. Articulate spokespersons of the movement have presented the anti-cult rationale and program in numerous books, pamphlets, and articles for popular periodicals. Persistently cultivating the media, the anti-cult movement has received widespread coverage in both magazines and newspapers, which have featured accounts of life in and out of the cults by former members. Alerted to the cult issue, the media have been quick to seize upon stories of improprieties of cults and their leaders. Thus, the movement has created both directly and indirectly a vast body of literature that will haunt the new religions for many years.

This massive attack through the media has alerted several government agencies, particularly the Internal Revenue Service, to the existence of nonconventional religions. Spurred in part by the negative image of cults, the IRS has investigated several newer religions. Prosecutions have led to the denial of tax-exempt status to several groups and the conviction (in a highly controversial case) of Rev. Sun Myung Moon, leader of the Unification Church, for tax evasion. The anti-cult movement has claimed partial credit, and rightfully so, for government actions against cult groups and has welcomed each success as a step in its overall goals.

The Rationale of the Anti-cult Movement

The program of the anti-cult movement required a means of transforming the purely familial and religious concerns of the parent groups into a secular public issue and turning the personal hurt felt by families into the aura of potential harm threatening all of society from the cults. Only by accomplishing such a transformation, the parent groups quickly learned, could they hope to influence either courts or legislatures, both of whom tended to dismiss their petitions as strictly family concerns and to reject suggested actions against the cults on grounds of religious freedom. In the crucible of controversy, the groups experimented with various approaches and by the late 1970s produced the dominant rationale to which the movement could adhere.

In the early 1970s, parents reported significant and unexpected changes in the behavior patterns and attitudes of sons and daughters who joined the cults. They concluded that the cults had somehow changed their otherwise normal son or daughter into a different person, one who would follow a weird, idiotic, foreign religion. Often unaware of or choosing to ignore their offspring's internal turmoil or period of religious experimentation prior to encountering the cult, they searched for a mechanism to explain what they saw as a sudden change. They toyed with hypnotism and talked of the pressures of adolescence. Nothing proved satisfactory until the "brainwashing" rationale emerged.

According to this hypothesis, cult groups and leaders are seen as entirely manipulative toward their members. Cults recruit impressionable youth through deceit, typically by inviting them to a harmless-looking event which is actually a carefully staged recruiting event for the group. Once involved, the prospective member is subjected to a number of mind-control techniques designed to destroy his/her rational faculties and subtly manipulate the person into ever-greater involvement in the group program. These techniques include the application of intense peer pressure, the frequent repetition of group beliefs, low-protein diets, sleep deprivation, denial of privacy, control of the immediate environment, the manipulation of language (jargon), the use of rituals to induce mystical trance-like states, and the wholesale condemnation of established structures (family, school, church, etc.). With their critical abilities reduced, victims are psychologically coerced into converting to the cult.

Having joined, the person continues to suffer the brainwashing techniques until completely united with the group and is unable to act or think apart from the leader's will. Prolonged existence in the cult environment, in a state of mental control, is believed by many anti-cultists to cause mental and emotional disorders, and a few theorists have suggested that permanent brain or nervous system damage will result from prolonged membership.

The discovery of brainwashing, or thought reform, in the literature on former Chinese prisoners of war of the 1950s facilitated the necessary transformation of the familial concerns into a public issue. Parental concern became a threat to public health, and a radical solution was necessary if further damage to individuals was to be prevented. The public threat demands government action while the harm being done to individuals requires immediate psychological treatment (i.e., deprogramming).

Deprogramming has been understood by anti-cultists to be a means of reversing the effects of brainwashing. During the deprogramming process, the individual is bombarded with all the reasons to disaffiliate from the group and at some point snaps back, i.e., regains the ability to think for him/herself apart from the constant pressure of the group. When that event occurs, the cultist immediately sees the mistake in joining the group, comprehends the process of brainwashing and mind control through which s/he went, decides to leave the group, and expresses gratitude to all involved in the deprogramming for their rescue.

Even as the techniques employed by deprogrammers were being refined, parents discovered that their deprogrammed children suffered from varying degrees of emotional distress. At first given the popular label, "information disease," by anti-cult writers Conway and Seigelman, the symptoms were eventually identified as those of the very common traumatic stress syndrome. Psychiatrists such as Margaret Singer, who worked closely with the anti-cult movement and counseled many deprogrammed ex-cultists, attributed the syndrome to membership in the cult group. More recent studies have pointed out that the syndrome is largely confined to those cult members who withdraw as the result of a deprogramming. It does not show up among the far larger number who leave voluntarily. Such evidence suggests that the trauma of deprogramming, not membership in the cult, produces emotional distress among former cult members.

The testimonies of successfully deprogrammed cultists became the prime piece of evidence which could be presented to both the public and the movement to demonstrate the truth of the anticult position. Having accepted the deprogrammers' redefinition of life in the cult, new ex-cultists frequently joined the anti-cult movement and regularly testified publicly about their experience. Critics of the anti-cult movement quickly attacked the testimonies of the ex-cultists noting the distortion which had entered into their accounts due to the deprogramming process and the infusion of the anti-cult rhetoric into the ex-member's story. The sameness of stories told by public apostates derives in part from the ex-member's molding the account of the actual experience in the group into conformity with a pre-existing script. The distortion caused by the traumatic withdrawal from a cult through deprogramming has been clearly demonstrated under the rigors of examination during legal proceedings.

The Future of the Anti-cult Movement

After a decade of activity, the anti-cult movement has one significant accomplishment to its credit. It has succeeded in creating a pervasive negative image of cults and spreading a popular public prejudice against several groups which are well known as cults. However, it has shown itself incapable of implementing any of its major program goals, which sought to severely regulate, inhibit the growth of, and eventually eliminate the cults altogether. This overall failure casts doubt on the future of the movement.

First, in spite of its success in creating a negative image of cults among both the media and the general public, the movement has been totally unable to stop or even slow the growth of the so-called cults. While the membership in various groups fluctuates year by year, the number of alternative religions and of people involved in them continues to grow. Many former members retain a positive appraisal of the group(s) with which they were affiliated and form a base of positive support in the larger culture. In fact, the anticult movement seems to have doomed itself to failure in that it set itself the task of reversing a major trend in American society toward religious diversity.

While it is difficult to access the overall effect of anti-cult efforts on individual groups, it is possible that it has inhibited the growth of some of the more vulnerable groups such as the Children of God (which has largely withdrawn its members from the United States) and those groups which have suffered successful prosecution by the government on various criminal or tax charges (Unification Church, Church of Scientology, Synanon). On the other hand, the anti-cult movement has given many obscure groups the publicity without which they would never have been able to reach a large audience of potential members. The movement has done as much to spur the growth of cults as inhibit them.

Second, the vast amount of time and energy expended to pass anti-cult legislation has completely failed, and with its loss of this area, the movement has also lost a prime instrument in mobilizing public support and media attention.

Third, the growing critique of deprogramming has forced many exponents of deprogramming to adopt less coercive (and hence less effective) methods of forcing cult members to disaffiliate. While deprogrammings will continue to be attempted, the withdrawal of support (as well as the increased cost due to legal complications) will further weaken the movement's ability to attract and hold their main support, distressed parents of cult members.

Fourth, while both sides in the cult wars have won and lost battles in the courts, the anti-cult movement has been unable to win any significant victories. Their few victories have come in lower courts where juries have tended to support parents and have been persuaded by the testimonies of deprogrammed ex-cultists. However, on appeal, judgments have tended to be reversed on Constitutional grounds. The reversal of the Christofferson decision in Oregon (in which an ex-member had been awarded a large sum from the Church of Scientology) was a severe loss. More recently, a federal court reversed the Peterson decision. In this case, a Minnesota court had ruled that when a person undergoing deprogramming begins to cooperate with the deprogramming, they by that action release the deprogrammers from any liability.

While also unable to win decisive victories, cult members have brought suits which have measurably hurt the anti-cult movement. Court victories have (1) forced the closing of anti-cult facilities (such as the Freedom of Thought Foundation in Tucson, Arizona), (2) yielded court orders against further active participation in deprogramming and other anti-cult activities by various anti-cult leaders, (3) exempted specific groups from further deprogrammings through class action decisions, and (4) driven individual deprogrammers (included Ted Patrick) from the field by depleting their financial resources in civil suits.

Thus the future of the anti-cult movement remains questionable. There is little doubt that it will continue active in some form for the foreseeable future. It is headed by a core of dedicated individuals, many of whom are either the deprogrammed ex-cultists themselves or their parents. They possess an extreme dedication to the cause. The only question, given the movement's failures, its loss of media attention, and the steady growth and acceptance of alternative religion, is the level at which it will be able to function. It is not unlikely that by the end of the decade the movement will be reduced to a number of small isolated groups whose major activity will be the circulation of anti-cult propaganda.*

Listed below are the major sources representative of the secular anti-cult position. Not included on the list are the many items directed toward a single cult.

1. Appel, Willa, *Cults in America*. New York: Holt, Rinehart and Winston, 1983. 204pp.

2. Conway, Flo and Jim Siegelman, *Snapping*. Philadelphia: Lippincott, 1978. 254pp.

3. MacCollam, *Carnival of Souls*. New York: Seabury Press, 1979. 188pp.

4. Patrick, Ted, *Let Our Children Go!* New York: E. P. Dutton, 1976. 285pp.

5. Rudin, James and Marcia Rudin, *Prison or Paradise*. Philadelphia: Firtress Press, 1980. 164pp.

6. Streiker, Lowell D., *The Cults Are Coming!* Nashville: Abingdon, 1978. 127pp.

7. Verdier, Paul A., *Brainwashing and the Cults*. No. Hollywood, CA: Wilshire Book Company, 1977. 118pp.

---

*The future viability of the movement may be tied to the outcome of the Robin George case, under appeal as this book goes to press. In 1983, Robin George, who had been deprogrammed from the International Society for Krishna Consciousness, was awarded $23,000,000.00 by a jury for actual and punitive damages. Though the judge lowered the judgment to $9,000,000.00, the case, if lost, will both seriously cripple ISKCON on the West Coast, and provide the movement with funding never before available for it. If reversed, it will provide a significant obstacle to further attempts to implement movement goals in the civil courts.

VI.
Violence and the Cults

VIOLENCE AND THE CULTS

The most serious charges leveled at new and unconventional religions concern their great potential for violence or the additional denunciation that such religions in fact have been and are the source of an inordinate amount of violence. As evidence, cult critics have pointed to the incidents of violent activity associated with nonconventional religious groups: the murder/suicides at Jonestown, the Manson Family killings, the takeover of three buildings in Washington, D.C., by the Hanafi Muslims, and the beating death of a child in the Michigan-based House of Judah.

This chapter broadly examines cult-related violence in order to isolate substantive issues concerning the potential for violence within the nonconventional religions, some five to six hundred of which currently dot the American landscape. Unfortunately, prior attention to this question has almost entirely focused upon the Peoples' Temple, a group so different from typical American cults as to offer little insight on the problems. In contrast, this chapter is based upon a survey of cult-related violence conducted in 1983–1984 by the Institute for the Study of American Religion. The survey led to the compilation of a file of reported incidents of violence regarding cult groups. Both newspapers and magazines, especially those published by anti-cult groups, were scanned and knowledgeable people were solicited for accounts of violent incidents. Some stories of cult violence that had received attention in the media were examined at greater depth and the groups involved asked to comment upon them. The results of that survey appear below.

The issue of cult-related violence is fraught with emotion and requires great care in the use of data. In merely cataloging the reported incidents, as was done in the early stages of this survey, one could easily come to the *false conclusion* suggested by many cult critics that *cult life is inherently dangerous and threatening*. The evidence, however, fails to support such a conclusion. Overwhelmingly, nonconventional religious groups have been free of reported incidents of violence. Most groups in the survey were quite similar to the more familiar and established mainline church bodies; they experienced one or two scattered incidents atypical of their day-to-day life. Those few nonconventional religious groups which have suffered a history of violent interaction with society are very much the exceptions of those groups which have been labeled "cult."

Most of the groups which have shown a long-term tendency for a violent interaction with society have received little or no attention from the anti-cult media. This lack of attention is due, in part, to the primary focus of anti-cult groups upon those cults that concentrate their energy in the recruitment of young adults. The more violent groups have been either predominantly black in membership (anti-cult cult groups tend to be upper-middle-class white) or older in membership.

However, certain groups do have a reported history of violence and, as a result, are a matter of legitimate concern. Groups which show a confirmed and continuing pattern of violence need the attention of religious scholars, psychologists and social scientists, the legal authorities, and the general public.

Some Preliminary Considerations

The survey established some necessary guidelines for evaluating the reports of violence. First, previous definitions of "cult-related violence" need to be considerably broadened. Levi, in his introduction to the only book-length treatment of the subject, defines it as "intentional homicide and intentional suicide initiated with a religious group."[1] That definition should be broadened to include (1) violent actions short of homicide which result in significant bodily injury or unintentional death. Violent acts reportedly perpetrated by cults include rape, beatings, and child abuse. Further, it should also include (2) practices that in themselves might not be considered violent but which may nevertheless lead to injury or death of the public or members of the group. Such practices might include, for example, unusual diet restrictions or the denial of necessary medical attention.

Inadvertently, Levi's definition also assumes a conclusion very much contradicted by the evidence, that all cult-related violence is initiated from within nonconventional religions. The survey has shown that violence directed toward nonconventional religions by outsiders is equally important and equally extensive though the object of only scant attention by the media. Thus the definition must also be enlarged to include (3) the very real violent activity directed against groups labeled cults. Anti-cult actions include the assassination of leaders, the bombing and burning of buildings, assaults upon groups by night riders, and the abduction of group members for coercive deconversion (i.e., deprogramming). Only one step from actual violence is (4) the threat of violence and terrorism against groups which are isolated either in a rural center or by public prejudice in an urban center. The effects of threats of violence are multiplied when reports of such threats are disregarded by legal authorities and groups are left on their own to face the possibility that threats foreshadow violent actions. It should be noted that the experience of threatened violence has led many rural religious groups, especially those isolated from efficient law enforcement structures, to initially develop an internal security system. Such systems, which often include a modest cache of weapons, are almost the sole basis of the frequently heard charges of religious groups stockpiling weapons. In like manner, the necessary training of security officers is transformed into an image of preparation for urban warfare upon society.

In this report, cult-related violence shall be defined as *violent behavior which leads to bodily harm or death (homicide and suicide) of individuals or the significant destruction of property due to actions initiated within a nonconventional religion against either members or the general public and also actions by the public against nonconventional religions' members and property.*

Second, the treatment of cult-related violence must attempt to filter the many unconfirmed reports and even malicious rumors from verified accounts of violent activity. Within the hostile climate that has pervaded the public consideration of cults, numerous false reports and rumors have been circulated. That problem was vividly illustrated in the midst of compiling the data for this report. Based upon the accusation of excessive child abuse made by ex-member Roland Church against the Northeast Community Church, the State of Vermont conducted a massive raid and took all of the children of the group into custody. Though a judge had ruled the raid illegal and dismissed most of the cases, two months after the June 1984 raid, Church confessed that he had lied in making the charges in order to justify his defection from the group.[2] Similar distortions have been regularly uncovered in the accounts of ex-members of groups who left with a grudge against the group or who have gone through the experience of deprogramming. Hostile reports of the defectors from nonconventional religions must be double checked against independent sources, and unverified claims either rejected or, at best, put aside for possible future verification.

The most pervasive unverified reports have concerned the stockpiling of weapons and the training for guerrilla warfare. For example, in 1978 reports began to appear in the press that the Hare Krishnas were stockpiling weapons at their farm community in West Virginia. Not reported were the several attacks upon the community by armed intruders or the fact that the entire stockpile consisted of several 22-caliber rifles which have to date (1984) never been used. Then in 1980, a cache of weapons was found in a car parked at the Krishna farm in California. News accounts heralded the discovery of a stockpile of Krishna-owned weapons, the arrest of Srila Hansadutta Swami (one of the organization's initiating gurus), and plans to search other California properties of the group. Again, not widely reported, were other facts: the guns found in the car were not owned by the Krishnas, rather, they were owned by several members who had purchased them in spite of the group's belief in nonviolence. Hansadutta was released by the authorities when it was discovered that there was no substance to the charges of possession of illegal weapons. Most importantly, no coverage was given to the disciplining and removal from positions of authority of Hansadutta and those deviating from the nonviolent stance of the Krishnas.

Unfortunately, in the case of Hansadutta, the problem continued after his reinstatement, and in 1983 he was excommunicated from the organization. He took the former Berkeley, California, temple of the International Society for Krishna Consciousness and formed the Vedic Cultural Society. In his own publications he has advocated the right to bear arms in self-defense and use them to protect members of his community. Subsequent to his establishment of an independent center, he was arrested as the result of a shooting incident in Berkeley.

The media coverage of the Krishna's problems, which has wedded images of Krishnas and guns in much media treatment of ISKCON, fades beside the space devoted to reports of military training supposedly accorded members of The Way International at The Way College in Emporia, Kansas. For three years in the late 1970s the College was one of several institutions of higher learning which offered a course in hunting safety initiated by the State of Kansas. This program, which used state money in its implementation, was carried out under state guidelines and did not include any military tactical training or the familiarization of pupils with military weapons. It did, however, generate numerous rumors of The Way's training members for urban guerrilla warfare, rumors which have continued to be repeated, even in the major news media, in spite of the lack of evidence to verify them.[3]

But as shall become obvious here, even the removal of such unverified and demonstrably false reports from the catalog of violent incidents leaves a substantial list. The existence of these several widely reported stories concerning violent activity, however, should serve as a warning against the confusion of mere charges of violent activity (which are far too numerous to present individually) with verified accounts. It is to the harm of all that some have crusaded against nonconventional religions with unverified stories of weapons stockpiling and child abuse. Their actions, which amount to a sophisticated form of crying wolf, distract attention from those individuals and individual groups which might, in fact, be stockpiling weapons, conducting military training, or abusing children.

Third, cult-related violence must be placed in the larger context of violence in American religion. While no attempt was made to survey violence in mainline churches, the survey of cult violence led to reports from mainline denominations concerning child abuse, mistreatment of residents of church-run homes for the elderly, shootings, and sexual mistreatment of members. No attempt to catalog these reports, which cover the range from Catholic to Protestant to Free Church congregations and structures, has been made, but such incidents, some equally as spectacular as those involving cults, rarely received national news coverage. There was one exception, of course.

Jim Jones' Peoples' Temple, labeled a "cult" after the deaths in Jonestown, was in fact a congregation within mainline Christianity. It was a full member of the Christian Church (Disciples of Christ), which in turn is a member of the National Council of Churches. Liberal Protestants heralded it for its social action program, and during the mid-1970s, several denominations such as the United Methodist Church devoted an entire adult church school lesson to extolling its virtues. The Peoples' Temple was not a cult in any traditional sense; it was a representative of an

unnoticed class—the mainline church which has degenerated into some-
thing not recognizable by reference to its parent body. As shall be noted
below, the Peoples' Temple is not the only recent representative.

Fourth, different nonconventional religions can and should be separated according to the differing levels of violence associated with them.
Most cults have had no serious charges of violence leveled against them.
Some have had some violent interaction with society. Only a very few
have passed through a period in which violence was a real factor in the
group's life (the Church of the Lamb of God, the Black Muslims, Faith
Assembly, etc.). This last-named group should be sharply distinguished
from the rest.

Cult critics, when discussing the issue of violence, continually yield to
the very attractive temptation to lump all cults together and brand all with
the guilt of any one. Such guilt-by-association, which unfortunately has
been integral to the media treatment of cult issues, is no less deplorable
than the racism and anti-Semitism from which it has been copied. Such a
tactic is, however, especially disheartening when adopted by an individual
or organization otherwise publicly identified with the fight against group
prejudices.

Violence Against Cults

Early one morning in 1978 the devotees at the Hare Krishna Community, New Vrindvan, in rural West Virginia, gathered for the worship
which begins each day. Suddenly, the barrels of several shotguns appeared
in the window and the sound of chanting was interrupted by buckshot
tearing through the air. The gunmen entered the temple. One forced the
leader of the group to walk up a nearby hill and ordered him to begin
digging his own grave. Others forced devotees to destroy one of the
statues of the deity. Fortunately no one was killed and eventually the
intruders left. Shaken by the events, the leaders of the community finally
agreed that a minimum of security must be established and so they
purchased several 22-caliber rifles.

The incident did not go unnoticed by the press, but in the resulting
coverage emphasis was shifted. It became a story of the purchase of the
weapons by the Krishnas and rumors of reprisals on the local community.
The coverage of the incident illustrates the lost element in discussions of
cult-related violence: violence inflicted upon cults.

In its most aggressive form, violence against cults has led to the
assassinations of cult leaders. Most are aware of the shootings of Mormon
leaders Joseph Smith (by a mob) and James Jesse Strang (by several
assassins). Less well known are the murders of Eric Jansson of the Bishop
Hill commune and Krishna Venta by angry ex-members of their groups.
In the past two decades the list of assassinated nonconventional religious
leaders would include:

Malcolm X
the family of Hamaas Abdul Khaalis
Joel LeBaron
Rulon C. Allred
Swami Nityananda

This set of deaths most clearly illustrates a major distinction among nonconventional religious groups in relation to violence, i.e., the distinction between those few groups whose members seem willing to resort to violence to further the group's goals and the overwhelming number of nonconventional religions which avoid violence except in self-defense. In each case cited above, the assassin of the cult leader was a member of a rival cult group. Malcolm X and the family of Hamaas Abdul Khaalis were both killed by men later identified as members of the Nation of Islam headed by Elijah Muhammad. Followers of Ervil LeBaron, leader of the Church of the Lamb of God, killed both Joel LeBaron and Rulon Allred. A member of the Ananda Marga lured Swami Nityananda to his death. With the exception of the Hanafi Muslims led by Khaalis, whose case is considered below, none of the afflicted cults took violent action against the rival group beyond demanding the prompt response of law-enforcement agencies.

Slightly different in kind was the shooting of San Diego Sikh Dharma leader Jagat Singh Khalsa by a man who broke into the San Diego Temple brandishing a carbine. This isolated 1978 incident ended fortunately without anyone being killed but served to heighten the fear among members of nonconventional groups which had been subjected to lesser forms of violence.

More numerous than the assassinations of leaders, of course, have been attacks by individuals and small groups upon cult members and property. While contemporary groups seem to have been relatively free of the kind of mob violence such as that which in the last century was directed against Roman Catholic convents and/or monasteries and against the Mormons, there have been repeated incidents of attacks upon members (simple assault) and buildings (arson, shootings, bombings). Few of the assault cases have been reported in the media, unless coincidental with a deprogramming attempt, but several attacks by armed night riders have become known. For example, once the people in and around Dimmitt, Texas, became aware of the presence of the Coven of Arianhu, a Witchcraft group associated with the national Church and School of Wicca, teenagers selected the isolated farm of leaders Louise and Loy Stone as a popular spot for late night visits. On several occasions the Stones reported harassment by truckloads of young people driving around their property, trespassing and shouting their disapproval of the Stones's religion, which many confused with Satanism. On Halloween 1977, a truck full of youths appeared. A short time later a shotgun appeared. Shots were fired. One youth was killed and another was wounded. (The death may have been partially due to the delay in getting the wounded girl to the nearby hospital. For some reason the driver of the truck took over an hour to drive the short distance). Loy Stone, arrested for the shooting, was found not guilty in the trial.

Less ambiguous was the burning of a building at Camp New Hope owned by the Unification Church in Ulster County, New York. Prior to the burning, the camp was the target of numerous rockthrowing and several shooting incidents. The Metropolitan Community Church, a church whose members are predominantly homosexuals, has had several of its church structures destroyed by arson. A pipe bomb was exploded in the campus of The Way College in January 1981. The San Diego temple of the Hare Krishnas was bombed in 1979. These violent actions against property seem to be an extension of the frequent incidents in which rocks, along with the occasional threatening note, are thrown through windows, a common complaint of owners of occult bookstores and supply houses.

Of the several reported bombings of nonconventional religious centers, none have shown more vicious intent than the incident in 1984 at the Philadelphia temple of the Hare Krishnas. Early one morning, a bomb exploded. A few minutes later, a second bomb exploded in the same location. The first bomb, the weaker of the two, had been meant to attract people to the site. The second, larger bomb was timed to kill or seriously injure any assembled Krishnas. Fortunately, the temple residents were slow to respond to the first bomb, and no one was injured.

These more-or-less sporadic acts against cults are the most extreme form of violence against nonconventional religious groups. The seemingly random pattern of their occurrence radically contrasts with the most prevalent form of violence against nonconventional religions: deprogramming. This practice of abducting and physically detaining members of cults began in the early 1970s. Though the number of incidents peaked around 1980, deprogramming continues as a popular practice (The Way International reported approximately 100 attempts in 1983) and has spawned a core of professional deprogrammers. The number of total deprogrammings and deprogramming attempts during the past decade runs into the thousands.

Each case of deprogramming, it should be noted, involves the abduction and forced detention of the cult member, and, in most cases, the physical violence is limited to those two actions, though the process of deprogramming involves a massive assault upon the psyche and value system of the victim, as traumatic for some as a physical rape. On occasion, however, the deprogramming has become even more violent. If the deprogramming victim attempts resistance and escape, s/he will almost surely be physically assaulted and often restrained with ropes and/or handcuffs. On several occasions deprogramming of female victims has led to sexual assault. In one case the husband of a woman undergoing deprogramming was severely cut with a razor while trying to free his wife from her abductors.

It should be noted that the number of violent assaults on noncoventional religious groups and their members have been as underreported as the number of violent incidents initiated by cult members have been exaggerated. Most incidents, especially incidents of threats, minor assaults and property damage, go unnoticed until they have been compounded and erupt into a major violent confrontation or even homicide.

Cult Against Cult

Review of the list of cult-related violence clearly exposes the location of the single most violent activity initiated by nonconventional religious bodies: where two or more closely related groups allow intense religious polemics (a very common characteristic of groups undergoing a process of splintering) to escalate into open warfare. Such incidents form a transition in the discussion of cult-related violence as such conflict finds a cult inflicting violence, but equally a cult as victim of that violence. Two prominent examples from recent decades immediately stand out—the Mormon polygamy-practicing groups of the Southwest and the Black Muslims.

During the 1970s, Ervil LeBaron left the polygamy-practicing Church of the First Born of the Fullness of Times, founded and led by his brother Joel. With his followers he organized the Church of the Lamb of God. He then declared himself leader of all of the polygamy-practicing groups and demanded that the other leaders acknowledge his new role. When they ignored him, he threatened violence. They still refused to accept him. He ordered executions. Joel was murdered in 1972. In 1973 Ervil ordered a raid on the town of Los Molinos where many of Joel's followers and family lived. The raiders set fire to several buildings and killed two people. In 1977 Ervil ordered several members to execute Dr. Rulon Allred, the leader of one of the largest polygamy groups. Allred died in his office of multiple gunshot wounds. The violence ended in 1979 with the arrest and conviction of Ervil LeBaron.[4]

Even more violent was the case of the Black Muslims. The Nation of Islam, which had been founded in the 1930s, grew rapidly in the years after World War II (during which time its leader Elijah Muhammad had been in prison for encouraging draft evasion). Then in the mid-1960s it began to splinter. Malcolm X, one of the Nation's most charismatic leaders, defected, organized a rival Muslim Mosque, and criticized his former leader for his departure from orthodox Islam. In 1965 Malcolm X was assassinated by members of the Nation of Islam. The murder of Malcolm X signaled the beginning of a decade of violence that left bodies lying on the streets from Brooklyn to Pasadena. The blood bath even touched Elijah Muhammad's family when his son-in-law Raymond Sharieff was shot as he left the offices of the Nation's periodical.

Most deaths in the Islamic wars occurred in fighting between the Nation and the Hanafis. On January 19, 1973, several men, later identified as members of the Nation of Islam, broke into the home of Hanafi Muslim leader Hamaas Abdul Khaalis, a friend of Malcolm X and former Nation official. Several weeks earlier Khaalis had circulated an open letter in

which he called Elijah Muhammad a "lying deceiver." Not finding Khaalis
at home, the invaders took their toll among other residents. Four were
shot and killed. Khaalis' wife survived but is paralyzed for life. His three
children were drowned. The men convicted for the crimes were given
what many, including Khaalis, considered a relatively light sentence. In
1977, partially in response to his anger and frustration over the incident,
Khaalis demanded, among other terms, that authorities produce the men
convicted of the 1973 murders. Presumably he would have killed them if
given the opportunity.[5]

Violence Initiated by Cults

In spite of the attention given to cult-initiated violence, little systematic effort has been made to analyze the data and to address the substantive
questions they raise. Commentators have been content merely to list
reported incidents in the attempt to support a prior conclusion that the
level of cult violence is sufficient to warrant suppression of nonconventional religions by society and the government. The cataloging of reported
acts of violence now allows examination apart from anti-cult polemic
which has treated all violence as symptoms of a single cult phenomenon.
Such previous amalgamations of data, gathered only as ammunition with
which to assault the cults, have provided no useful assistance in, for
example, locating potential pockets of future violence or preventing their
occurrence.

The specter of cult violence centers upon the possibility of a cult,
motivated purely by some "religious" ideal peculiar to itself, randomly
attacking innocent people. Occasionally, the specter grows into an image
of violent revolution and urban warfare. Of course, the Manson Family,
and extremist groups (from the Ku Klux Klan to the Symbionese Liberation Army) have supplied some verification of such possibilities. One
less-heralded case of a nonconventional religion also supplies material to
ponder: the "Zebra" killing involving the Nation of Islam in the San
Francisco Bay area.[6]

During 1973 and 1974 a series of random shootings occurred in San
Francisco. The perpetrators turned out to be members of an informal
group which had been organized within the Nation of Islam. Though the
members of this small group kept their activities secret from the rest of
the Temple, they assumed that they had been brought together on direc-
tives from the highest level of Muslim leadership in Chicago. Their
mission: translate the violent anti-white rhetoric of the Nation of Islam
into action by killing selected white victims. While there is no evidence
that Elijah Muhammad and/or the formal leadership of the Nation of
Islam either authorized or knew of the group, there is no doubt that the
anti-white theology articulated by the Muslims provided the fertile ideological ground out of which the group could emerge. That is to say, the
Nation of Islam created a group of people organized around their hatred of

white oppression of blacks and a religious doctrine of divine disapproval of whites which justified action against them. While the Zebra killers found their roots in the history of Black oppression in the United States, they have their precedents in those groups throughout recorded history who have called down divine sanctions to justify their anti-social actions. Historically, quite apart from warfare between rival religions, radical religious groups have committed robbery, rape, torture and even murder against non-members whom they define as evil, outside of God's chosen people or realm of law, or otherwise deserving of the violence inflicted upon them.

While some call upon the divine to sanctify antisocial action, others revel in what society calls evil which they redefine as their "good." They take the Lord of Evil as their God, and what society calls sin as their path. Such Satanic groups, though rare, small in membership, and shortlived, do nevertheless exist. Much of the genuine fear surrounding Satanic groups originates in their secretive nature, in the descriptions of what they do.

Possibly the first actual Satanic group, a group who took the Christian devil as their deity, was the seventeenth-century cult built around La Voison, a figure in the court of Louis XIV of France. With the aid of defrocked priests, La Voison led black masses and dispensed potions to keep followers in their positions of power and influence. When discovered, the group, by the extent of its infiltration to high places close to the king, threatened to topple his government. While it is not known if the number of Satanic groups has increased in recent decades, certainly the reports of their existence have.[7]

Satanic groups, at least in the past two decades, have been of two distinct varieties. The milder Satanic groups which have grown out of the work of Anton LaVey have propagated a rather mild form of allegiance to His Infernal Majesty. His Satanic Church and other groups such as the Temple of Set have had a high profile and have been careful to conduct their rituals and other activities within the law. La Vey and other leaders have frequently cooperated with police on cases involving an occult angle. The second type of Satanist group is a small, closed group consisting primarily of either (1) young teenagers experimenting with the occult and/or drugs, or (2) sociopaths and psychopaths. Illegal and violent activity arises from this latter type of group.

Even in milder forms, Satanic rituals may use two hard-to-obtain items—the bones of the dead and the consecrated hosts from a Roman Catholic Eucharist. Satan is perceived by his worshipers to be the ruler of dead souls and the archenemy of what Christians would consider most sacred. Roman Catholics believe the Eucharistic host to have been transubstantiated into the very body of Christ. Most Satanic groups, particularly those consisting of young occultists, thus signal their presence by (and limit their anti-social activities to) the desecration (vandalism) of religious buildings and theft of objects from churches and graveyards.

Most Satanic groups come and go very quickly as they release whatever psychopathic or sociopathic urge that led to the formation of the group in the first place. Occasionally, however, the pathology goes much deeper, and the activity of the group can lead to the torture and sacrifice of an animal (usually a cat or dog) or to the ritual murder of an individual. If a human victim is chosen, it will usually be an ex-member of the group, a personal enemy of the leader(s) or an attractive young female. A recently discovered group in New York, for example, targeted German shepherds for ritual death and mutilation.

While an encounter with a Satanic group can be extremely traumatic, if not fatal, to an individual, their small number has, with one exception, limited their larger social impact to the fear they engender. Since the early 1970s, the rural west has been plagued by a series of cattle mutilations. Researchers dismissed one early hypothesis which blamed the mutilations on Satanists as few signs of ritual behavior were associated with the dead cattle. More important in discounting the Satanic cult theory was the massive number of cultists which would have to exist to accomplish the large number of reported mutilations. However, more recent thorough examinations of the cattle mutilation reports have found that the over-whelming number of reported cattle mutilations were attributable to natural causes (primarily to predator damage on cattle killed by such hazards as lightening, snake bite, poison weeds, disease, and simple acci-dents). The modest number of cases which emerged as attributable to human causes were those associated with ritual activity: their number was small enough as to be readily assigned to the activity of the few known and hypothesized Satanic groups.[8]

The warfare between two groups touches a relatively confined sphere, and even the rare incidents of assaults or death from Satanic groups seem remote. And yet, on several occasions, a large, stable, and relatively visible group becomes involved in an intensely hostile situation, which over a period of time yields to violence. Such situations become the focus of legitimate public concern and law enforcement agencies. But, in each of the several prominent cases which have emerged during the 1970s, violence was preceded by a decade or more of antagonism, heightened rhetoric, and hostile actions (just short of violence) by both members and non-members which created a climate of distrust, misinformation, and latent hostility which worked against more peaceful resolutions to problems.

The Synanon Foundation, now the Synanon Church, moved into Marin County, California, in 1964. Almost from the beginning, hostile attitudes began to be expressed within the community. As it acquired more land and expanded several times the size of its original 65-acre purchase, complaints were voiced that it was taking an increasing amount of land off the county tax rolls. Adding fuel to the controversy were complaints that the county was lax in enforcing zoning laws (which would have slowed construction) and ignoring environmental impact. New build-ings were supposedly being constructed without the issuance of required permits. On occasion, problems with neighbors, especially one through whose property Synanon had an easement, led to arguments. Stories circulated of children left by parents in Synanon's care running away and complaining of cruel treatment. Several negative media articles critical of

Synanon had been met with lawsuits, at least one of which had been won for a sizable amount. The growing tension between the community and Synanon erupted into a series of violent incidents in 1978.

As community hostility grew, the Synanon community, which was somewhat isolated in the most rural section of Marin County, began to experience some direct violence in the form of nightriders. Guns were fired into buildings on several occasions. By the time the sheriff's office could respond, the perpetrators were far from the scene. To protect itself, early in 1978, Synanon purchased a supply of guns and ammunition for the use, if necessary, of its security force. Several weeks after the announced purchase, with their concurrent rumors of weapons' stockpiles, a county grand jury issued a report criticizing (1) officials for not making Synanon abide by county regulations and (2) Synanon for disregarding the regulations and doing little to correct the problem with the children in its care. In the midst of these events, an ex-member was awarded $300,000 in a lawsuit against Synanon.

The increased anger against Synanon, about which the residents of the county were choosing sides with most opposing, and Synanon's own beleaguered condition, set the stage for events to follow. Someone, and it may never be known exactly who, placed a rattlesnake in the mailbox of the attorney of the former member who had won the $300,000.00. Synanon founder Charles Dederich and two residents were arrested. Before the case could go to trial, Dederich suffered three strokes. The three defendants decided to plead no contest. Not only was Dederich's health a consideration, but significant public feelings, generated by media reports, called the possibility of a fair trial into question. The two residents were sentenced to a term in prison, and Dederich was ordered to cease any active role in the running of the community. Soon after, The Synanon Church sold its Marin County property and moved its offices and community to Badger, California.

Since the move, no further incidents of violence have been reported, however, the fallout from the rattlesnake incident has been enormous. Over forty people associated with Synanon received widely publicized grand jury indictments; then all of them were quietly dropped before going to trial. As a result of the attention, Synanon became involved in a series of litigations which, it appears, will be some years in the adjudication process. It is the opinion of Synanon that it has been the victim in the whole process, and it has sought vindication by initiating lawsuits against the people it feels were responsible for damaging its program and image.[9]

Another group which developed an image permeated with violence is the Ananda Marga Yoga Society, though almost all of the violent incidents, including the death of 17 Ananda Margis at the hands of a Calcutta mob in 1982, occurred outside of the United States. Trouble began in 1971 when Anandamurtiji, the leader of Ananda Marga, was arrested in India for murder. Anandamurtiji, who was also a political theorist and founder of a political party, had previously accused Indian Prime Minister Indira Gandhi of corruption. His trial was denounced by international human rights groups as purely political and in 1978 his sentence was reversed and he was released. Meanwhile accusations of violence piled up and were lent credence by the conviction of two members in Australia for murdering a politician and the presence of numerous documents in law enforcement agency files linking Ananda Marga members to a variety of violent crimes. (It should be noted that Ananda Marga has denied the many accusations against it and attributes their proliferation to the same persecution that originally sent their leader to jail; and apart from the Australian case none of the accusations have led to arrests and/or convictions.)[10]

Though not reaching a level of violence of such as either the Nation of Islam or Ananda Marga, the history of the Church of Scientology follows a parallel path. Soon after its founding, the Church began to experience problems. In 1958 the Internal Revenue Service withdrew tax-exempt status. In 1963 the Food and Drug Administration seized a mass of books, tapes, and E-meters used in the Church's counseling procedure called auditing. As the United States government moved against Scientology trouble spread. Based upon information supplied by U.S. government officials, inquiries began in Australia which led to Scientology's banning in 1965. In response to these actions, the Church, in 1966, established the Guardian's Office, to which it assigned the task, among others, of safe-guarding Scientology and its organizations. Almost immediately, the Guardian's Office was forced to devote a major portion of its time to the continuing government attack and a new assault from several expose-type books which the Church considered libelous. It countered with lawsuits to force the books off the market.

By the mid-1970's the Church charged that a coalition of government agencies, ex-members and individuals who simply disliked the Church were combining to destroy it. They spent much of the decade in legal battles. They attempted to obtain government documents on the Church through the Freedom of Information Act and were frequently met with denials of the existence of the requested documents, only to have the said documents appear elsewhere. In the process both sides developed a war-like attitude, and both eventually sent spies and even *agents provocateurs* into the others' camp. In the midst of this war charges surfaced the Church had turned violent, that Scientologists had harassed, beaten, and even murdered some ex-members and individuals defined as "enemies," though no Scientologist was ever formally charged or tried. People in-volved in lawsuits against the Church accused church members of break-ing in and stealing files. Finally, members of the Church associated with the Guardian's Office were arrested and convicted on charges of stealing government documents from the Federal Bureau of Investigation and the Internal Revenue Service.

In the period since the conviction of top-level Scientology officials, the Church has taken significant steps to reorganize and to alter its polemic stance vis-a-vis society, but, as with Synanon, it will be many years fully disposing of the problems created during the 1970s. Major steps in chang-ing the past history occurred in 1983 when the High Court of Australia reversed all of that country's anti-Scientology acts. However, that was followed by a United States tax court ruling against the Church and a civil court decision against the Church involving a multi-million dollar case brought by an ex-member.[11]

One cannot leave the accounts of groups with a history of violence, without some mention of the Children of God (now called the Family of Love). While there have been no reports of violence towards the general public, ex-members have made repeated charges of member-on-member violence. Almost all of the reports originate within the circle of members in relatively close contact with David Berg, the leader. Very early in the life of the Children of God, a sex ethic which varied considerably from that generally accepted in society emerged. Most of the charges of violence, some well-documented, relate to sexual abuse and rape. The charges seem to have been a by-product of Berg's attempts to manipulate the social bonding within the higher echelons of the Family and to use sex as a proselytizing tool. The latter practice, called "flirty fishing," brought large-scale public reaction as well as an outbreak of venereal disease and has been discontinued in many places. The charges against Berg and his associates were largely responsible for their abandoning the United States in the mid-1970s. Charges of problems at the top of the organization, though not the violence of the early 1970s, have continued in the 1980s, most recently being confirmed by Berg's own daughter who left the group after many years.[12]

Again, lest the image be left that nonconventional religious groups are somehow unique in becoming associated with violent events, there is the case of a Santa Ana, California, parish—a case frightening in its parallels to the Peoples' Temple. During the 1950s the Church of the Way was a small congregation in the Free Methodist Church. Then several years after a new pastor came to the Church, denominational officials charged the pastor with deviation from Church doctrine. The congregation stood with the pastor and in 1959 withdrew from the denomination. It continued to grow through the 1960s, but slowly word began to spread that all was not well at the little church down the street, by now renamed Madeley Trinity Methodist Church.

Some have traced the trouble to the early 1970s when lay members began to speak out during the Sunday services. The "exhortations" took the form of accusations against other church members. Such verbal intimidation became the first step in leading the Church into a separatist stance, and, as separation from other Christians grew, a number of bizarre and not a few violent practices were introduced. Most of the conflict was expressed in an extreme form of the belief in "demon possession." First, pet animals were singled out as "possessed" and beaten to death. Then spouses were ordered to shun their mates identified as possessed. Eventually several members were physically assaulted as a part of an attempted exorcism. In 1977 two members who had been beaten sued and won substantial out-of-court settlements.

Then, suddenly, in the winter of 1979–1980, the Church abandoned Santa Ana and moved to Springfield, Missouri (over 100 members). It held one service in March 1980 in a rented building and then simply disappeared. Members scattered and have kept in touch by way of a set of postal boxes. (At the time of this writing, the Madeley Trinity Methodist Church remains in hiding, even to family members left behind at the time of the sudden move.)

The case of the Madeley Trinity Methodist Church, like the Peoples' Temple before it, manifests that other aforementioned potential for violence—the mainline Church gone bad. The reports of beatings at that Church also lead directly into the last remaining issue which has received substantive concern with regard to cult violence—child abuse.

During the last decade cases linking child abuse to a religious group appeared with a somewhat regular frequency. Thus, given the growing concern about child abuse as a national issue, it was only a matter of time before a substantive case would surface. That occurred in 1982 when a child died as a result of a beating by a parent. The mother, later convicted of involuntary manslaughter, was a member of the House of Judah, a small Black Jewish group headquartered in Allegan County, Michigan. William A. Lewis, the leader of the group, believed in strong discipline for children and advocated corporal punishment in response to childish disobedience.

In the wake of the House of Judah case, other reports of child abuse were quickly assembled as further evidence of the violent tendencies present in cults. Yet, upon close examination, the child abuse charges did not come from the major nonconventional religions (i.e., those most identified as cults in the public mind) but from conservative evangelical Christian Church groups which took Biblical admonitions (Hebrews 12:6) about chastising children as literal fact. These included the Gideons (Ocala, Florida), the River of Life Tabernacle (Montana), the Stonegate Christian Community (West Virginia), the Northeast Kingdom Community (Vermont), the Covenant Community Fellowship (Rennselaer, Indiana), the Church of Bible Understanding (New York and Pennsylvania), and the Church of God in Christ through the Holy Spirit (not to be confused with the large Pentecostal denomination the Church of God in Christ).

The strict adherence to literal Biblical admonitions has also led to other problems besides child abuse. Throughout the twentieth century, some conservative Protestant sectarian groups have turned against doctors and the medical profession, frequently as part of a general adoption of an emphasis on faith healing, a belief that if a member's faith is strong God will restore that member to health from all diseases and keep them in a perpetual state of health. During the 1970s, the Faith Assembly, led by Pentecostal minister Hobart Freeman, emerged as a strong new sect group with congregations across the Midwest and into the South. Members followed Freeman in denouncing medicine as a derivative of Pagan religion and refrained from the use of medical service. Home childbirth became standard, but leaders frowned upon attendance at natural childbirth classes. As a result, the Faith Assembly has experienced a large number of deaths which could have been prevented by a minimal amount of proper medical care. Deaths have resulted from diabetics discontinuing their insulin intake, mothers giving birth at home, and infants being denied medical care. In the wake of the exposure of the problem, the state of Indiana moved against the Assembly. Several members whose children had died were convicted. Leader Hobart Freeman, also indicted, died before his case could come to trial.

Finally, a discussion of the major incidents of violence initiated from within a "cult" body leave a residue of isolated cases. Some relate to an individual's religious pathology. Individuals on occasion adopt a religious format to express their violent and aggressive urges. Such is the case of Lindberg Sanders, a black man and former mental patient. He gathered a small group around him and preached that police (mostly white) were Satan. In Memphis in 1983, he took a police officer hostage and killed him. In a raid on the house where the hostage was held, Sanders and his small band were killed. Similar is the case of Keith and Kate Haigler who intercepted a Continental Trailways bus in rural Arkansas. At the end of the hijacking incident, the pair asked state troopers to kill them—they believed they would be resurrected in three days. The troopers only wounded them, so the two shot each other.

Of course, a few incidents related to the major cults do appear. For example, a violent incident involving members of the Divine Light Mission of Guru Maharaj Ji was occasioned by a young man who disliked the guru and tossed a pie in his face. While the Guru asked that no retaliation occur, a week later the pie-thrower was severely beaten. The case of Walter Wallace who joined the Kripalu Yoga Ashram of Yogi Amrit Desai is similar. Desai teaches vegetarianism and advocates occasional fasts. Wallace starved to death, seemingly as the result of a long private fast. While one of the ashram's physicians had warned Wallace not to fast, no one seemed to recognize that he was slowly starving to death.

The Church of Armageddon, recently disbanded, also known as the Love Family, is one of several groups that emerged out of the drug culture of the 1960s. At one time in its life its practices included the ritual sniffing of the chemical toluvene. In 1972 two members of the group died as a result of their use of the substance. The fact that they used it in contradiction to group practice, i.e., unsupervised, and that one had been specifically ordered not to use the substance, does little to lessen the responsibility of the leadership of the Church for their deaths. The Church did, however, discontinue the practice after the incident and no other reports of violence from that group emerged, though charges of corruption against the leader led to the group's dissolution.[13]

A Note About Suicide

Within the reports of violence are a small number of suicides. For example, on August 5, 1974, Robert J. Williams shot himself in the parking lot of the Law Enforcement Center at Wichita, Kansas. The previous November, Williams had confided to a newspaper reporter that he was a practicing Witch. The reporter, in return for an account of contemporary Witchcraft, agreed to keep Williams' name and identity confidential. He broke his promise, and Williams' story, complete with name and picture, appeared on the front page of the newspaper. Williams was fired from his job as psychologist at the state reformatory. Though later reinstated, he remained in a tense situation.

Like child abuse, suicide is a national issue. Unlike child abuse, the actual number of cases is miniscule. However, even with the case of Williams, where much more information has been made available than in most cases, the causes of an individual suicide remain difficult to discern under the best of circumstances and impossible from a few newspaper clippings. Unless more cases should emerge, we must judge that no pattern of cult-related suicide exists and dismiss suicide from our discussion as it constitutes no present discernible danger relative to religious groups.

Conclusions

The Correlates of Cult-Related Violence. The causes of cult-related violence discussed above are very complex. They cannot be separated from the generally high level of violence within American society as a whole and the continuing theme of seeking violent solutions to social problems.[14] As one researcher noted, social violence ". . . is highly complex, involving the deep-seated tendencies in the personality with processes in the immediate situation, in the face-to-face group or organization, and in the larger society."[15] Much more work is needed before the final appraisal of the origins of cult-related violence can be fully disclosed. This chapter can only offer some tentative observations concerning potential areas of future cult-related situations and some immediate steps which could be taken to reduce or eliminate possible violence. First, *it is to be expected*, in spite of all measures to the contrary, *that some cult-related violence will continue into the foreseeable future.* Cults participate in the general theme of religious violence. Religion has, in the past, been the cause of wars and innumerable acts of violence upon individuals. Only with the greatest difficulty have populations learned to fight their religious battles with words instead of guns and instruments of torture. Just as religion has been used to sanction slavery and the sexual exploitation of women, there is every sign that it will continue to be used to rationalize the impulses of religious leaders.

Religious people also inherit the violence transmitted by families from generation to generation. Given the high level of family violence in the United States (from child abuse to neglect), it is unlikely that cults will be able to exclude people who carry those deep-seated tendencies to violence from joining them and even rising to positions of leadership, just as they do within mainline religious groups. Further, given the high level of tension with society under which some nonconventional religious groups have been forced to operate, it is not surprising that the violent tendencies of some cult leaders have emerged. What is possibly more surprising has been the relative infrequency of such violent outbursts.

However, violence does occur, and even relatively few incidents cannot be condoned. Does the review of the prior cases of cult-related violence suggest (1) new ways to understand it and (2) actions that could be taken to lessen its occurrence? In answer to that question, four correlates to cult-related violence have been discerned and several suggestions for long-term action proposed. The correlates of violent activity can be seen as indicators of potential for future violence.

First, *some cults have given and continue to give direct sanction to violent activity.* Both the Black Muslims and the Church of the Lamb of God called upon the tradition of holy war to legitimize the killing of the group's (i.e., God's) enemies. The belief that certain times and situations not only allow but demand the faithful to take up arms was articulated powerfully in the Old Testament and from there was transmitted to Jews, Christians, and Muslims alike. It has been used in this century to justify full-scale military operations, the assassination of political leaders, and the killing of random enemies of the faith.

Great potential for future violence can be found in the several conservative Christian groups who have adopted a militaristic program along with pro-Caucasian policy undergirded with anti-Black and anti-Semitic rhetoric. Some of these groups (which include the Christian Conservative Church of America; the Church of Jesus Christ Christian of Aryan Nations; the Covenant, the Sword, the Arm of the Lord; the Mountain Church and the New Christian Crusade Church) have strong ties to the Ku Klux Klan. The Covenant, the Sword, The Arm of the Lord, the members of which live together in a community at Zaraphath-Horeb, Arkansas, for example, describes itself as a "peaceful people" who "live with guns." It offers training to both members and others of like mind in urban warfare, "Christian" martial arts, and "the use of firearms for military purposes." This group actually puts into practice what others, such as The Way International, have merely been accused of doing.[16]

Less publicized during the 1970s, but possibly the source of more real damage to individuals, have been the numerous cases of child abuse. Occurring most frequently in conservative evangelical Christian groups, the practice has found its sanction in Biblical passages such as Hebrews 12. Violent tendencies within parents who were themselves abused children can be nurtured by a group's belief in strict discipline and an advocacy of corporal punishment as proper means of controlling behavior.

Second, while some groups and group leaders have given direct sanction to violence, *more cult-related violence grows out of the indirect sanction of violence from belief systems which intellectually undergird group members' violent tendencies.* For example, beliefs held by one group which stereotype another group and hence dehumanize its members are easily adopted by individuals as a rationale for action against members of the despised group. The Church of Scientology, for many years, designated people as "enemies," "potential trouble sources," or "suppressive." It went so far as to suggest someone could be considered "fair game." Within the Church and certainly in the literature, these terms are part of a vast body of technical language with specific meanings and correlative action guidelines. However, they are also highly emotive words which in the heat of controversy can convey, and undoubtedly have conveyed, their emotive charge in spite of the precise technical usage.

Such terms as "enemy," "Satanic," "Gentile" (as used by Mormons), "counterfeit" (as used by evangelical Christian counter-cult ministries), "heretic," and other terms used by one group to express their contempt of others and to assign them a status outside the realm of God's chosen, and hence of lesser worth, is the religious equivalent of secular terms such as "nigger," "kike," or "wop." Each serves to direct group prejudice against various minorities in a community. They denigrate the member of the group and give tacit legitimation to the flogging of a black man, the defacement of a synagogue, the telling of ethnic jokes and the deprogramming of a religious believer.

The sanctioning of violence, both directly and indirectly, in a cult-related situation is vividly illustrated in the philosophy of the militant secular anti-cult movement. In its promotion of deprogramming, it has given direct encouragement to the necessary violence connected with each incident (in which a person is forcefully detained and physically confined for a period of days or weeks). It has lightly dismissed, thus indicating the unimportance in its eyes, of the very real cases of physical abuse heaped upon people who strongly resisted their captors. Further, underlying the whole anti-cult movement and providing the intellectual sanction for deprogramming, both to those who practice it and those who merely promote it, the brainwashing hypothesis has been used to create a pervasive negative image of nonconventional religions by stereotyping them as manipulative destructive cults. Drawing upon the traditional tactics of group prejudice, the movement has pictured leaders as wealthy, selfish and exercising undue control on members, and attacked groups as threats to the social order. Individual members have been assigned the role of "helpless victim" and referred to as "zombies" and "puppets" to imply their position as the robot-like tools of cult leaders. Ted Patrick, who developed deprogramming, claimed cult members were so changed by their life in the group as to be incapable of independent thought and thus not suitable objects of civil rights. More recently, anti-cultists have spoken of the need of "repersonalization" of cult members, implying, at least partially, the loss of personhood. Patrick, in what is obviously an extreme statement for the movement, drew the logical conclusion, that any act is justifiable in efforts to extricate a person caught in a cult.

The secular anti-cult movement has drawn strength from the popular prejudices which have historically been directed against groups holding nonconventional opinions and following unpopular practices. In prior generations such prejudice brought America waves of anti-Masonry, anti-Catholicism, and anti-Semitism and raised the specter of the Yellow Peril, the Turbaned Tornado, and the Red Scare. In each case, the attempt was made to mobilize the public and the legislative machinery to squelch a rising threat by an "un-American" and "leprous" social group.

In response to the sanctions of violence, it should be noted that *the denial of any sanction to violence by people concerned with a cycle of violent activity can short circuit it.* Among the Black Muslims, no such denial existed, as all sides accepted the legitimacy of violence in given situations. However, when attacked by the Church of the Lamb of God, leaders of both the Church of the First Born and the Apostolic United Brethren, brought strong sanctions to bear against any retaliation. Little doubt remains that had they joined in the hostilities initiated by Ervil LeBaron, the death toll could have been much higher and, like the Hatfield-McCoy feud, gone on for decades.

Third, *much cult-related violence must be traced to the youthfulness of the leadership.* Typically, first-generation movements draw leadership from among the early talented followers of the founder(s). If the organization spreads rapidly, young adults still in their twenties can find themselves the managers of a large national movement. Should that movement come under attack by elements in the society or face severe tensions from within, they must guide the believers often without any assistance from older individuals who have expertise in conflict resolution, public relations, or legislative lobbying. Youthful leaders require time to learn the seriousness and consequences of violent outbursts. That learning process may have to proceed concurrently with a period of violence surrounding the group in which they have assumed leadership. The inexperience of youth seems to be a contributing factor in the occasional incidents of violence such as that illustrated in the conviction of the Divine Light Mission leader in Winterthur, Switzerland, for attempted murder, and in the various actions planned and executed by the Guardian's Office of the Church of Scientology in the 1970s.

Fourth, *violence erupts, in most cases, only after a period of heightened conflict between either different factions of a religion of a nonconventional religion and the community.* In such cases, both sides must bear responsibility when and if verbal violence turns to physical violence as both sides will have inflicted damage upon the other and each will have had multiple opportunities either to withdraw and refuse to perpetuate the conflict or seek a satisfactory alternative solution.

The presence of a long-standing conflict, either in the form of heightened rhetoric of one religion against another or community criticism of a particular religious group should alert observers to a situation in which a potential for violence exists. Such rhetoric and/or criticism is by no means a sure indicator, as almost every group goes through one or more periods of conflict, and very few allow conflict to erupt into violence. If, however, strong violent tendencies appear within some members and if a group sanction for violence is present, the potential is markedly increased. Most groups choose to respond to conflict by seeking non-violent solutions—through secular legal alternatives—or, in most cases, simply and patiently waiting out the conflict. For example, most cults have reacted and continue to react to the anti-cult pressures either (1) by seeking redress in the courts (an offensive action) or (2) blocking anti-cult legislation and building aggressive public relations programs (both defensive actions), or (3) nothing (an often effective passive solution). They have, with few exceptions, refrained from physically attacking deprogrammers and other leaders in the organized anti-cult movement.

Towards a Reduction of Violence. The Peoples' Temple alerted the public to the potential for violence surrounding religious conflict. While the Jonestown situation is a unique case in many ways, both in the situation of the groups (a Black American group isolated on a rural farm in a foreign country) and in the aura of secrecy which surrounds it (most of the papers collected in the investigation committee have not been released under the Freedom of Information Act due to matters of national security), it points to other occasions of violence. Also, while yet reluctant to pinpoint the causes of religious violence, whether it be the more elusive incident of the Peoples' Temple or other cases closer to home, the discernment of the several correlates of cult-related violence leaves, in the meantime, considerable room for remedial action. First, *the necessary role played by groups and their leaders in sanctioning violence suggests that efforts to counter such sanctions could produce marked results.* Such an effort has already begun to stop child abuse by exposing family dilemmas which allow it to exist and bringing legal structures to bear on traditional sanctions to its continuance. An additional effort by evangelical Christian ministers to disavow interpretations of Scripture that sanction child abuse could add weight to secular initiatives. In like measure, a rejection by public leaders of such coercive measures as deprogramming coupled with the advocacy of non-violent alternatives for families disturbed by the membership of one person in a nonconventional religion could hasten the adoption of family counseling measures which could in turn alleviate the single most controllable area of cult-related violence.

Second, *the general commitment to eradicate the structures of religious group prejudice could be strengthened.* The common practice of generalizing about nonconventional religions could be replaced with the more accurate and profitable alternative of discriminating between the various groups and judging each on its individual merits and weaknesses. Toward this end, the promotion of dialogue between members of nonconventional religions, church leaders, and the public could create situations in which cult-based stereotypes held by non-members could be confronted and eliminated. Certainly such attempts at dialogue, especially with groups that have separatist tendencies, would be difficult, but hardly more so than those initial dialogues that began the process of eliminating derogatory stereotypes of Blacks, Jews, or the poor. In each case the value received by the culture has been more than ample reward for the effort.

Third, *processes of intervention in potentially violent situations could be developed and improved.* Some violence-prone religious groups do exist and others will most likely emerge in the future. The proper agencies of the society should be prepared to mobilize at the first signs of potential violence. However, emphasis should be placed upon the prevention of violence as opposed to dealing with its consequences after the fact. Situations with a violent potential, especially those which involve a nonconventional religious group, do not always respond best to pressures of law-enforcing agencies.

More adequate responses come through community pressures: the full exposure of the potentially violent situation to public scrutiny and the active intervention of knowledgeable individuals who can assist opposing parties to seek non-violent solutions are more likely to defuse potentially violent conditions than the application of an outside force.

Fourth, *the recognition of the increasingly pluralistic religious environment of the West and the movement to include the so-called "cults" into the larger religious community should proceed with all due haste.* The cults, most of whom are representatives of the massive wave of Eastern and Middle Eastern religious groups, which migrated to the United States during the past two decades, have become permanent residents of the United States, indeed of all the Western world. Their presence can be seen as but one aspect of the shift in American society from a predominantly Protestant Christian country to a religiously pluralistic society in which the Roman Catholic Church is the single largest religious body and in which Islam has grown larger than Judaism.

The religious diversification of America will be met with dialogue and attempts to understand, or a steadily increasing level of religious conflict can be expected. Given the precedence of several generations of Jewish-Christian dialogue, the amount to be gained from a general shift of perception of the so-called cults seems enormous. The values to be gained from dismantling the structures of hostility and building bridges of insight and discernment could be highly educational to both sides, and, while conserving the energy now put into polemics, result in the creative solution to some common problems. Given the present trends, the development of higher levels of acceptance and understanding of people with different, even radically different, religious outlooks is fast becoming a necessity of cultural survival.

Notes

1. Ken Levi, ed., *Violence and Religious Commitment* (University Park: Pennsylvania State University Press, 1982).

2. Don Nori, "Persecution at Island Pond." *Charisma* 10, 4 (November 1984), 68–78.

3. Cf. Schwatz, Alan M., "The Way International." *ADL Research Report* (Spring 1982), 1–17.

4. For a more detailed account of the Church of the Lamb of God, see Ben Bradlee, Jr., and Dale Van Atta, *Prophet of Blood* (New York: G. P. Putnam's Sons, 1981) and Verlan M. LeBaron, *The LeBaron Story* (Lubbock, TX: The Author, 1981).

5. On the Black Muslim incidents, see C. Eric Lincoln, *The Black Muslims in America* (Boston: Beacon Press, 1961) and George Breitman, Iterman Porter, and Baxter Smith, *The Assassination of Malcolm X* (New York: Pathfinder Press, 1976).

6. Clark Howard, *Zebra* (New York: Berkley Books, 1980).

7. Cf. H. T. F. Rhodes, *The Satanic Mass* (New York: Citadel Press, 1955) and Arthur Lyons, Jr., *The Second Coming: Satanism in America* (New York: Dodd, Mead, 1970).

8. Daniel Kagan and Ian Summers, *Mute Evidence* (New York: Bantam Books, 1984).

9. I am grateful to members of Synanon's staff for their response to the accusations of violence at Synanon made in such books as Dave Mitchell, Cathy Mitchell, and Richard Ofshe, *The Light on Synanon* (New York: Seaview Books, 1980).

10. N. K. Singh, "Anand Marg's Lust for Blood." *The Illustrated Weekly of India* (October 10, 1977), 8–14.

11. For a detailed listing of Scientology's litigation, see *What Is Scientology?* (Los Angeles: Church of Scientology of California, 1978).

12. Deborah (Linda Berg) Davis, *The Children of God* (Grand Rapids: Zondervan, 1984).

13. See the discussion of the Church of Armageddon in Steve Allen, *Beloved Son* (Indianapolis: Bobbs-Merrill, 1982).

14. Richard Hofstadter and Michael Wallace, eds., *American Violence, a Documentary History* (New York: Alfred A. Knopf, 1970).

15. Nevitt Sanford, "Going Beyond Prevention." In Nevitt Sanford and Craig Comstock, eds., *Sanctions for Evil* (San Francisco: Jossey-Bass, 1971).

16. *Hate Groups in America* (New York: Anti-Defamation League of B'nai B'rith, 1982).

INDEX